PRAISE FOR
Spies in the Fa

"A riveting true-life thriller . . . astonishing."

—*Wall Street Journal*

"Intimate and chilling. . . . Whereas most coverage of CIA strategy can only present recorded events, Dillon can provide motivations, offering a more intimate, humanizing look at both sides of the Iron Curtain."

—Mary von Aue, *Vice*

"A beautifully written, profoundly moving account of one of the most important U.S. Intelligence sources ever run inside the Soviet Union. A cliff-hanger from beginning to end, Dillon's account is filled with espionage tradecraft and family drama—essential reading for anyone fascinated by how spying really works."

—Peter Earnest, Executive Director, International Spy Museum

"With detail and technique that are almost novelistic, Dillon weaves the personal stories of the two families: her own and that of Polyakov. . . . Reads like a fine spy novel whose ending we know but whose story transports us nonetheless."

—*Kirkus Reviews* (starred review)

"Dillon's book is a poignant portrait about how espionage touches personal lives. An intriguing work with a touching narrative. . . . Cold War historians and espionage aficionados will be delighted."

—*Library Journal*

"A well-researched book depicting two families on either side of the Cold War."

—Mackenzie Dawson, *New York Post*

"A masterly interweaving of subplots and layer upon layer of detail, which add up to a remarkable crystallization of the many forces and personalities that made up this significant chapter in Cold War foreign relations."

—Sarah Mansfield Taber, *American Scholar*

"A riveting read. Dillon creatively weaves the narratives of her CIA father's career and family life with those of Dmitri Polyakov, one of the Cold War's most valuable Russian assets. An untold and important story that's been a long time coming, this book is worth the wait."

—The Honorable John Lehman, former Secretary of the Navy and member of the 9/11 Commission

"This spellbinder spans lives, families, and politics on opposite sides of the Cold War, combining suspenseful accounts of two intelligence agents deeply committed to avoiding nuclear war with each family's unique—and heartbreaking—experiences. This moving story is gripping from start to finish."

—Jacqueline Leo, President and Editor in Chief, *Fiscal Times*; former Editor in Chief, *Reader's Digest*

"Riveting. . . . In her rigorously researched account, Dillon shares enthralling insider glimpses of Soviet-era espionage."

—Maura Hogan, *Charleston Magazine*

"Interweaving details of daring tradecraft with moving human elements, Dillon tells the fascinating story of two agents and their families with differing experiences and perspectives, and very different outcomes. This mesmerizing book will appeal to historians, spy buffs, intelligence professionals, and everyday readers alike."

—H. Keith Melton, author of *Ultimate Spy* and coauthor (with Robert Wallace) of *Spycraft* and the Spy Sites series

"Eva Dillon expertly tells an untold chapter of Cold War espionage from a front-row seat. It was her father, after all, who was the Spymaster. This is a warm, riveting, great read."

—Joe Drape, *New York Times* bestselling author, *American Pharoah* and *Our Boys*

SPIES IN THE FAMILY

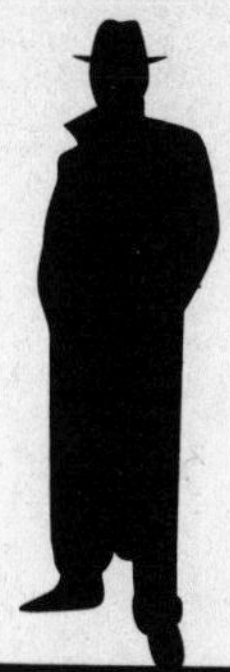

SPIES IN THE FAMILY

AN AMERICAN SPYMASTER, HIS RUSSIAN CROWN JEWEL, AND THE FRIENDSHIP THAT HELPED END THE COLD WAR

EVA DILLON

HARPER

NEW YORK • LONDON • TORONTO • SYDNEY

HARPER

A hardcover edition of this book was published in 2017 by Harper, an imprint of HarperCollins Publishers.

HarperCollins books may be purchased for educational, business, or sales promotional use. For information, please e-mail the Special Markets Department at SPsales@harpercollins.com.

FIRST HARPER PAPERBACK EDITION PUBLISHED 2018.

Designed by William Ruoto

Library of Congress Cataloging-in-Publication Data has been applied for.

ISBN 978-0-06-238590-1 (pbk.)

18 19 20 21 22 LSC 10 9 8 7 6 5 4 3 2 1

To Dmitri Fedorovich Polyakov

CONTENTS

CONTENTS

PROLOGUE

SO CLOSE

In May 1988, in his eighth and final year in office, President Ronald Reagan traveled to Moscow for his fourth summit with General Secretary Mikhail Gorbachev. No other American president had held as many summits with a Soviet leader.

By then the Cold War was winding down. Gorbachev had shown his reformist colors early in his tenure as general secretary, and by 1988 there was far more openness in what had been, since its founding, a grim police-security state. Soviet citizens were beginning to enjoy freedoms (of speech and religion, for instance) that were unheard of in earlier times. Reagan and Gorbachev had struck up a civil relationship that grew friendlier as they made progress on arms reduction. "A certain chemistry does exist between us," Reagan wrote in his diary. At one of their meetings, Reagan gave Gorbachev a pair of cuff links engraved with the figure of swords being beaten into plowshares, a traditional symbol of peace.

Walking with Gorbachev on the Kremlin grounds during a break from meetings, Reagan was asked by a reporter about his famous "Evil Empire" speech of five years earlier. "I was talking about another time, another era," he replied. His optimism for the future of the Soviet people was evident in a speech he gave on that visit to students at Moscow State University.

> Your generation is living in one of the most exciting, hopeful times in Soviet history. It is a time when the first breath of freedom stirs the air and the heart beats to the accelerated rhythm of hope, when the accumulated spiritual energies of a long silence yearn to break free.

In between formal summit meetings, Reagan pulled Gorbachev aside for a private conversation. The United States would be appreciative if the USSR would pardon a prisoner who had been arrested as an American spy, or trade him for a Soviet spy incarcerated in America.

Gorbachev sent an assistant to look into the prisoner's status. When the assistant came back, Gorbachev turned to Reagan. "Mr. President," he said, "I will have to disappoint you. The man you are asking us to pardon is dead. His sentence for spying was carried out two months ago."

INTRODUCTION

PULVEREM PULVERI

I was heartbroken to miss my father's funeral. His death at an early age was a shock, and away on a semester abroad during college, I didn't make it back in time. Listening to the details a few days later from my six brothers and sisters, I was struck by the description of the size of the crowd as they arrived at the Cathedral of St. Matthew the Apostle in Washington, DC, that October 1980 morning. The church's majestic nave was nearly filled.

My siblings wondered who all these people were, they told me later, most of whose faces they did not recognize. As mourners came up to offer their condolences, it began to sink in that all these people were Dad's friends and colleagues from CIA headquarters and from his postings in Berlin, Mexico City, Rome, and New Delhi, all the places we had lived growing up. We had never guessed he had so many contacts, so many associates, that so many people might want to see him off. He had kept that side of his life secret.

Mom and Dad had been married at St. Matthew's twenty-nine years earlier, and only a small wedding party had been present back then. At the funeral, hundreds of people were crowding in. My father had been such an unassuming, humble person. Could all this really be for him?

The coffin was a simple one, a plain pine box with no

ornamentation, and it stood in contrast to the splendor of the cathedral as the pallbearers carried it down the aisle. It had been my father's wish: no frills, no adornment, his body to be wrapped in ordinary white linen. *Pulverem pulveri*: dust to dust.

My three teenage brothers carried the coffin along with five of my father's "State Department" friends, all of whom we had known well growing up. It was only later that we found out who they were in their own secret CIA lives: David Murphy, chief of Soviet operations; Gus Hathaway, chief of the Counterintelligence Center; Ben Pepper, branch chief, Soviet Bloc counterintelligence group; Bill Friend, Western European Division, then retired; and George Walsh, Dhaka Station chief.

On the floor directly in front of the altar was a large engraved inscription inside a circle: HERE RESTED THE REMAINS OF PRESIDENT KENNEDY AT THE REQUIEM MASS, NOVEMBER 25, 1963, BEFORE THEIR REMOVAL TO ARLINGTON WHERE THEY LIE IN EXPECTATION OF A HEAVENLY RESURRECTION. The coffin was placed on top of the engraving.

George Walsh, Dad's best friend from his Boston childhood, delivered the eulogy. "We shall remember that he was forthright and direct when he spoke," he said, "and yet was kind and gentle. He was scornful of pretension and vanity. We shall remember that he was called upon to shoulder responsibility at an age when most are free to play, yet from childhood, with many occasions to be sad, he was nevertheless known for his enduring good cheer, his unflagging good spirits, and diligence in his many duties to family, to church, to country. Strong in conviction, firm in his faith, his faith inspired faith in others."

Sitting in the front pews of the cathedral listening to George speak, in their daze of bewildered grief, my brothers and sisters were unaware that something strange was happening behind them. Years later, colleagues of Dad's told me that two men had appeared with cameras at the side door of the church and started snapping pictures. Someone rushed over and hustled them out. Then, during the Communion, a disturbance took place near one of the confessional booths. Another of Dad's colleagues told me that she and a CIA workmate noticed a slight movement of the curtain in the booth. When her companion opened the door, he found a man with a telescopic lens peeking through the latticework; he grabbed the man's arm and marched him out the back of the church.

The picture takers, we later found out, were working with Philip Agee. Agee was a former CIA officer who'd become disgruntled with the CIA, left the Agency, and published a book, *Inside the Company: CIA Diary*, which had blown my father's cover, as it had those of hundreds of other officers. After the book's publication, Agee fled to Cuba and founded a magazine, *CovertAction Quarterly*, infamous for its Naming Names column, dedicated to further exposing undercover CIA personnel. Such a large collection of high-level CIA people at my father's funeral was too rich a target to ignore, so Agee's men were identifying as many as they could, a windfall for their KGB sponsor.

We didn't know any of this back then. It would be years before the curtain came up enough for us to understand.

★

We were pretty sure Mom knew some of Dad's secrets, but throughout their lives together she was as silent about them as he was. Occasionally, after he died, she would tell us a few things, but she was never comfortable talking about it, and took most of what she knew to the grave with her when she died in 1997, seventeen years after my father.

We weren't completely naïve. We had known definitively that Dad was with the CIA ever since the tell-all book *Inside the Company* identified him five years before his death. But we had all been busy with our lives, and hadn't pursued finding out more about it then. Besides, over our childhood years, moving from country to country, we had become conditioned to accept things as they were explained to us. And why not? There was something wonderful and reassuring about my father. He was calm, warm, trustworthy, and confident, and gave off a sense of steadiness. Even his name was solid: Paul Leo Dillon. We were content with our lives, a happy family moving around the world on Dad's assignments over the years.

In 1997, I was forty and well into a career with Condé Nast Publishing in New York City. My brothers and sisters had their own families and careers, and after we buried our mother with Dad at the Culpeper National Cemetery in Virginia, we started clearing out the house in Vienna, Virginia, where we had lived between Dad's overseas assignments.

There, up in the attic, we found cardboard boxes full of letters and memorabilia that spanned the entire course of our family's life, over decades and continents. And what we found was astonishing.

My husband, James, started to look through one of the boxes and pulled out a magazine. "Hey, guys," he said to my brothers, "did your dad have any fancy shotguns in the house when you were in India?"

"Oh, yeah," said Jacob, the youngest in the family. "He had a few. Very fancy ones."

"Do you know if he ever went hunting or fishing on the Yamuna River?"

"Yes," said Paul, the middle boy. "He let me go with him once. It was funny because he hadn't had an interest in hunting or fishing before India. Why do you ask?"

"Look at this," said James. "Your dad's name is in here. He handled this Soviet general."

My interest was now piqued, too. "James, let me see that."

James had found an issue of *George* magazine, the "Spy Issue." Inside was a photo of a middle-aged man at a party of some sort—the women were wearing festive tiaras, and the man was smiling broadly and sporting a white top hat. I started to read:

> His code name: TOPHAT. His mission: to use his position as a Soviet intelligence officer to spy on the Russians for the United States . . . [He] served this country for 18 years as the CIA's highest-ranking Soviet agent. Then he was betrayed.

I read on:

> TOPHAT was sent as a military attaché to India, where Paul L. Dillon, an ex-marine from Boston, was dispatched to serve as his CIA case officer.

Dillon, the article said, was "an unsung hero of the Cold War." My father? An unsung hero of the Cold War? I continued reading:

> In the Pantheon of super-agents, TOPHAT occupies a special place.

I set the magazine down and sat back, my mind a little blown. This clandestine life that my siblings and I knew so little about was suddenly taking form, my father's hidden career becoming visible.

The boxes revealed other items my mother had collected over the years: magazine and newspaper articles, letters, pictures. It seemed as if she'd left it all behind for us to find. When she was alive she wasn't going to reveal much, but she wanted us to know all the same.

So, my father had been intimately involved with the longest-running, highest-ranking Soviet asset in the history of the Cold War. This was incredible news to take in. But who was this general, this top Soviet spy? What was the nature of his relationship with my father? What political impact did their collaboration have? I wondered, too, what kind of life the Russian general had led. Did he have children our age? What was it like for them to grow up in the Soviet Union with a spy for a father? And what was the betrayal the magazine spoke of?

Discovering my father's partnership with a Russian spy opened a door for me. The early loss of my father had left a void that I hadn't fully processed. My siblings and I didn't speak to each other about it much—we preferred to bring to mind the joyful memories of him in our young years rather than dwell on the regret of his absence in our adult lives. But enough time had passed, and this new evidence of my father's past gave me an opportunity to dispel that regret by learning more about my father's secret life, and the life of this top Soviet asset who had been his partner in espionage.

The story that follows is the result of my efforts to find out. It's drawn from interviews with more than eighteen of my father's former CIA colleagues and other intelligence professionals; from research by investigative reporters, spy book writers, and other specialists; from CIA and FBI reports; and from various media from Russia and the former Soviet Union. By far my most cherished source was TOPHAT's son, Alexander, who, I discovered, had immigrated to the United States and was willing to share his memories with me.

This, then, is a story about families and heroes, and about one of the Cold War's enduring, and important, secret histories.

SPIES IN THE FAMILY

CHAPTER 1

AMERIKA

Captain Dmitri Fedorovich Polyakov, artillery officer, near the end of World War II. *(Courtesy of Alexander Polyakov)*

In the spring of 1951, a Soviet battle cruiser, the *Molotov*, slid into a berth on the Hudson River on New York's Upper West Side. Once she was fully docked, a small group of Russian military and diplomatic officials disembarked, among them Lt. Col. Dmitri Fedorovich Polyakov; his wife, Nina; and their three-year-old son, Igor.

They were among the privileged. With the Iron Curtain firmly in place since the end of World War II, only certain Soviet citizens were allowed to travel, and they tended to be the best and the brightest. Some, usually the athletes and artists, were carefully watched so they wouldn't defect. Others, the diplomats and official representatives, were more trusted. The Polyakovs were among the latter.

In his first foreign posting with the Soviet military, thirty-year-old Lieutenant Colonel Polyakov was a newly appointed member of the Soviet Mission to the United Nations Security Council Military Staff Committee. At least, that was his official role. His real job was as a spy.

Polyakov was a military intelligence officer in the Soviets' largest foreign intelligence agency, the GRU. The Glavnoye Razvedyvatel'noye Upravleniye, or Main Intelligence Directorate, complemented and sometimes rivaled the better-known KGB.

While the KGB and GRU both employed spies, each had its own distinct mission. The KGB's primary task was internal security, that is, spying on and suppressing domestic dissidents and closely watching foreigners who might express anti-Soviet sentiments or commit anti-Soviet activities: journalists, tourists, but most of all the diplomats and intelligence personnel of the capitalist enemies. The GRU, conversely, focused on external threats and stealing military technology. Like the CIA, it deployed its agents overseas in an ongoing endeavor to gather external intelligence. As a result, its force of spies working foreign targets was far larger than that of the KGB.

In the 1950s, with the wartime alliance between Russia and the West abandoned, the tension and mistrust that ruled the relationship between the Soviets and Americans pervaded their societies as well. Soviet propaganda portrayed America as a cesspool of drugs, crime, and sinister capitalist exploitation. In America, McCarthyism was at its height and the term *Communist* was fast becoming a slur. By the early 1950s, the GRU was focused like a laser on what was then being called the "Main Enemy," the United States of America. Dmitri, Nina, and little Igor Polyakov had landed in this alien world, one that was both alluring, with its bustle, its skyscrapers, and its abundance of consumer goods, and ominous as the nucleus of international aggression and anti-Soviet subversion and hatred.

The Polyakovs were assigned a small apartment on Manhattan's Upper West Side, in a building occupied mainly by Soviet families from the United Nations. Exploring their new neighborhood, they were fascinated by the food stores, shops, and restaurants, the bright lights and electric energy of the city, such a contrast to the dismal gray of Stalinist Moscow.

Polyakov's English was good but not fluent. Although he'd been preparing for this assignment for years, he spent his first months in America working with a special tutor to sharpen his language skills and become more familiar with the customs and habits of American life—what clothes to buy and how to wear them, questions of etiquette, even how to make small talk. He would need those skills for his work at the United Nations, attending General Assembly meetings, advising Russian diplomats on military affairs, and interacting with his counterparts in other countries' delegations. But he needed them even more for his real job: stealing secret information.

Lieutenant Colonel Polyakov's undercover GRU assignment was to run a network of "illegals," spies the Soviets had slipped into the country with forged or stolen passports and identification. Posing as U.S. citizens, they came with fabricated backgrounds, life stories, or "legends," about who they were, where they'd grown up, where they'd gone to school, and where they'd worked, all of it memorized. They kept low profiles and acted like ordinary citizens, integrating themselves into the fabric of American life.

Illegals had instructions to get access, especially, to technology industries, universities, and laboratories. Through the information they stole, Russia made quick progress copying America's advanced technology. The designs of Soviet bombers, submarines, missiles, and weapons systems were accelerated and improved by access to stolen American technical designs, saving tens of billions of rubles in research and development.

Dmitri Polyakov's diplomatic cover didn't fool the FBI, which had identified him as a probable intelligence officer from the moment he arrived. The Bureau knew that the Soviet delegation's military attaché position would likely be filled by a GRU officer, and therefore a spy. For the FBI's Counterintelligence Division, Dmitri Polyakov was a person of considerable interest from day one.

Polyakov worked out of the stately redbrick Soviet Mission at 680 Park Avenue, across the street from Hunter College. One of the floors within the mission contained the clandestine offices of the GRU *rezidentura*, its base in New York. (Polyakov was the GRU's deputy *rezident*, or deputy chief.)

Among the second-floor classrooms and offices of the Hunter College building across the street was a sealed room with an unobstructed view of the entrances to the Soviet Mission. The FBI rented the room from the college, no questions asked. From there, the agents could look down on and photograph everyone who came and went through the mission's doors, including Polyakov, whose arrival each morning was recorded by his FBI watchers. Whenever he left the building, a radio call went out from the sealed room to watchers on the street, and tails fell into place behind Polyakov. In fact, hundreds of FBI agents in surveillance and investigative teams worked the Soviet target, which included others from the United Nations Mission as well as Polyakov.

One of those watchers was Ed Moody, a young FBI special agent who had been assigned to cover Polyakov. This was Moody's first major assignment, and he was determined to make his mark by catching Polyakov in the act of espionage. Accordingly, Moody followed Polyakov everywhere, noting where he went and when, learning his habits and timing, keeping track of any contacts he made, all the while trying to distinguish innocent encounters and activities from suspicious ones.

Special Agent Moody was also trolling for vulnerabilities. FBI counterintelligence looked for Russians who might be susceptible to recruitment. Getting a Soviet intelligence officer to give up or sell precious secrets didn't happen often, but when it did, it was considered a major coup.

Counterintelligence agents were keenly attuned to behavior that might signal that a Russian could be turned. At home, Russians were used to standing in line to buy standard consumer items or scarce food commodities, whereas in New York, market shelves were full and liquor and luxury goods were widely available. Had a Russian been buying things (gold earrings for a wife or girlfriend, a stereo system for himself) that were beyond his means? If he had, where was the money coming from? Was he gambling, stealing from office accounts, or in debt? Was the Russian an alcoholic, visiting prostitutes, cheating on his wife, or a homosexual? Could he be blackmailed? And to keep his superiors from learning of these susceptibilities (a situation that would surely result in an immediate return to Moscow and likely the loss of his job or worse), would he become an agent for the Americans? Approaching someone who might be responsive was, in FBI terms, a "courtship." Could Dmitri Polyakov be courted?

Special Agent Moody scrutinized Polyakov's movements, looking for signs of tradecraft: a quick brush pass handoff in a crowd, a surreptitious exchange of a small item at a coffee shop counter, picking up an envelope from one of his illegals at a dead drop (a hiding place where messages or intelligence could be left or collected). But Moody saw nothing. As a well-trained intelligence officer, Polyakov knew when he was being tailed, and was skilled at hiding his tradecraft. Moody noted another thing: Polyakov was particularly good at "going black," that is, giving the FBI the slip. Also, to all appearances, he was a devoted family man who didn't smoke and rarely drank. All this Moody noted in his file on Polyakov.

The Polyakovs, c. 1957. *Left to right:* Alexander, Dmitri, Petr, and Nina. *(Courtesy of Sandy Grimes)*

★

Three months after the Polyakovs arrived in New York, tragedy struck the family. With their husbands at work, Nina and the other Russian women in the residential building would go to Central Park where the children could run around and cool off in the summer heat, wading in the little corners of the lakes and ponds. One day in August, three-year-old Igor began to throw up. He also had a fever, and complained that his neck hurt. It was polio. In the late 1940s and early '50s parents lived in fear of the summer polio season. One way the virus was thought to be contracted was through stagnant water in ponds or lakes. Two major outbreaks took place in 1951 and 1952, when more than fifty thousand cases were reported in the United States, resulting in thousands of fatalities. The polio vaccine was still five years away.

Igor's symptoms were grave, and over time they worsened. His muscles weakened, and his cognitive ability seemed to be affected. Nina and Dmitri had all the medical assistance they needed, but there was little anyone could do other than to make him as comfortable as possible. (Years later it was widely reported, in both the American and Russian press, that Igor died shortly thereafter in New York City. But, in fact, he lived to the age of seventeen.)

Despite this period of personal misery, Polyakov's career as a spy handler was going well. His illegals were producing, and he was regularly channeling useful reports back to Moscow Center. In 1953 he was promoted to full colonel.

Also that year, the Polyakovs celebrated the birth of a second son, Alexander, named after Dmitri's mother, Alexandra. Another baby boy was born two years later, named after Nina's father, Petr Kiselev, a colonel who had been Polyakov's commander during the war. Colonel Kiselev and Polyakov had fought side by side in the frozen forests of Finnish Karelia, and again during the war's last major German offensive, the Nazis' Operation Spring Awakening, on the shores of Hungary's Lake Balaton. The two men had created a bond then that only the desperation of war can forge.

Polyakov and Petr Kiselev came home from the war as heroes—the colonel with the Order of Lenin, the Soviet Union's highest medal for valor, and Polyakov with the Order of the Patriotic War and Order of the Red Star for gallantry in action. Dmitri Polyakov had not only proven his courage, but demonstrated an ability to think creatively under pressure and to lead men in battle. As a result, he was offered a place in the Frunze Military Academy, Moscow's prestigious general staff college. One of his class's top graduates, he was then recruited into the GRU for advanced training as an intelligence operative, which readied him for clandestine warfare against his country's new enemy: the United States of America.

★

By 1956 the Polyakovs had been living in the United States for five years. Their youngest sons, Alexander and Petr, had never been to Russia, and Dmitri and Nina had become acclimated to American life. Nina had studied English at Moscow State University; Polyakov's language skills were improving, and he had deepened his knowledge of American history and political culture. But as Polyakov's tour in the United States was coming to an end and the family prepared to return to Moscow, the seeds had likely been planted for what was to be the most momentous decision of his life.

FBI special agent Ed Moody registered Polyakov's return to the USSR in July 1956. Without having collected any incriminating evidence on him, Moody closed his file and put it away.

CHAPTER 2

REDSOX

Mom and Dad (Anne and Paul Dillon) at a fair in Kempten, outside Munich, Germany, 1951. Dad's army uniform was part of his cover. At the time of this picture he was working for the CIA on REDSOX, an operation that recruited Soviet refugees to be parachuted back into their homelands as informants. *(Author's collection)*

In the early fall of 1951, Dad had some news for my mother: We're moving to Kempten, Germany, he told her, a little town not far from Munich, in the Bavarian Alps.

This was a year after my father had been recruited by the CIA and a few months after their wedding. He was twenty-five years old and had spent an exhaustive year training in spy craft:

surveillance, counterintelligence, evasion and escape, infiltration-exfiltration, and paramilitary operations. He had also been taking intensive Russian classes at the Navy Language School in the Anacostia neighborhood of DC. For months, Mom and Dad had been awaiting news of an assignment, Dad's first overseas posting, and now the day had arrived.

★

Dad had joined the Marine Corps in 1944, right out of Boston College High, the Jesuit preparatory school to which his parish had given him a scholarship. He had needed the scholarship because his family had financial problems. Dad's father was a well-educated accountant, but also an alcoholic who would disappear for weeks or even months. Worse, following one of his binges, he was accused of armed robbery and spent six years in jail, beginning in Dad's junior year in high school. As a consequence, my father worked to support the family with a job delivering ice and milk in the mornings before school. The oldest of five children, he was a father figure to his brothers and sisters, and his mother's essential partner as she struggled to keep the family afloat.

The Marine Corps posted Dad to Hawaii, but it was toward the end of the war, and he never saw action. The most exciting thing we children heard about his military experiences was when he had to outrun a tidal wave that hit the Hawaiian Islands and killed 159 locals. He ran as fast as he could, he told us, and climbed on top of a parked train, the water rushing underneath. We were fascinated, of course, imagining a hundred-foot-high wall of water smashing the train off its tracks and Dad swimming for his life past uprooted palm trees and floating cars.

In 1946, Dad came home and entered Boston College on the GI Bill, continuing with the Jesuit education that would set his life's moral compass. He excelled in languages, especially Latin; he also studied philosophy and theology, and attended Mass every

Sunday and Wednesday. He told his parents he wanted to become a priest, but in his senior year he was recruited by the CIA, a lay career perhaps more fitting for a man who would go on to father seven children.

My parents met at a cocktail party in Georgetown. She was proper, well mannered, and quiet, with a soft southern accent she was trying to lose; he was charismatic, charming, and outgoing, with a strong Boston accent he wasn't aware of. They married in 1951. The *Savannah Morning News* noted that my mother "made a charming picture in an afternoon dress of white embroidered organdy over pale yellow with a yellow sash." The paper said nothing about the bridegroom's employment. "If you have to say anything," Mom had advised her parents earlier in a letter, "you may say he is employed by the Defense Department, which isn't true, confidentially, but is what he is supposed to say."

★

Despite having to resign from her work at the *Middle East Journal*, a job she'd enjoyed since moving up from Georgia, Mom loved living in Germany. Settled in Kempten, she wrote home about the beautiful Bavarian countryside, the quaint and charming German towns, the friendly neighbors who helped her settle in and shop. "Kempten is surrounded by dairy country," she wrote to her mother. "On Paul's days off we take drives out on the mountain roads, or take picnics and go swimming in the big green rivers along the valley floors."

Still, it wasn't all picturesque. When they drove into Munich, eighty miles northeast, Dad and Mom could see evidence of the ugly cost of the hard-fought war. Mom was shocked at the sight of bombed-out buildings being rebuilt and the rubble-strewn areas yet to be cleaned up.

Like the other CIA officers he worked with, my father was under army cover and wore an army uniform. His brother, who actually *was* in the army, once came to visit from his post in Frankfurt, and Dad picked him up at the train station. On the crowded platform, Uncle Dick started teasing his civilian brother. "Nice uniform, Paul. How'd you earn it?" Dad quickly hushed him up.

Unlike the experienced and sophisticated Russian and British intelligence services operating in one form or another for over fifty years, in 1951 the CIA was still a new organization. President Harry Truman had created it in 1947 after he closed down the Office of Strategic Services (OSS), the nation's World War II clandestine service. My father was one of many new officers the CIA was aggressively recruiting to get up to speed against the increasingly adversarial Soviet Union.

By the time Dad was posted to Kempten, the Soviets had consolidated control over the countries they had fought through during the Red Army's push toward Berlin, and had replaced local governments with Communist regimes. Masses of refugees were fleeing to the West. Almost 170,000 crossed the West German border the year Dad arrived, almost 200,000 the year after. The Allies (Americans, British, French) set up special camps in West Germany to house and process the human tide of the bewildered and displaced.

Most of these refugees simply wanted to get away from the grim police-state regimes that had descended on their homelands. Yet others were open to going back to do something about it. These were the people the CIA was looking for as it monitored the refugee camps, the people my father had been sent to Kempten to train as spies for America. The newly minted CIA viewed the suppressed and embittered refugees as potential recruits for its plans for subversion, propaganda, and armed resistance against the Communist states. Individuals and teams could be inserted into the Soviet Bloc, even into the USSR itself, to gather intelligence, stimulate dissidence, support and even, perhaps, provide leadership to developing anticommunist, anti-Soviet resistance cells.

Coincidentally, Dad's first intelligence assignment was the same as Polyakov's: training illegals and inserting them into the enemy's country. But while America's open society made slipping Soviet spies into the United States relatively easy, the closed borders and secret police forces of the Soviets and their satellites made sending U.S. spies into Soviet territory not just more difficult, but mortally dangerous.

Despite the dangers, the CIA developed an operation codenamed REDSOX. My father's job was to train suitable candidates recruited from the refugee centers in paramilitary skills and tradecraft (methods he had so recently learned himself) and send them back into their native lands. He would then be their liaison for radio communications back and forth. Unlike Polyakov's illegals, who had little trouble entering the United States using expertly forged passports, REDSOX agents would have to parachute in by night or be smuggled across heavily patrolled borders.

CIA recruiters in the Munich-area refugee camp sent candidates down to Kaufbeuren, a town half an hour's drive from Kempten, for the operation. Small groups of Russians, Belorussians, Moldavians, Estonians, Poles, Latvians, Lithuanians, and Bulgarians were vetted for their suitability. In the mornings, Dad would drive the half hour from the house in Kempten to an abandoned Luftwaffe airbase outside Kaufbeuren that housed the REDSOX program. In one of the airplane hangars, the Agency had installed a high platform for parachute jump training. In nearby houses, the agent trainees took classes in operating radios for communicating with their handlers, transmitting Morse code, and encrypting messages.

The CIA recruits faced a full curriculum that included map reading, compass runs, unarmed combat, and weapons skills. One class was called Introduction: Personal Qualifications of a Conspirator, which included instruction in creating alibis and cover stories, understanding concealment methods and surveillance techniques, and learning how to create credible disguises. The recruits studied

Soviet organizations they would be expected to know about (the Party, the army, sports teams) and were instructed in the advantages of democracy and freedom so they could muster recruitment arguments if and when they needed them.

During the actual operation, the agents would be dropped near forests, where they would hide until they could change clothes, bury their extra gear, and emerge as normal citizens. Accordingly, the recruits trained for a week in the German forests of Grafenwoehr. There, they were expected to jump and land wearing 130 pounds of equipment: two radios and a pedal-driven generator to provide the radios with power; an air force survival vest containing three days' rations; a first-aid kit; a shotgun and a pistol; a mosquito head net and mosquito repellent; dog repellent; a razor, compass, maps, and a pocket knife; pills with special ink for secret writing; pencils and a notebook; a shovel; Soviet clothes to be put on before leaving the woods; Soviet cigarettes; and a well-worn suitcase to carry their radios.

Like Polyakov's spies, the Americans' agents-in-training also had to learn their fabricated biographies until they knew them inside out. A declassified secret CIA report described the training and experience of one of the parachute teams: One agent trainee had supposedly been a truck driver on a kolkhoz collective farm who had turned his truck over in a ditch, lost his license, and was granted permission to leave the farm so he could look for work elsewhere. Now he was trying his luck in Moscow. Another was posing as a gardener who'd been working on a collective farm in Ukraine, where he'd had an affair with the daughter of the head of the kolkhoz, who released him when his contract expired. Now he was heading back to his native Belorussia in search of employment. A third trainee would try to get to Leningrad and enter its underworld. His *carte d'entrée* was his expertise as a forger, and he was carrying the tools of his trade with him: inks, drawing instruments, tracing papers, and sample blank documents. Once established, he was to send back information on how to live illegally in Russia. Along with the necessary IDs and other documentation, all agent trainees were equipped with a money belt with rubles and a small bag of gold coins for bribing officials.

The CIA report explained what happened when that team of three agent trainees was launched. The drop site was to be a forested area in Belorussia. The three men were going to parachute in together; then each would head for his target city: the unemployed "truck driver" to Moscow, the "gardener" to Minsk, and the "forger" to Leningrad. As soon as they landed, they would bury their parachutes and get as far away from the drop zone as they could. One of them would radio back a one-letter Morse signal, indicating that all was well. At daylight, they were to lie low, then break up at night and head in their respective directions.

When the departure time came, they were driven at night to an army airfield outside Wiesbaden where they boarded a Douglas C-54 Skymaster. On the plane, they donned their parachutes and gripped their bundles. "We've entered history," one of them said to the jumpmaster.

The C-54 flew eastward, crossing East Germany, Czechoslovakia, and Poland, finally entering Soviet airspace over what is now Belarus. For six hours they went undetected, even when they crossed the Poland/USSR border. Then, somewhere between Slonim and Baranovichi, the side doors of the big plane opened and the three men jumped into the night.

Back at the REDSOX base, radio operators listened intently for the "all is well" signal, but none came. No one panicked; there was more than one likely explanation. The radios may have broken loose from the pack boards and been lost or smashed; or perhaps the team had landed too close to habitation and couldn't move. One of them might have been hurt in the jump. The plane had flown six hours to the drop zone and six hours back with no interference: no scrambled fighters, no flak, no sightings of anything out of the ordinary. No one had tracked them; no one could have anticipated the drop zone or seen the jumpers in the dead of night. The three were most likely hunkered down and waiting to move.

Yet time passed, and they were still not heard from. What had happened to them, or where they might be, was a mystery.

Meanwhile, the agent preparation continued. REDSOX and its related programs were viewed as long-term operations. It might take months, perhaps years, for inserted agents to establish themselves and begin sending back intelligence. My father and the other CIA trainers worked with team after team, through three months of hard preparation and then the insertions, mainly by air, with the big Skymasters lumbering unnoticed through Eastern Bloc nighttime skies and delivering the jumpers.

Ominously, though, not a single one of those teams was ever heard from. Over a two-year period, at least fifty agent teams were trained and sent off, and the Agency listeners heard nothing. What had happened to them?

"I was puzzled," said John Bogart, a REDSOX colleague of Dad's. "It bugged me, and I didn't quite understand that of all the agent groups that were being dispatched into the Soviet Union, I never heard of a single success."

Agent training was an intense and intimate experience, one in which handlers and trainees became very close. And every three months or so, my father was sending a new team off into what must have increasingly seemed like a black hole.

I asked Bogart why, if they never heard back from the agents, did they keep sending one team after another, for months? For years?

"It was hoped that these guys were getting established," he told me. "It would take time for them to get integrated into a community and go out and seek the information we wanted. So, we were giving them the benefit of the doubt."

I had a hard time imagining my father giving his refugee agents the benefit of that kind of doubt—these men he'd trained, whose faith and trust he'd fostered, whom he'd presumably grown close to and who had then simply disappeared. The silence must have weighed heavily on him.

In a report attached to one of my father's CIA job evaluations from that period, he had written his own assessment. There, under the heading "Mental Demands," Dad had reported: "It is my opinion that the mental demands of my position have been considerable for the following reasons: ████, ████, and ████."

Dad's explanation had been redacted—hidden by CIA censors. So, while I can't know for certain why my father felt that the mental demands were "considerable," I think he was agonizing over what his lost agents might have been going through. He was sensing, if not knowing, the worst.

★

My father standing before Haus der Kulturen der Welt (House of the World's Cultures) in Tiergarten Park, Berlin. *(Author's collection)*

Years later, in 1963, the CIA found out definitively what had happened, and the news sent shock waves through intelligence agencies around the world. During the time of the agent drops, at the Agency's Washington headquarters, James Angleton, the soon-to-be head of counterintelligence and then deputy of the Special Operations Office overseeing the REDSOX program, was sharing all the REDSOX details with his British Secret Intelligence Service counterpart, Harold Adrian Russell "Kim" Philby. There was nothing untoward in this, except that Kim Philby was not what he seemed.

Information sharing between the CIA and Britain's Secret Intelligence Service, known popularly as MI6, was customary. The British and American spy agencies worked closely together on most operations against the Soviets, and the British were sending their own agents behind the Iron Curtain to collect intelligence and attempt to destabilize Communist governments. Because the British and American agencies were running parallel programs in overlapping regions, they needed precise information about each other's activities. The liaison person between the two agencies for the flow of this information was MI6's Kim Philby.

Angleton and Philby had become friends during World War II, when, as a young OSS officer, Angleton was sent to London to train with the much more experienced MI6. The Americans were intelligence amateurs then, and MI6's veterans were their teachers, including the already prominent Philby, by then a highly accomplished professional, having run wartime spy networks against the Germans in Spain, Portugal, Italy, and North Africa. Philby was a scion of the upper class, charming, cheerful, well mannered, and immensely likable. His career was on the fast track. Some believed he was being groomed to be head of MI6.

The Americans coming for intelligence training were beholden to their mentors, absorbing the Britons' advanced tradecraft methods and techniques. James Angleton was highly intelligent, with an intense, exotic personality. Among the neophyte intelligence officers who had shown up for instruction in the MI6 offices, he stood out, attracting Kim Philby's attention.

Like Angleton, Philby possessed a subtle, searching intellect, one drawn naturally to the jigsaw-puzzle world of counterintelligence. It was no wonder, then, that he and Angleton would be attracted to each other. Philby was Angleton's main tutor in counterintelligence, and Angleton looked up to him.

In May 1949, Kim Philby was posted to Washington, DC, to work with Angleton on shared British-American intelligence matters. And share they did. Philby and Angleton lunched regularly at Harvey's, famous as the favorite watering hole of Washington's power elite. Their long martini-doused lunches were taken up with the mutually enjoyable exchange of secrets and spy gossip. Philby's relationship with Angleton put the former in a position to know everything about American operations against the Soviets, including REDSOX. And what Philby knew, the KGB knew almost as quickly. For at least fifteen years since the early '30s, MI6's Kim Philby had been an agent for the Soviets.

"Philby was responsible for passing on the timing and geographical coordinates from one intelligence agency to another," wrote Ben Macintyre in *A Spy Among Friends*, and James Angleton was unwittingly giving Philby the dates, times, and parachute drop coordinates of the CIA's Kaufbeuren-trained refugee agents.

That knowledge sealed the fates of my father's spy teams and those of his colleagues. "I do not know what happened to the parties concerned," Kim Philby later wrote in his memoir, *My Silent War*, from the leisure of his retirement in Moscow, "but I can make an informed guess."

John Bogart was more direct. "They were met by Soviet security people and shot on the spot." Then, more bitterly, he added, "They cleaned our clocks."

CHAPTER 3

THE GENERAL AND THE SPY

Dmitri Polyakov with son Alexander, New York, 1960. The blue Ford Fairlane was purchased by the Soviet UN Mission for Polyakov's personal use in his covert mission of managing Soviet illegals. *(Courtesy of Edward Moody)*

One day in October 1959, in his New York City field office, FBI special agent Ed Moody picked up his phone to hear the excited voice of one of the watchers monitoring the Soviet Mission from the secret room at Hunter College across the street.

"He's back!"

"Who's back?" Moody asked.

"Our old friend Dmitri Polyakov," replied the watcher.

Since Polyakov's July 1956 return to the Soviet Union, Moody hadn't expected him to return to America; the GRU and KGB didn't often send their agents back for a second tour. They usually didn't trust their own people enough to risk their becoming too attached to the enemy's way of life.

Now Moody began tailing Polyakov again, even more determined to catch him out. This time around, the Soviet was driving a car, a new blue Ford Fairlane. Moody traced the license plate and tax records; the Soviets had bought it for him. This was truly rare: Russians from the mission were generally required to make their way around the city in groups, so they could keep an eye on one another. But Polyakov was moving about independently, and now, with a car, he could do so more widely.

Moody was impressed. This is a person they trust, he thought. In a memo to Director of the FBI J. Edgar Hoover, Moody noted, "Polyakov is an astute, intelligent, shrewd, and fully Americanized Soviet intelligence officer held in high esteem by his superiors. He is probably the most important Soviet intelligence officer assigned to the Soviet Delegation in the U.S. at this time."

The whole Polyakov family was back in New York, except for Igor. Too debilitated by polio symptoms to travel, he had stayed behind with his grandparents. Dmitri, Nina, Alexander, and Petr moved again into an apartment on the Upper West Side, this time in the Cameron, a stately older building on West Eighty-Sixth Street populated mostly by residents from the Soviet Mission. The new apartment was spacious, with two big bedrooms and an even larger living room.

At three, Petr was likely too young to appreciate the difference between this and the cramped Moscow apartment the family had shared with Grandpa and Grandma Kiselev, but six-year-old Alexander thought he was in heaven, especially because the apartment had a huge television set. In Moscow, Grandpa Kiselev had used his military connections to purchase a TV, but the screen had been so tiny that it needed a large water-filled lens attachment to magnify the image. Even so, propaganda programs and the talking heads of Party officials describing the fulfillment of the current five-year plan had been Alexander's only viewing options. Now there were cartoons and cowboy movies on a big screen. And on the street, so many cars. He'd never seen so many cars! He marveled at the difference between Moscow's dead-silent nights and the electric liveliness of New York City's evening clamor, the honking and sirens and the excitement of their new neighborhood.

Alexander attended the small Russian grade school attached to the Soviet Mission on Park Avenue, and on weekends his father took him and Petr to Central Park to practice shooting with the bow-and-arrow set he'd bought them, or to Macy's, where there was an entire floor filled with toys.

Polyakov took up the same UN diplomatic responsibilities he had handled last time, again a cover for his spymaster job of supervising the network of Soviet illegals. Special Agent Moody, in a memo to his supervisor, had no doubt about what Polyakov was up to:

> He has been identified as a Staff Officer of the Soviet Military Intelligence service (GRU), a member of the "Illegals Directorate" assigned . . . for the purpose of assisting illegal intelligence activities in the US. . . . It is felt that Polyakov is in possession of a vast amount of intelligence information concerning Soviet agents, their schooling, identity, and their operations both in the U.S. and abroad.

Moody's analysis was even more on target than he knew. During Polyakov's time back in Moscow, he had served as chief of the GRU department that trained illegals for America. Now that he had returned, he was running these agents in their fabricated American lives.

Among Polyakov's spies was one Ivan Egorov, and his wife,

Alexandra. Ivan had succeeded in getting himself hired as a personnel administrator at the UN Secretariat. Another husband-and-wife team of illegals, the Sokolovs, operated under the names of Robert Baltch and Joy Ann Garber. (The real Robert Baltch was a Catholic priest in upstate New York; the real Joy Ann Garber was a housewife in Connecticut.) "Robert Baltch" (whose father had been a White Russian Army officer who'd fled to France after the revolution) taught French at George Washington University.

The mission for both the Egorovs and Sokolovs was to obtain American defense secrets and pass them on to Polyakov, who in turn would forward them to Moscow Center. One of the locations Polyakov and his network used to post signals was in front of the iconic Tavern on the Green in Central Park. The restaurant kept a signboard next to the pedestrian walkway to post menus and announcements. It was easy enough for Polyakov or one of his spies to stroll by, stop for a moment to look at the signboard, and inconspicuously push in a thumbtack: red to signal that a dead drop was ready to be filled; white, that the drop was filled and ready to be picked up; or yellow (a danger signal), a tail had been spotted—abort the mission. "Later on, [the Soviet handlers] came by and just removed them real easy," Ed Moody said of the thumbtacks. "Nobody was interested in them; [it] wasn't unusual to see something on a sign in New York City. People were always messing up signs with graffiti or their own messages."

Polyakov's most prized spy was a man named Kaarlo Tuomi, an illegal whom he had trained in Moscow and sent to New York. Tuomi was born in Michigan to Finnish parents, and like many other Finns who immigrated to the United States at the time, his stepfather was a socialist who became a true believer in communism. In 1933, when Tuomi was sixteen, his stepfather moved the family to Russia, part of a large group of Finnish Communists who had immigrated first to the United States and then to the USSR to help build communism.

The family settled in Russian Karelia, on the border with Finland, and became Soviet citizens. Then, in 1937, during the height of the Stalinist purges, the KGB came in the middle of the night and took Tuomi's stepfather away, most likely because he had earlier lived in the United States. Tuomi never saw him again.

After a stint in the Red Army during the war, Tuomi enrolled in a foreign languages institute, in the hope of becoming a professor of English, but it was not to be. His colloquial, unaccented English, a rare ability for Soviet citizens, attracted the attention of GRU recruiters looking for potential illegals. As a former American who had lived for years in the USSR and had proven his loyalty, Tuomi was an ideal candidate. Also, he wasn't given much choice; the most sought after deep-cover trainee was a person who could pass for the enemy.

As an apprentice spy, Kaarlo Tuomi spent three years studying U.S. history, geography, politics, economics, and the military. He practiced the idiomatic American English that had evolved since he left the United States, watching American films, reading American popular authors, and absorbing American culture, politics, and sports. He was also trained in intelligence tactics: cryptography, photography, secret writing, and surveillance.

Polyakov, with his own recent experience living in New York City, was Tuomi's instructor during the final six months of his training in the USSR. Then he told Tuomi he was being assigned to New York, and that, once there, he was to concentrate on the waterfront, finding out what he could about the movement of military matériel and troops through New York Harbor. He helped Tuomi create his legend, using as much from his student's Michigan upbringing as they could. They worked together on Tuomi's legend for weeks, as the Finn memorized the details of where he'd supposedly lived and worked. Polyakov sent Tuomi on a trial run to Western Europe, to play the role of an American tourist. His performance was flawless. Of all the illegals coming through

Polyakov's deep-cover school, the American-born Tuomi came closest to being the perfect spy.

In the final days of 1958, Polyakov saw Tuomi off at Moscow's Sheremetyevo Airport. Tuomi would fly to Canada and take a train into the United States. The departure had been difficult. Tuomi was leaving behind his wife and three children, a painful sacrifice in dedication to his country. Many illegals served lifetime assignments; he was forty-one years old and knew it was likely that he would never see them again.

Once in the United States, Tuomi first spent time reacquainting himself with his old hometown in Michigan, visiting the locations where, according to his legend, he had lived and worked. Polyakov had instructed him to take his time, to get to know his fake American life like a new skin. He was told to get a driver's license, open a bank account, enroll in business classes, and get certification as a bookkeeper—all this before he made his way to New York.

Tuomi applied himself, closely following his instructions and building his bona fides as an American. Shortly after he arrived in New York he succeeded in landing a bookkeeping job on the Brooklyn waterfront with A.L. Burbank, a large shipping and handling corporation. It was exactly the kind of job his Soviet handlers had hoped for, both the business itself and the location. As planned, Tuomi could now watch the docks for the movement of military supplies.

By the time Polyakov returned to New York for his second tour, Tuomi had established himself. Now his instructor became his handler. Strict operational security meant that the two rarely met in person. Instead, they communicated via dead drops throughout the city.

Servicing dead drops and leaving signals for Tuomi and the others in his network of spies, Polyakov was a master of the cat-and-mouse game of shadowed and shadower. With his new car, it was easier for him to attend to dead drop and signal sites out in Fort

Tryon and in Queens under the Kosciuszko Bridge. If a personal encounter was necessary, Polyakov could drive to an isolated spot for a rendezvous.

FBI special agent Ed Moody and his squad followed Polyakov everywhere, but New York City's traffic, construction, and even stoplights often worked against them. Polyakov could make a quick turn in his blue Ford while his followers were caught at the light, or slip through an intersection just before it was blocked with traffic. His adeptness frustrated Moody and his colleagues, but the FBI agents had their own tricks. Given the opportunity, Moody would drop a rolled-up condom into the Fairlane's gas tank. In ten minutes or so, the condom would be sucked down into the fuel feeder line to stall Polyakov's car, giving the surveillance team time to catch up. Moody's people also regularly broke one of the car's taillights, making the Fairlane easier to spot at night in heavy traffic. They even got the police to write dozens of parking tickets while Polyakov was parked outside the Soviet Mission.

All the hassling exasperated Polyakov. He was, after all, a diplomat, with rights. He complained to the UN security officer about the treatment he was getting and asked for protection against the unlawful actions of the New York City cops.

While Moody and his squad did everything they could to track Polyakov, they were unaware that they themselves were being tracked. The Russians had discovered the FBI's radio frequency and were monitoring the chatter among the agents tailing their assets. Polyakov often knew how many agents were following him and where they were. Moody and his FBI bosses had no clue that their every conversation was being monitored, though they wondered how it was that their target seemed so often able to anticipate their moves and elude them.

Sometimes the chase took them out to Rye Beach, on the shore of Long Island Sound, north of Manhattan. Soviets in New York were not allowed to travel beyond a twenty-five-mile radius from the city, and the beach town of Rye was just within that limit. Polyakov negotiated the rental of a little beach cottage where Nina and the boys could go during the summer and he could come out on the weekends. After Polyakov met with the owner for an initial interview, Ed Moody, who had clandestinely observed this transaction, paid his own visit to the landlord.

Moody was intrigued by the landlord's account of his conversation with Polyakov. The two had discussed the recent July 1960 incident of an American RB-47 stratojet on a reconnaissance mission that had been shot down by the Soviets, who claimed the plane had violated their airspace. "Polyakov commented that he was very sorry about the death of the flyers," Moody wrote in his report on what the landlord told him. "He remarked that war was the last thing 'they' wanted, as he has experienced war."

Polyakov made other interesting remarks. He told the landlord that he was "very impressed with the U.S.," that he "liked the lay of the land," that he was "concerned about the thought of sending his boy back to Moscow to school," and that he "would like to keep the boy with him in the U.S." The landlord had noted, too, that Polyakov was driving a new American car and wearing stylish American clothes.

Moody was surprised that a veteran GRU officer would offer comments like these—Soviets were habitually circumspect and restrained around Americans. Maybe, Moody thought, he was getting a peek into the inner workings of the Russian's mind. Could it be possible that something was shifting in Polyakov's thinking, an ideological evolution that might affect his loyalty?

★

In the spring of 1960, Polyakov picked up a message from a dead drop. The message that day was from Kaarlo Tuomi. It contained, in code, the usual information about what Tuomi was seeing on the Brooklyn waterfront. Yet, scribbled in the cramped empty space at the top of the paper was an alarming note, written in haste: Tuomi had been caught and turned by the FBI. He was under its control, and it had forced him to become a double agent. The information he was supplying was being planted by the Americans.

Tuomi had in fact been arrested months earlier, only a few weeks after he arrived in the United States. In fact, the FBI had been waiting for him. Agents had followed and watched him as he went about familiarizing himself with the locations in his legend. On March 9, 1959, Tuomi was in Chicago after having spent time reacquainting himself with his birthplace in Michigan, and was approached on the street by two men. "Hello, Kaarlo," one of them said. It was the greeting he feared the most.

Tuomi's undoing was a letter he had sent during his training in Moscow, to his uncle in America, on orders of his supervisors. The letter asked his uncle for a copy of his birth certificate; it was thought that this document would deepen his legend. Yet the uncle never responded. The letter turned out to be a disastrous tactical error. The Red Scare of the 1950s was in full swing, and any letter from the USSR was suspicious, especially one from the son of an avowed Communist who had taken his family to Russia to help build the new socialist paradise. Tuomi's uncle, who had not followed his kinsmen to build the Communist utopia in Russia, had taken the letter directly to the FBI, and from that point on, Kaarlo Tuomi was on the Bureau's watch list.

Tuomi's arrest was followed by four days of intense interrogation. He tried to stick to his cover story, but it was no use—his interrogators knew too much. When he finally broke, admitting he was a spy, the FBI gave him two alternatives: go back to Russia or remain in the United States and work as an agent for the Bureau.

Going back to Russia, Tuomi knew, would be a terrible choice. "I would be convicted of treason," he wrote in the memoir he published later in his life, "the biggest crime of all . . . I would become a second-class citizen, lose my income, everything, my family would suffer. I would probably never be set free." He knew the fate of Red Army soldiers who had been captured by the Germans and repatriated after the war. Most had been sent to the gulag; many were never heard from again.

Still, the thought of taking the other option consumed Tuomi with guilt and remorse. "I struggled senselessly with myself," he wrote. "I was pressed to break my signed oaths of service to my country, which employed me and which took care of me and my family's welfare. I was pressed to surrender to the intelligence service of the country which fomented war and acted against the socialist world in every way; against the socialism that, as I had been taught, would inevitably bury the capitalist world. What could I do?"

What Tuomi did was cooperate with the FBI, which before long came to consider him one of its most valuable assets. He told the Bureau all about his training, the dead drop locations he was using in and around New York City, the codes to his secret messages, and who his controllers were, including his top controller who'd trained him back in Moscow: Dmitri Fedorovich Polyakov.

So, the Americans now knew formally what they had long assumed: that Polyakov ran illegals. Paradoxically, the confirmation of this fact protected Polyakov more than it threatened him. Because of his diplomatic immunity, the FBI couldn't arrest him; it could only expel him. Yet doing that would expose its valuable new source. Better to let Polyakov run Tuomi and allow the Bureau an inside view of the goings-on. As Tuomi explained in his memoir, "The double agent's life is, in fact, quite free. No one dares follow him too closely for the opposite party may get an inkling of the close surveillance and the utility value is gone." Tuomi was considered so important a source to the FBI that J. Edgar Hoover himself had signed off on keeping him protected and operating, in effect securing Polyakov as well.

The FBI did everything it could to make it appear to Polyakov, and Moscow Center, that Tuomi's cover and his spying efforts on behalf of the Soviets were in place and going well. Tuomi revealed to the FBI what the Soviets expected of him, and it was the FBI, rather than Tuomi himself, that had subsequently arranged the Brooklyn waterfront job at A.L. Burbank. (They'd visited Mr. Burbank personally, who'd cooperated, opening up the job for Tuomi.)

Tuomi was responsible for booking the loading and discharging of cargo, and for invoicing. He monitored the army terminal especially closely—the U.S. military shipped supplies all around the world from Brooklyn. He noted the containers and memorized the destination ports, and after work he went to the dockworkers' bars and drank with them as they talked about loading armaments, mobile weapons, and special technical equipment for observing Russian missiles. He sent regular reports back to Moscow Center, and seemed like its perfect spy, except that everything he sent was supervised by the FBI.

Moscow Center considered Tuomi a success; so did the FBI. But the misery he felt over deceiving the Soviets was tearing him apart. Finally, he decided he had to get a message back to Moscow Center somehow, telling them that he had been caught, that he was being controlled.

One evening, during a routine meeting with his handlers, the FBI dictated, and Tuomi coded, the usual message to Polyakov about what he was seeing on the Brooklyn waterfront, and the message was then sealed. The sessions with his FBI handlers sometimes involved extensive drinking, and the agents didn't notice when Tuomi excused himself to go to the bathroom and took the sealed envelope with him. Holding it over the running hot water faucet, he steamed the missive open, wrote out the emergency message in the constricted space at the top of the paper, then sealed it back up and slipped it onto the table in the meeting room without being detected.

Delivering it to the designated dead drop, Tuomi waited anxiously for the reply, but it never came. At first he was puzzled by this, but eventually he understood: Polyakov had read his message but hadn't sent it on. Doing so would have announced to his superiors that he had been running a controlled agent, that he had been relaying doctored information. The consequences of that wouldn't have been good, and Polyakov would have been putting his own career in jeopardy.

Yet, because of the nature of doubling sources, Polyakov now knew that the FBI was aware of everything in his communications with Kaarlo Tuomi. And he was going to have to play along.

With Tuomi doubled, Ed Moody's pursuit of Polyakov changed. He still tailed his asset, looking for his contacts and trying to catch him in the act, but to the FBI, Polyakov was now a letter carrier, passing Tuomi's spurious messages between the New York dead drops and Moscow.

On occasion, Ed Moody himself helped Tuomi fill Moscow Center's requests. When the Soviets learned that an American chemical company was experimenting with a special sodium-coated wire to conduct electricity, they directed Tuomi to acquire a sample. Determining that it would not harm U.S. interests, Moody obtained a piece of the wire through a contact at the chemical company, and Tuomi left it at a dead drop for Polyakov to send on to Moscow Center. The exchange made Polyakov look good. It made the FBI look good by keeping U.S. government agencies apprised of what the Soviets were after. It certainly made Tuomi look good.

It was a win-win-win all around.

★

Special Agent Moody's job was to know everything he could about Colonel Dmitri Polyakov. One way of doing that was to use "access agents," or informers, people Polyakov interacted with on a regular basis who would pass on to Moody what the Russian did and said.

One of Moody's most valuable access agents was Polyakov's American counterpart at the United Nations, Lt. Col. Paul Fahey, a military attaché to the American Mission. Fahey and Polyakov had gotten to know each other in the normal course of their UN activities. Each was an artillery officer, and this helped them develop something of a personal rapport. Fahey agreed to pass on details of his conversations with the Russian—he and Polyakov attended UN functions together and occasionally went out for dinner.

Fahey and Polyakov would sometimes discuss the state of relations between their two countries, and over time Polyakov began to trust Fahey enough to confide that he was not a fan of First Secretary Nikita Khrushchev. Fahey was surprised. Even considering their developing friendship, it was rare for a Soviet representative to offer any kind of criticism of his top leader to his American counterpart. Yet Polyakov was downplaying his real feelings about the Soviet leader: in truth, he was disgusted by Khrushchev.

Khrushchev, Polyakov believed, was responsible for the USSR's food crises, which were due, he thought, to unworkable agricultural planning and plain incompetence. In Polyakov's opinion, Khrushchev was an uncouth boor, prone to emotional outbursts and loudmouthed statements that threatened diplomatic relations and even the uneasy peace between the two Cold War powers. "We will bury you," Khrushchev had told a meeting of Western ambassadors. "We are turning out missiles like sausages," he bragged after the launch of Sputnik. Polyakov had been mortified.

Polyakov's childhood memories magnified his dislike of Khrushchev. Dmitri Polyakov grew up in Ukraine, and he and his family had barely survived the *Holodomor*, the famine Stalin imposed on Ukraine in 1932 and 1933, when peasants resisted collectivization. Millions had starved to death, and whole villages had disappeared. As a ten- and eleven-year-old, Polyakov had fished and foraged in the forest for wild foods and scavenged anything edible from the streets. The family might not have survived had it not been for Polyakov's father Fyodor's job in a sunflower oil factory, which entitled him to an allotment of three liters of oil a month. The family bartered the oil for potatoes or even, occasionally, eggs.

When the sanctions were lifted and Polyakov returned to school, only seven of his thirty classmates were alive to join him. But that wasn't the end of the misery inflicted by the central government. A few years later, when Polyakov was in his impressionable teens, the political purges of the Great Terror gripped Ukraine as Stalin arrested and executed many thousands. Polyakov's classmates would come to school with eyes red from crying, their fathers having been dragged from their homes in the middle of the night. Nikita Khrushchev was Ukraine's governor then, overseeing the purges as Stalin's chief lieutenant.

Khrushchev's treatment of Red Army veterans was especially offensive to Polyakov. After the war, Khrushchev downsized the army by over a million men, many of them former officers. These good and loyal men, who had been soldiers for years, were summarily dismissed, without retraining, and thrown out into a Soviet economy unable to absorb them. Polyakov was furious—so many of these men were his friends, his colleagues.

The tipping point, however, might have been Khrushchev's dismissal of Gen. Georgy Zhukov. Zhukov was perhaps the greatest Russian general of World War II. He had been the chief planner in the Stavka, Stalin's high command staff, and the only one capable of standing up to Stalin and changing the dangerously unpredictable dictator's mind. Equally at home in the field, Zhukov led the final destruction of Germany's Eastern armies and smashed his way into Berlin, putting an end to the Nazi Reich. Zhukov was adored by the military, including Polyakov, who considered him the Soviet Union's only truly outstanding general. When Khrushchev, fearful of Zhukov's immense popularity, forcibly retired him, Polyakov considered it an unforgivable insult, not only to Zhukov but to him and every other veteran.

If he needed anything further to feed his contempt for Khrushchev, Polyakov found it at the UN General Assembly proceedings in the fall of 1960. Sitting in the hall as part of the Soviet delegation, Polyakov saw Khrushchev lose his temper and pound the table in front of him with his fists. Then the Soviet premier famously took off his shoe and banged the table with it. Polyakov was horrified, embarrassed beyond words. "He couldn't bear the man," Polyakov's son Alexander said later, recalling discussions with his father. "He felt like vomiting every time he saw his picture."

Polyakov's shifting loyalties were beginning to show. He told Paul Fahey that, in his opinion, John Foster Dulles, the late hardline U.S. secretary of state, had advocated the only sensible foreign policy for the United States to follow. Being supportive of U.S. foreign policy was highly unusual for a Soviet military attaché, and Fahey duly reported this to Ed Moody.

Then, a few months later, on May 1, 1960, the Soviets shot down an American high-altitude reconnaissance plane flying over Soviet territory, the new, super-secret U-2. Khrushchev was both furious that the Americans had violated Soviet airspace for the purposes of espionage and embarrassed that they had the superior technology to do it. The pilot of the downed plane, Francis Gary Powers, had survived the crash and been jailed in Moscow. Khrushchev reluctantly attended a previously planned peace summit in Paris just two weeks later, but stormed out when President Eisenhower would not apologize for the Powers incident. Khrushchev then rescinded an earlier invitation for Eisenhower to visit the Soviet Union.

This prompted another surprising remark from Polyakov, one that came shortly after the summit collapse, when he and Paul Fahey attended the U.S. Armed Forces Day Parade in New York City. As the parade ended, Polyakov took Fahey aside for a private conversation, away from their departing colleagues. "I want to apologize," Polyakov said. "For what?" Fahey asked. "For the sonofabitch behavior of Khrushchev in Paris," Polyakov bluntly replied.

Fahey related this astonishing comment to Moody, who quickly reported it to his superiors. "Polyakov again made remarks to [Fahey] which, if revealed, would undoubtedly place him in serious trouble with his immediate superiors as well as [with] . . . Nikita Khrushchev," Moody wrote in his report.

There was more to Polyakov's growing frustration than personal pique at Khrushchev. Polyakov was a reflective man—an intelligence officer, but also a student of politics, military affairs, and international relations. By 1960, he and his family had lived in the United States for almost seven years. In the Soviet Union, he had studied the United States as the Main Enemy, his target. But in his years in New York, he'd observed the Americans close up and thought at length about Soviet values and their relation to the values he saw at work in American life. And he was coming to the unsettling conclusion that his political views were shifting away from the rigidity of Soviet orthodoxy and toward the ideals of social democracy.

This political evolution didn't translate into a desire to become an American—Polyakov's Russian roots went too deep for that—but he viewed the Soviet Union as an aggressor whose commitment to ideological confrontation might well lead to a cataclysmic war. He began to believe that he might, in some small way, prevent this by helping the Americans better interpret Soviet political, military, and economic actions and intentions. Polyakov did not believe the Americans would start a war against the USSR, but if the United States were threatened by a strongman personality with an essentially aggressive ideology, who knew what could happen?

★

In late July 1961, Col. Dmitri Fedorovich Polyakov made an unexpected request to Paul Fahey, one that would prove fateful. Lt. Gen. Edward O'Neill was commander of the American First Army based in New York and also the senior American military representative to the United Nations. Protocol did not allow someone of Polyakov's rank to approach such a person directly, so he discreetly asked Fahey if a private meeting could be arranged with O'Neill.

Fahey brought this intriguing information to Ed Moody, who in turn went to General O'Neill. At the United Nations, it was common for countries to host cocktail parties or dinners to interact socially with other countries' delegations. As chance would have it, O'Neill was hosting just such a party a few days later, and he sent an invitation to Colonel Polyakov and his wife, Nina. All invitations to diplomatic occasions were scrutinized by Polyakov's superiors, and a last-minute one like this would ordinarily have drawn suspicion. It wasn't questioned.

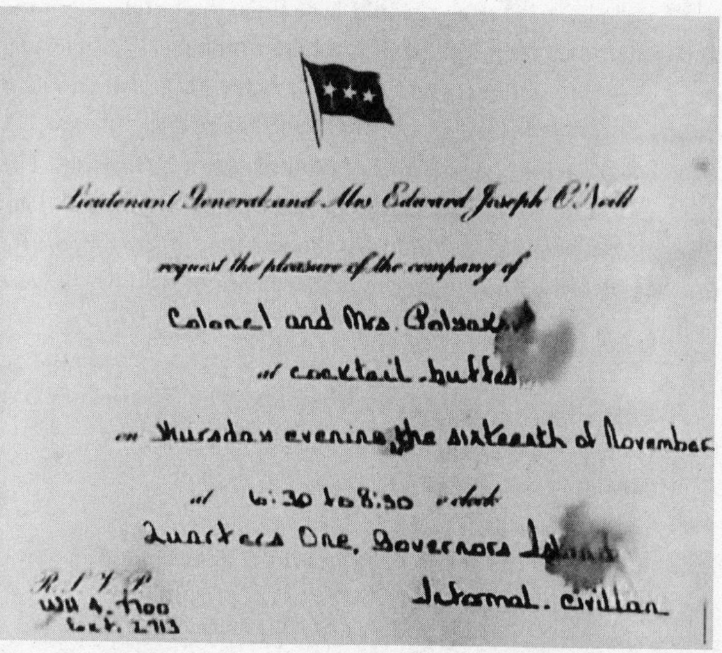

Lieutenant General and Mrs Edward Joseph O'Neill

request the pleasure of the company of

Colonel and Mrs. Polyakov

at cocktail buffet

on Thursday evening the sixteenth of November

at 6:30 to 8:30 o'clock

Quarters One, Governors Island

R.S.V.P.
WH 4-1100
Ext. 2113

Informal . civilian

Lt. Gen. Edward O'Neill's invitation to Colonel and Mrs. Polyakov for cocktails, November 16, 1961. This is one of two invitations to O'Neill's residence as cover for Polyakov's request to meet clandestinely with a U.S. intelligence offficer.

On August 9, Dmitri and Nina arrived along with the other guests at General O'Neill's official residence on Governors Island, off the southern tip of Manhattan. Hours earlier, two other guests had arrived: Ed Moody and an FBI technician, bringing boxes full of recording equipment and tools. Setting themselves up in the basement, the two FBI men ran a wire to the general's study and installed a hidden microphone. It was there that O'Neill planned to meet privately with Polyakov.

With the party under way, Special Agent Moody and his colleague listened intently on their earphones from the basement. For a while there was only silence. Then people came into the study. The agents heard three voices: Paul Fahey's, General O'Neill's, and Dmitri Polyakov's.

"I was pleased that you would have enough confidence in me to talk with me," said O'Neill, "as soldier to soldier. I was pleased, and I hope you will feel entirely free to talk with just the three of us here."

Polyakov replied in his thick accented, limited English. The mike picked up only part of the conversation: "I talked to Paul [Fahey] . . . I would like to . . . confidentially . . . my support for the cause . . . you know what would happen to me if this talk were to be known."

O'NEILL: Dmitri, this is just the three of us.
POLYAKOV: We can talk . . . two of us. One to one.
PAUL FAHEY: Want me to go?

The FBI men in the basement heard the door close. Fahey was out of the room.

POLYAKOV: I want to talk to General . . .
O'NEILL: I'm pleased you think I'm the right man, Dmitri.
POLYAKOV: I have thought of it . . . much what I've come here

about is to give information . . . like maybe you will talk to some officials. Maybe you organize it.

O'NEILL: What do you mean by officials, Dmitri?

POLYAKOV: Men.

O'NEILL: I'm a little puzzled as to who? I'm puzzled as to who you want to talk to.

POLYAKOV: CIA.

O'NEILL: What?

POLYAKOV: CIA. I talk to you in your office because I know that there are, maybe there's some trouble for me if I talk . . .

O'NEILL: In other words, you would like for me to arrange for you to talk to a CIA man. Is that right? Where could it be done?

POLYAKOV: Maybe you have some party.

O'NEILL: Alright, alright . . . So suppose, in order to make it appear completely official I would ask the French secretary, how about that?

POLYAKOV: Fine.

O'NEILL: The English one doesn't stay here all the time, he comes up from Washington . . . I could ask Paul, of course. Do you want the Chinese here?

POLYAKOV: Da, that would be okay.

O'NEILL: I will work up a party of our foreign friends.

POLYAKOV: Alright.

O'NEILL: Alright. Let me see what I can do.

Listening in the basement, Ed Moody fought to suppress his excitement. He had been following the Russian for years, knew his movements, and had intuited his thoughts, but he hadn't had any idea what Polyakov wanted to talk to General O'Neill about, and he had been burning with curiosity to find out. Now it appeared that Polyakov had made a major decision. Meeting with a CIA officer would be a momentous move for Polyakov, a giant risk. If he followed through, such an action would be irrevocable.

As Moody strained to hear the conversation upstairs, Polyakov abruptly changed the subject. What would happen, he asked O'Neill, if the Soviet Union were to invade West Berlin and take it by force?

General O'Neill responded instantly. "War," he said. "It would mean all-out war."

Moody now had on tape something more momentous than the Russian's request to meet with a CIA officer. It was obvious his superiors had ordered him to ask O'Neill about Berlin.

Three years earlier, Nikita Khrushchev had given the United States six months to evacuate its forces from West Berlin. President Eisenhower had rejected the ultimatum out of hand, and nothing had happened. Recently, Khrushchev had given John F. Kennedy the same message, at their summit in Vienna, trying to intimidate the young, newly elected president. Clearly the Russians wanted the Western nations out of Berlin and were planning *something*, and Polyakov's question to O'Neill was in all likelihood one of many attempts to get an answer. It also explained, Moody thought, why Polyakov's bosses had so readily approved the last-minute invitation to General O'Neill's: the Soviets needed information quickly.

After Polyakov and the other guests left O'Neill's party, Moody sent the tape to Washington, DC, where it first went to J. Edgar Hoover's office, then to the White House. Four days later, on the night of August 13, 1961, East German guards and workers started installing barbed-wire entanglements all along the boundary line between East and West Berlin. A week after that, concrete emplacements went in, the beginning of what would soon be a twenty-seven-mile-long wall separating the city's two sides.

In the years to follow, Moody would often wonder if the interchange he heard between Polyakov and O'Neill might have played a role in persuading Nikita Khrushchev to build a barrier rather than attempt to take West Berlin by force. Building a wall would solve the problem of the massive flight of East Germans to the West. It would frustrate and anger the Americans, but they weren't likely to go to war over it.

CHAPTER 4

THE WALL

My sister Maria with Grandmother Dillon at the Brandenburg Gate in West Berlin. The sign reads, Attention! You Will Be Leaving West Berlin in 40 Meters. *(Author's collection)*

In September 1961, Dad took my two older sisters and me to see the Berlin Wall. I was four years old.

The wall had gone up a few weeks earlier. Holding Dad's hand, I was afraid of the barbed wire, the mean-looking soldiers with guns, and the huge German shepherds. Dad said no one would hurt us, that we shouldn't be frightened. I was too young to understand the wall's meaning, but I sensed that whatever this was, it wasn't good.

We'd been living in Berlin since Dad returned to Germany in 1955. In between his two postings to Germany, he and Mom and baby Maria, who was born just before they left Kempten in 1953, had come back to Washington, DC, headquarters, where part of Dad's job had been debriefing Soviet defectors escaping the power grab and bloodbath following Stalin's death.

By the time Dad returned to headquarters, it was widely suspected within the Agency that MI6's Kim Philby had been spying for the Soviets. James Angleton, now the CIA's counterintelligence chief, had been traumatized by Philby's duplicity. His friend, teacher, and intimate sharer of secrets had duped him, going all the way back to his training days.

Philby's deception was a cruel vindication of Angleton's increasingly paranoid worldview. It spurred on what he believed was a vast Soviet master plan to send fake defectors to control and confuse the Americans by offering up false information carefully prepared to appear real and valuable. According to Angleton, no Soviet sources could now be trusted, and his trepidations were spreading a dark cloud over the Agency's operations, especially over the Soviet Bloc (SB) Division, where Dad worked. Angleton's followers who bought into the Soviet plot theory soon had a nickname within the Agency: the "Black Hats." Dad hadn't embraced their way of thinking, of believing that all Soviet sources were controlled. "Paul thought it was all bullshit," Gus Hathaway, then a case officer like my father but later chief of the Counterintelligence Center, remembered.

My father and his like-minded colleagues probably had a taxing time at headquarters during that period, given all the suspicion and contentiousness generated by Angleton and the Black Hats. Angleton was hyperintelligent and, to many, charismatic, but he was also Machiavellian and suspicious of every recruited Soviet, and since my father's and his colleagues' job was to recruit Soviets, they couldn't have enjoyed working in that atmosphere.

Before long, though, Dad was posted back to Germany, away from the epicenter of Angleton's dark theories. Notably, it was David Murphy, a leading Black Hat who'd been Dad's boss back in Munich, who arranged for Dad to go to Berlin with him when he was posted back to Germany himself. This irony—that Murphy and my father got along despite their ideological differences—perplexed some of my Dad's friends. "I always wondered how your father could be friends with Murphy," Hathaway said. "We'd ask him that. But he was his own man. He had integrity, no BS. 'This is the way it is,' he'd say."

"I'm enchanted to be back in Germany," Mom wrote to her parents shortly after their arrival in Berlin. After the quaint little house with a garden in Kempten, the family was now assigned a small apartment on the American base. Mom longed to be out in a German neighborhood experiencing the local life, something my parents strove for in each of our overseas postings. "Unfortunately, the new ruling is that no one below a grade 12 will get a house," Mom wrote home. "We're just 11s, so we'll have to have one of the American apartments. They are more than adequate, but I'm spoiled now and want a house with a garden."

Many of the CIA case officers working in Berlin were in their twenties and early thirties, young marrieds like Mom and Dad, and the nature of their work meant their social circle was restricted. Given the pressures of intelligence work, the young officers needed a way to blow off steam, and there were lots of parties with plenty of drinking and smoking. But Mom was always trying to expand their experiences outside the American enclave. "Tomorrow night," she wrote home, "some friends and we are jointly giving a mammoth square dance. We are inviting, in addition to the office people, a batch of British, several German couples, State Department people, and some Scotch officers who have promised to come in kilts and bring a bag-piper!"

Besides Dave Murphy and his wife, Mom and Dad forged strong bonds with three other Berlin Base couples who would remain lifelong friends: Ben and Perky Pepper (Benjamin Franklin Pepper was a descendant of the Founding Father and had a large portrait of him in his Virginia home), Gus and Marjorie Hathaway, and Bill and Louise Friend. In the years to come, our stays in the United States and other countries would occasionally overlap with theirs.

★

Though my mother was enjoying being overseas again, Berlin in 1955 was far from idyllic. The city was a cauldron of Cold War political tension. The post–World War II division of the city into four sectors—American, French, British and Soviet (East Berlin)—was a constant irritation to the East German leadership and their Soviet masters. The Soviets wanted control of West Berlin; they wanted the American, British, and French out.

West Berlin was surrounded by Soviet-controlled East Germany, stranded one hundred miles from the borders of West Germany and accessible from West Germany only by a single narrow rail and highway corridor. The contrast between the bleak, economically lifeless East Germany and the thriving, expansive West Germany was highlighted in Berlin, with its lively free sector butted up against its moribund Communist one. After going to a party one evening at a downtown hotel, Mom wrote home, "The cocktail party was given in the 'roof garden' where the view is particularly noteworthy, or downright startling. Surrounding the hotel and looking toward the West Berlin side is all bright lights, lit streets, automobile lights winding around. But looking over into East Berlin there is nothing but a black patch out in the distance."

Mom and Perky Pepper (whom Dad called "Perko") loved walking around Berlin, in and out of the American, British, and French sectors, though they were careful to avoid the Soviet sector. Dad and his CIA colleagues were under army cover, and without diplomatic immunity, the Soviet sector was an unwise place for them or their wives to be. At the larger crossings, big signs in German read, "ATTENTION! You Are Now Leaving West Berlin," but if you didn't know the city well, you could cross elsewhere into the Eastern sector by mistake. One of Mom's letters home described their new environment. "We went down to the Brandenburg Gate one day, and saw East-zone communist demonstrations. The one disadvantage of being in Berlin is that we are not free to travel, being completely surrounded by the Soviet sector."

Berlin was the Iron Curtain's last remaining open border crossing, and for the time being, most who wanted to come into West Berlin from the East were allowed to do so. Many East Berliners worked in West Berlin, and vice versa. Families visited back and forth. But by far the largest movement comprised the tens of thousands of refugees streaming into West Berlin.

Khrushchev was facing an embarrassing situation. The number of East Germans fleeing to the West through Berlin's open border grew so large that the destabilizing exodus threatened to undermine East Germany, for the flood of escapees was heavy with talented professionals—doctors, lawyers, scientists, teachers, and engineers.

"West Berlin," Khrushchev told visiting Senator Hubert Humphrey in 1958, was "a cancer," "a bone in my throat." Everyone thought that war could break out over Berlin, and if it did, American, British, and French troops faced a Soviet Army so superior in numbers that it could roll over them in a matter of hours.

Most of the Soviet military and intelligence activity was directed from a huge complex in Karlshorst, a suburb of East Berlin in the Soviet sector—in fact, the largest KGB station in the world was located there. To combat this, West Berlin's CIA base was also the Agency's largest outpost, with more than 150 agents. The big questions that CIA case officers such as my Dad were tasked to answer were: what were the Soviets' military plans, and would the USSR invade West Berlin at some point?

To find out, the CIA base was focused on recruiting and running agents who had access to Karlshorst: maids, tradesmen, technicians, contractors, secretaries, garbage collectors—anyone who either worked there or who was allowed in. Sometimes they were East or West Berlin citizens, sometimes they were refugees recruited from Marienfelde, the large refugee-processing center in the American sector. Through these informants, Berlin Operations Base was drawing a detailed picture of how Karlshorst operated, what it looked like inside, who worked there, and what its procedures were. Every bit of information was being assembled in what was called the "target room," where analysts were fitting the puzzle pieces together, trying to get the most thorough understanding of how the opposition worked. And the ultimate targets of all this work were GRU or KGB people who might have firsthand knowledge about classified information.

Since it was relatively easy for German and Soviet citizens to go back and forth over Berlin's East/West boundary line, Dad and the other case officers would meet their spies in safe houses in one of the Western sectors, almost always at night. The CIA cars all had American-identifying license plates with special screws that allowed the plates to be removed and screwed back on in one turn. The Americans would drive around for a while, watching carefully for anyone following. Then they'd stop in front of a blackened, rubble-strewn area left over from the bombings, change their plates to be less conspicuous, and take a circuitous route to the safe house.

It was serious business. Yet some of the situations Dad was involved in had their humorous side, too, such as when he was involved in an operation that went farcically awry.

A classic recruitment technique used by both sides is the "honey trap," in which a target is lured into an incriminating liaison with an attractive sex partner for the purpose of blackmail. Gus Hathaway and Ben Pepper identified an important Karlshorst-based GRU officer who seemed likely to be susceptible to the charms of a beautiful woman. They set out the bait, a beguiling prostitute hired by Pepper, and the GRU man took it.

The GRU officer was a prime catch, so the base set up a foolproof trap for him: a fancy apartment equipped with cameras and recording equipment behind false mirrors. It planned to record its target in flagrante delicto, confront him with its evidence, and take him straight to a safe house, where my father would lead the interrogation meant to blackmail the officer into giving up secrets or (the hoped-for prize) turn him into an asset. A group of officers, including Hathaway, Pepper, and Dave Murphy, would hide in the apartment to run the equipment and spring the trap. They were all armed, in case the startled Russian got violent, and nervous—Dave Murphy tried to load his bullets in backward, and dropped them on the floor.

After the GRU officer arrived at the apartment, the two were just getting down to business when, inexplicably, a junior officer jumped the gun and barged through the door for the "a-ha" moment. Not enough had happened to blackmail their victim, and the surprised and angry GRU officer, buttoning up his shirt, yelled that they had nothing on him and left. Hathaway, Pepper, and Murphy were so embarrassed and so overwhelmed by the debacle that they forgot about their partner, Paul Dillon, back at the safe house. It was two whole days before anyone remembered that Dad was still there, patiently waiting to find out what was going on. "Your dad was pipin' hot mad when we finally went out there and got him," recalled Gus Hathaway. "But we had a good laugh about it back at the office."

★

Even though my father had avoided the paranoid machinations of the Black Hats at headquarters by accepting a job overseas, he couldn't evade them altogether. Dad's boss, Dave Murphy, who eventually rose to become the SB Division chief, was himself a Black Hat and suspected almost every Soviet source of being a provocation (an agent deployed by the opposition who pretends to be sympathetic to the other side). "Paul had a good case," recalled Hathaway, referring to a Soviet whom my father was trying to recruit, "and Murphy insisted on sticking his nose into it, and told the possible source he was a fake, and the guy walked out."

Back at DC headquarters, Angleton's counterintelligence operation had emerged as the most powerful fiefdom within the CIA. Angleton was close to CIA director Allen Dulles, who gave him unparalleled personal access. From his darkened, cluttered office, Angleton had his eye on everything—most of all on the SB Division's cases—which caused more than a little resentment among the field officers.

"We had another great case," recalled Hathaway. "A Soviet with, in my opinion, good bona fides. But Angleton insisted he was controlled and sent [CIA case officer] Jim Flint to tell the Soviet that he was controlled and we didn't want him. The officer was so insulted he punched Flint in the face."

Aware of its vulnerability, the KGB tightened the security at Karlshorst, replacing many of the East German workers in the compound with special KGB security guards. One of their electronic sweeps revealed a microphone embedded in a chandelier, planted by a CIA-recruited East German electrician, and this prompted the KGB to expand its surveillance on CIA officers, like Dad, working out of the Agency's Berlin Base. Knowing he was being watched and needing to get a package to an asset immediately, Dad once persuaded Mom to deliver it to a dead drop site in a Berlin park. She did it, but the experience made her so nervous that she told him never to ask her to do it again.

Not that she would have had much time to be a part-time spy anyway. By the summer of 1955, she was pregnant with their second baby. "I hope that news of Leo or Clare will be reaching you in a few days," she wrote to her parents that summer.

Clare was born in September, and a year later, Mom again wrote to her parents. "A baby is due mid January. We are planning on Leo or Eva." Clearly, they kept hoping for that baby boy named Leo, Dad's middle name. But the next letter home proclaimed my arrival: "Little girls are, fortunately, irresistible, but one would like a son occasionally!"

The next year, carrying out their Catholic duty, Mom was pregnant again. Following a pattern, she wrote to her parents that the upcoming baby would be named Julia if a girl or Leo if the hoped-for boy. Julia, however, was born in April. Mom and Dad loved having another girl, their fourth, but they weren't going to give up trying for a boy, either.

Just before Julia's birth, Dave Murphy was promoted to Berlin Station chief, and he soon promoted Dad to head up the Berlin Soviet Branch. "They used to kid him," Dave Murphy told me years later, speaking of Dad's colleagues in the office, "because they used to say he was the chief's pet." Dad and his boss were certainly close; perhaps it was their Irish-Catholic bond. Every year, Dave Murphy and my father would together give up drinking for Lent.

With Dad's promotion, our family finally qualified for a house. Mom was overjoyed. "Paul's raise came through," she wrote, "then through a wonderful stroke of luck we got a house immediately, and it is a perfect one. Not an army-built house in the American community, but a German house in a very nice neighborhood, Dahlem, with fruit trees, nut trees, berry bushes, and a sand pile for the children."

My father and mother attended the wedding of their friends, and Dad's colleagues, Bill and Louise Friend in a wartime Quonset hut in the British sector that had been converted into an Episcopal church. The reception was at the Army Officers' Club. "We had to do what was de rigueur," Louise told me, "which was to cut the cake with a sword. We had to follow the army custom, which we didn't want to do . . . the problems of cover, you see."

★

Prior to my father's promotion, he had been recruiting agents, running spies, and vetting defectors. Now, as head of the Berlin Soviet Branch, his duties were more administrative. One deviation from his usual work came in 1958, when he was sent to the Brussels World's Fair as part of the CIA's effort to infiltrate copies of the great Russian writer Boris Pasternak's novel *Doctor Zhivago* into the Soviet Union.

My father in front of the American Pavilion at the Brussels World Fair, 1958. He was sent to Brussels to distribute Russian-language copies of Pasternak's book *Doctor Zhivago* to Soviets attending the World Fair. *(Author's collection)*

Doctor Zhivago is a humanist, individualistic novel, a love story in which the emotional lives of its characters rise above the ideological battleground they are forced to endure. That by itself made it anathema to the Soviets. Pasternak's implicit criticism of Stalinism, collectivization, and the Great Purge resulted in the novel's being banned in its home country.

Then, in 1957, *Doctor Zhivago* was smuggled out of Russia by an agent of an Italian publisher. The publication of an Italian translation enraged the Soviet leadership, and a smear campaign was launched against the book.

The CIA quickly picked up on *Doctor Zhivago*'s potential as a weapon in the ideological war against the Soviets. The goal was to find some way of distributing it into underground samizdat channels in the Soviet Union so that Soviet citizens could read the work of one of their own literary masters, a work that reflected the truth about their lives under Communist oppression.

The chance for this came in 1958, with the opening of the Brussels World's Fair. The first world's fair since World War II, Expo 58, as it was also known, was a showcase for the USSR and the United States to demonstrate competitively the superiority of their respective systems. It was also the first time a large number of Russians would be allowed to go to the West as tourists—though their KGB minders would be keeping tabs on them.

The Agency, for its part, saw those Russian tourists, all fourteen thousand of them, as a channel to get *Doctor Zhivago* into the Soviet Union, and arranged for a Russian-language edition to be shipped in bulk to the fair. Copies of the book, housed in the Vatican Pavilion, were handed out to visiting Soviet citizens. My father's job at the fair was to quietly distribute copies to curious Russian visitors.

There was intense interest in the book, and many copies did get smuggled back into the USSR by Soviet fairgoers. Officials in Moscow were infuriated when, a few months after the World's

Fair, Boris Pasternak was awarded the Nobel Prize for Literature. He died less than two years later. It wasn't until Gorbachev's glasnost reforms thirty years later that *Doctor Zhivago* would see a Russian publication and its author would be rehabilitated.

★

By late 1959, Mom and Dad had been in Berlin for five years. Maria and Clare were going to a German Catholic school, and we all spoke German, as Erika, the housekeeper Mom employed when we moved into the house in Dahlem, spoke no English. "Eva is learning to talk by leaps and bounds," Mom wrote home. "She can say Wiedersehen, and Ich komme gleich! (I'm coming right away), when Erika calls her."

In December of that year, Mom was expecting again, their fifth. By now, it appeared, pregnancy was old hat for her, as seen in a postscript to a letter she wrote home: "I think I've forgotten to tell you that we're having another baby in April. The name will be Leo or Jane."

In April 1960, Leo finally arrived. Mom and Dad were ecstatic, and my sisters and I were full of curiosity over this new sibling who wasn't a girl.

While the new babies were welcome distractions at home, the tension between the East and West over control of West Berlin continued to build for Dad at work. At the 1961 summit with Kennedy in Vienna the following summer, Khrushchev threatened to sign a unilateral peace treaty with East Germany. Such a treaty would, in effect, give the East German regime control to cut off free-world access to the Western enclave, which would have disastrous consequences for the American, British, and French occupiers, since Berlin was a hundred miles from Allied territory. "Berlin is the testicles of the West," Khrushchev menaced. "Every time I want to make the West scream, I squeeze on Berlin." The Western allies refused to respond, but everyone knew the Russians themselves could simply invade, crushing the Western forces there, which would have meant, as General O'Neill had told Dmitri Polyakov, "all-out war." Kennedy replied to Khrushchev's threat, saying, "It's going to be a long, cold winter."

Sometime in July 1961, a KGB defector walked into the American embassy in Vienna and was sent to Berlin, where Dad debriefed him. He knew the plans, the defector said. The Soviets were going to build a wall that would split Berlin in half, cutting the two sides off from each other. To Angleton, however, hunched over the dispatches in his office back at headquarters, it was clear: the so-called defector was yet another KGB plant sent to throw off the CIA with false information and lies. My father and the others were instructed to ignore the man. "If we had listened to him," Hathaway told me, "we might have known about the wall going up."

On August 10 a woman came through the Marienfelde refugee reception center. She told her interviewer that she had access to the Karlshorst compound, and further talks with base agents seemed to confirm this. Two polygraph tests were inconclusive, however. When a third polygraph was also questionable, my father and other base officers confronted the woman with a fabricated story: A source, they said, had seen her name on the desk of the chief security officer at Karlshorst, suggesting she was an active agent. How could she explain that? The interrogation went on for hours, and then into the afternoon of the twelfth. Finally, when they told the woman they would have to polygraph her yet again, she broke: She was, indeed, working for East German security, the Stasi. She was controlled, and had been sent to give false information to the CIA.

The woman was now deeply compromised. (If the Stasi found out she'd broken under interrogation, the ramifications for her would have been grave.) So, she agreed to go back to Karlshorst, gather specific information on the Soviets' immediate plans (the Americans hoped), and bring it to the CIA.

It was a major triumph, turning an agent for the Stasi, doubling her, possibly breaking the mystery about whether something was about to happen. She went back to East Berlin, due to return to the CIA on August 13.

★

At midnight on August 12, 1961, thousands of East German workers and guards brought equipment up to the boundary line between East and West and began tearing up the streets on the East side, just inches away from the border line. Dawn broke on barbed-wire emplacements going up on the cleared track. At the wire, panicked East Berliners sprinted through openings or tried to climb or jump over. By midday, it was impossible to get through. East German security troops lined the construction, facing east, ready to shoot anyone trying to cross.

Berlin was now divided, with West Germans in the West, East Germans in the East. Every one of the base's Eastern sources, including Dad's newest agent, was trapped on the other side with no way of getting back across.

"It was pandemonium," John Bogart said, "because the officers had agents that they were running in and out of East Berlin and very few had contingency communications plans for staying in touch if something like this happened. Nobody even gave it a thought!" The Berlin Operations Base was suddenly blind.

"We had one hundred eighty officers in Berlin," Hathaway said, "and we didn't predict a wall was going up. We all thought we would be fired because one hundred eighty guys didn't know about the wall."

As soon as the twenty-seven miles of barbed wire were in place, cinder block and concrete construction began. Over time, a wall twelve feet high, with wire, sentry towers, and mine fields, emerged from what before had been a simple boundary line.

Meanwhile, Mom was in a room at the U.S. Army Hospital waiting to deliver her sixth baby in eight years, bedridden for two weeks with minor pregnancy complications. "You can cut the tension with a knife," she wrote home as hospital staff came and went with updates on the turmoil in the streets.

For days, nothing happened. West Berliners were caught between fear that war would break out and despair over being cut off from family and friends in the East. Then, on August 19, retired general Lucius Clay and Vice President Lyndon Johnson arrived at West Berlin's Tempelhof Airport, sent by President Kennedy to demonstrate the strength of America's commitment to West Berlin. (Thirteen years earlier, Clay had been military governor of the American sector, and he was still a trusted and immensely popular figure in the city.)

That same day, an American armored column crossed the border between East and West Germany, a hundred miles away, and began moving up the autobahn to reinforce the Berlin garrison. East German security did nothing to stop it. When the first tanks rumbled into West Berlin, exultant West Berliners swarmed around them, adorning the gun barrels with flowers. And though the situation was threatening, the Soviets did not challenge the American reinforcements. The two sides of the city remained firmly sealed off, the wall a fait accompli. "It's not a very nice solution," President Kennedy concluded, "but a wall is a hell of a lot better than a war."

The next day, my mother gave birth to my brother, Paul, her sixth child, our second brother.

★

The previously open city and its tide of refugees had created a steady stream of intelligence opportunities. Now, with the wall in place, East Berlin was a "denied area," CIA lingo for a closed and hostile operational environment. Many of Berlin's CIA staffers were now being assigned elsewhere, including Dad, who was transferred back to the new CIA headquarters, in Langley, Virginia.

So, in December 1961, my father and his family of seven sailed home, across the Atlantic on the SS *America*.

CHAPTER 5

MOODY AND MABEY

Dmitri Polyakov *(right)* with Russian colleagues aboard the RMS *Queen Elizabeth*, June 1962. *(Courtesy of Edward Moody)*

After rushing the tape of Colonel Polyakov and General O'Neill's clandestine meeting on Governors Island to FBI headquarters and the White House, Special Agent Ed Moody focused on the part of the conversation that had really grabbed his attention: Polyakov's request to meet with a CIA officer. Asking for a secret meeting with the CIA was an extraordinarily dangerous thing to do. If the Soviets found out, it could mean only one thing for Polyakov: a charge of treason.

O'Neill and Polyakov had agreed that another social occasion would be the best cover for a second meeting. O'Neill was already planning one in mid-November, for the United Nations' military delegations, and Colonel and Mrs. Dmitri Polyakov were invited. Several other Soviet couples were also invited as further cover.

On the evening of Thursday, November 16, 1961, Dmitri, Nina, Alexander, and Petr drove down to Battery Park, at the southern tip of Manhattan, for the short ferry ride out to Fort Jay, on Governors Island. On the ferry, the Polyakovs watched the lights of the boat traffic dotting New York Harbor. The Statue of Liberty was illuminated in the twilight, encircled by tourist boats. As they disembarked on the island, they were greeted by a U.S. Army sergeant, who led them to a squad car for the short drive to O'Neill's residence, where all the children would be babysat for the evening while the adults mingled. For the boys' amusement, the sergeant turned on the cherry-red revolving beacon on the car's roof. Eight-year-old Alexander was fascinated.

What Polyakov didn't know was that the CIA man he was about to meet was in reality an FBI man. The Bureau had not informed the CIA about Polyakov's request. From the beginning, Polyakov's case had been in the hands of the FBI, the agency that had jurisdiction over domestic activity, not the CIA, which by law operated only outside America's borders. Each agency jealously guarded its turf, and in fact, the two rarely collaborated.

Ed Moody wanted the job, and asked for it. Polyakov was his case, and he knew more about the GRU colonel than anyone else, but his bosses thought he appeared too junior. Moody's supervisor, John Mabey, was therefore chosen to be Polyakov's "CIA contact." Moody would remain behind the scenes, monitoring the case and never letting a moment of Polyakov's actions go unnoticed or undocumented.

John Mabey arrived at General O'Neill's that evening with a

woman from the office posing as his wife. The fake couple circulated until General O'Neill found a safe moment to introduce Polyakov to Mabey. They quickly agreed on a meeting for later that evening, at midnight near Manhattan's Columbus Circle, where they could talk unobserved.

A cold rain was sheeting down when John Mabey arrived at Columbus Circle. Watching nearby were Ed Moody and another agent, Mabey's security detail. A few cars passed by, but in the frigid downpour, few pedestrians were out. Eventually, Dmitri Polyakov walked toward Mabey bundled in a heavy overcoat and wearing a fedora.

Standing in a doorway alcove for cover from the rain, Mabey told Polyakov he needed to provide the Agency with information to establish his bona fides. Polyakov had anticipated the request. The Americans wanted solid evidence that he wasn't a GRU provocation.

Mabey asked what Polyakov's true role in the United States was.

"I am a military intelligence officer, a colonel, conducting illegal work here," Polyakov said.

This was a promising start. Mabey told Polyakov they'd need to meet again, and that he wanted something from Polyakov: the names of the cryptographers in the *rezidentura*, the GRU's Washington headquarters.

Polyakov agreed to supply the names at their next meeting. It was a test. The Soviets would never give up those names voluntarily, not even to lure the FBI into accepting a plant. But the FBI already knew the names of the cryptographers. If Polyakov gave Mabey the right names, he was genuine; if the names he gave were fictitious, Mabey would shut the case down immediately. Wanting to get out of the cold rain, the two men agreed to meet a week later, at Grant's Tomb, a national memorial site located between Riverside Park and Columbia University.

After years of studying Dmitri Polyakov, Ed Moody was already convinced of the Russian's bona fides. "He knew what the consequences were," Moody said years later. "He entered into this thing with eyes wide open and never backed out. He wasn't doing it for himself. He was doing it for the common, ordinary Soviet citizens who were being abused because of these people that occupied the Kremlin." Despite Moody's opinion, Polyakov was new to John Mabey—the FBI needed concrete proof.

Ulysses Grant's hulking neoclassical tomb was deserted the night Mabey and Polyakov next met. Sitting in Polyakov's car, Mabey produced photographs of Soviet diplomats and suspected KGB and GRU intelligence officers. Polyakov looked through them, identifying who was a true diplomat and who was a spy. Then he gave Mabey the names, the true names, of six intelligence cryptographers.

Mabey left Grant's Tomb elated: a defector in place, "and in deep place," as he put it later. "It was the first time we had ever developed an inside agent able to give us information from within a Soviet establishment. The dream of every kind of intelligence agent."

On the way back to his office, Mabey invented a code name for Polyakov: TOPHAT. It was a play on the name "Top Cat," a character from a cartoon his children watched at the time.

TOPHAT was the biggest penetration of Soviet intelligence the FBI had ever made. Back at FBI headquarters, when Mabey told his colleagues about his meeting, the room exploded with backslaps and congratulations. This was a real coup—a colonel, highly connected in military intelligence, with access to very substantial secret military information and knowledge of every illegal operating in the United States.

Mabey and Moody understood, though, that this new relationship was going to have a fairly short life span. Polyakov had told

Paul Fahey, his American army friend, that he was scheduled to be posted back to Moscow in June. This gave him just six more months in New York. Moody and Mabey had to get their plan moving, and quickly.

On January 2, 1962, Dmitri Polyakov went through the end-of-day routine in the *rezidentura*, closing up his files and placing all the classified material in his safe, and left for home. As usual, the FBI watchers radioed that he was leaving, and the tails fell into place behind him. By the time Polyakov arrived at his apartment, Ed Moody, John Mabey, and several other FBI agents had positioned themselves around the building. Polyakov parked his car and entered the lobby. As he got into the elevator, John Mabey stepped in behind him. In the elevator, Mabey told Polyakov that he had arranged a safe apartment where they could meet, on the seventh floor of that very building, one floor above Polyakov's own apartment. Polyakov nodded his head and stepped out of the elevator on his own floor.

A week later, during their first meeting in the seventh-floor apartment, Polyakov promised he could identify all the illegals operating on the East Coast, and the Americans the Soviets had recruited to spy for them. He also had access to Soviet military plans and philosophy, including information on Soviet nuclear plans and strategies.

This was as rich a trove of information as Mabey could expect so early in the relationship. Mabey figured that there had to be a correspondingly heavy demand from Polyakov for what he was offering.

Polyakov's reply was extraordinary. Beyond expenses, and some gifts for his colleagues and superiors which he could trade for favors or information, Polyakov's motives were not about the money. They went far deeper, as his American handlers were to learn over the years.

"It would be inaccurate to characterize his comments on motivation as an emotional catharsis," Sandy Grimes, one of my father's colleagues who worked on the Polyakov case at headquarters for over twenty years, later wrote in her book, *Circle of Treason*. "Polyakov was and remained a circumspect individual whose character and military training never would have permitted such a display."

The balance of the Cold War, Polyakov believed, was tilting toward the Soviets, a danger considering Khrushchev's bullying and erratic temperament. Polyakov wanted to level the playing field by helping the Americans understand Soviet strategies and intentions and, perhaps more important, the character of the USSR's rulers. He had personally witnessed the courage and sacrifice of the Russian people during the war, and had been part of it himself. Now, Grimes explained, Polyakov "began to view the Soviet leaders as corrupt thugs who subjugated the common man for personal power and to line their pockets and those of their sycophants." As Polyakov saw it, the leaders were "mocking the sacrifices of the Russian people."

As their relationship developed, Polyakov began to open up to Mabey. He had no trust in the idea of "peaceful coexistence," a Kremlin ploy, he believed, to lull the United States into a false sense of security. Polyakov wanted Americans to understand that any policy of peaceful coexistence that Khrushchev advocated was disingenuous. In the face of the ever-growing stockpiles of nuclear weapons, peaceful coexistence was doomed, Polyakov said. Global conflict was far more likely.

Polyakov reminded Mabey of what Khrushchev had said: that the Soviet Union was going to bury American imperialism. Khrushchev believed that the United States was weak militarily and politically—America hadn't been able to win the Korean War, and had done nothing to aid the Hungarians in their revolt.

Polyakov was putting himself at risk so that the Americans would see Khrushchev and the Politburo for who they were, so that the United States would stand up to the Soviets' policies and counteract them. "I want to warn you," Polyakov told Mabey, "you Americans are arrogant and careless. You don't always see how what the Soviet Union does militarily and politically is aimed at weakening you."

Polyakov's motives were complex. He was deeply concerned about the potential for war between the superpowers, and he wanted to do what he could to lessen the inevitability of a disastrous clash. But that didn't mean he was a champion for "the cause of freedom, justice, and democracy," as Grimes later put it. "Quite the contrary, these were lofty ideals that did not matter to him and his daily life." Polyakov was Russian to the core. John Mabey asked Polyakov if he would ever consider defecting, to come over with his wife and children. Polyakov's answer was no. He was born a Russian and would die a Russian. Both Mabey and Moody understood that and deeply respected Polyakov's loyalty to his country.

★

That first seventh-floor meeting was followed by several more. Once the relationship deepened, real information began to pour out of Polyakov. He told Mabey that the GRU and KGB were monitoring the FBI's radio communications. Listening to the FBI's radio talk, they had learned, among other things, that the FBI had bugged the car of the deputy KGB *rezident* in Manhattan. To conceal the source of the information, the Soviets waited until they knew the FBI was watching. "Then they made a big show of kicking the tires of the KGB officer's car," David Wise, in his book *Nightmover*, later reported, "pulling out wires, and pretending to have 'discovered' the transmitter."

The Soviets, Polyakov told Mabey, also monitored microwave phone calls coming out of Washington or New York. They could listen in on Defense Department calls, National Security Agency calls, FBI calls. The technological side of this information wasn't a revelation—the NSA had the same capability—but neither Mabey and Moody nor anyone else at the FBI knew that the Soviets had this monitoring technology up and running in New York and Washington. The forest of antennas on the roof of the Soviet mission, which housed the GRU, had never been adequately analyzed. "If you ever took an aerial view of the top of any Soviet establishment, be it the embassy in Washington, the Soviet Mission in the United Nations or the San Francisco consulate, there were so many antennae you would think that you were sitting in a radio or TV studio set up," Mabey later told an interviewer. Polyakov's information, he said, "completely changed the counter-intelligence activities of the FBI."

In their earlier meeting, Polyakov told Mabey that he was in charge of handling Soviet illegals in the United States, that he had trained them during his posting back in Moscow. Now he identified those agents: Among others, he told Mabey about Ivan Egorov, the personnel manager at the United Nations, and the Sokolovs, who were operating in Washington, DC, under the names of Robert and Joy Ann Baltch.

These names were all new to the FBI, but one name Polyakov brought up was well known to them, and both Polyakov and Mabey knew it: Kaarlo Tuomi. Spying was a tricky business, Ed Moody thought as he listened to the tapes of Mabey and Polyakov talking about Tuomi. Polyakov had been running Tuomi before he was caught and turned. When he found out Tuomi was doubled, Polyakov had continued to run him as if he didn't know. And now Polyakov was working for the FBI as an agent, which was something Tuomi, an FBI source himself, didn't know. A very tricky business indeed.

When Polyakov turned over "the whole kettle of information," as Mabey told an interviewer many years later, "we had the whole thing [all the illegals] in our hand." From the moment Polyakov identified them, the Bureau put each of the illegals under close surveillance. Yet Mabey and his colleagues didn't arrest them immediately, so as not to reveal that Polyakov was leaking information; the FBI needed to protect its new crown jewel. So, rather than arrest the illegals, the FBI just watched them, waiting until it could spring the trap without casting suspicion on the asset who was giving the Bureau such a rich flow of secrets.

Polyakov also gave Mabey samples of the chemicals that Soviet intelligence used for disappearing ink, enabling the FBI to read intercepted communications. He also revealed the content of the Soviet Mission's code books and encryption tables, the organizational structure of the GRU, and a long-term plan to create a new GRU illegal structure in the United States.

Yet they couldn't meet in the apartment above Polyakov's forever; there were too many other Soviet families in the building. So, after about a month, the meetings moved to a building on Madison Avenue, across the street from a store that sold sporting goods and outdoor gear: Abercrombie and Fitch. The store included an entire floor dedicated to hunting rifles, shotguns, and ammunition, complete with a shooting range. Other floors featured a golf school, a watch repair desk, a kennel for dogs and cats, and a pool for fly- and bait-casting instructions. Long before Abercrombie and Fitch became a clothing brand, its midcentury store in Manhattan was Dmitri Polyakov's favorite, a place where he could browse for hours, indulging his love for hunting, archery, and the outdoor life.

Given Polyakov's reputation as an avid outdoorsman, no one in the *rezidentura* questioned his frequent visits to Abercrombie and Fitch. The store had a side door, and directly across the street from that door was the side door of the office building Special Agent

Moody had chosen for the meetings with Polyakov. "He could go in the store," Moody said, "and boom, he's off the street, in an elevator, and he's in our office."

The new "safe house" in the Madison Avenue building was Room 642, just off the elevator. It wasn't perfect—a large glass window fronted the hallway, and anyone coming off the elevator could see who was inside. The office was empty, and Moody was told there were no funds available to furnish the space. J. Edgar Hoover's Bureau was "cheap, cheap, cheap," Moody grumbled to himself. So, with his own money, he bought drywall, nails, and two-by-fours and built a partition wall to cover the front window. Then he brought carpet and furniture from his own house. Once he had set the place up, Moody installed a hidden mike that connected through the telephone line to the recording equipment in the Bureau's downtown office.

Listening to tape after tape after tape of Mabey's and Polyakov's meetings, Ed Moody came to see Polyakov the human being beneath the veneer of the professional GRU officer. For Moody, who had covered Polyakov from his first New York assignment, TOPHAT was not just another counterintelligence job. Moody had invested much of his career in this man he had never met face-to-face and whose comings and goings filled his work life day and night. Moody believed Polyakov to be a true hero, selfless, fearless, and, most of all, dedicated not to America, but to the Russian people. "He did it for what he saw went on in the Soviet Union," Moody told me. "How they slaughtered people, mistreated his friends. He saw so much of it; it just got to him."

★

With the prospect of Polyakov going back to Russia, the FBI now needed to let the CIA in on their big catch, and get the Agency's help to devise methods of communicating with him in Moscow (where the FBI had no jurisdiction) so he could continue his revelation of secrets. Once back at GRU headquarters, Polyakov's information would be even more valuable.

Yet, communicating with Americans in Moscow was significantly more dangerous than in the United States. The fabric of Soviet society was infested with KGB officers and their informers, and no one was watched more closely than Americans operating out of the U.S. embassy. Any Soviets who interacted with them quickly came under suspicion.

Polyakov told Mabey he'd be willing to continue reporting while he was in Moscow, but only under very strict rules: his own. Polyakov was not at all convinced of the CIA's competence in tradecraft. A year earlier, Pyotr Popov, another GRU officer who had been spying for the Americans, was arrested on a Moscow bus as he was meeting with his CIA contact. The CIA man had been kicked out of the country; Popov was lying in an unmarked grave with a bullet in his head.

Polyakov also told Mabey that in Moscow he would not meet with any CIA officers in person, and he insisted that dead drop sites be used one time only. (If the KGB were on to him, a drop site could be under surveillance.) Most important, Polyakov didn't want anyone to come looking for him or to do anything rash if he didn't fill a dead drop on schedule or comply with some other prearranged plan.

Polyakov was to leave the United States on June 6, a month after Nina and the children. In May, John Mabey and Ed Moody went to the new CIA headquarters in Langley, Virginia. In an unusual arrangement, the Agency and the Bureau agreed to each have a role in running Polyakov while he was in Moscow: the CIA would equip him with communication materials and service the dead drops and signal sites in Moscow; the FBI (still under the ruse that it was the CIA) would initiate and oversee the messaging from New York.

The CIA prepared the communication plan: onetime pads

(printed pads of random numbers to encrypt and decrypt messages, used only once, rendering the codes unbreakable), substrate chemicals for disappearing writing, microdot instructions for using the onetime pads and for the chemical formula, a high-tech camera, and a specialized miniature lens for reading the microdots. The Agency would also provide suggested locations for Moscow dead drops and signal sites incorporated in microdot writing, an encyclopedia about hunting with a hidden slit under the cover for concealing letters, and instructions on intelligence gathering priorities.

INVENTORY OF TOPHAT ITEMS

1 Cipher pad 1 3/4 by 2 1/8 inches, printed by offset printing on flash paper.

~~1 Dummy pad as above, untrimmed.~~

Blank sample sheets of flash paper. + printed pages #002 + 006 - 011 + 016

1 Cipher pad of soft film in brown plastic case, each page 35mm frame size. Pad is 3/16 by 1 by 1 1/2 inches.

1 Sample page (#001) like above pad.

1 ~~Sample of blank soft film~~.

1 Cipher pad of soft film in black plastic case, each page 35mm size, containing 15 cipher pages per frame.

1 Sample page containing cipher pages number 001 through 015.

1 Cipher pad on soft film in rool 1/8 inch in diameter and 7/8 inch long, each page 35mm size, containing 15 cipher pages.

1 Cipher pad in roll 1/4 inch in diameter and 7/8 inch long, containing 2 pages per 35mm frame size, each page 5/8 by 3/4 inches.

1 Sample page as above, Page 061.

1 Strip of type 649 film 1/4 by 2 inches, containing 100 microdots in an area 1/8 by 1 3/16 inches, each dot representing one page of 100 five digit groups.

All cipher pads contain 100 pages of 100 five digit groups, each number 001 through 100.

Inventory of tradecraft items issued to TOPHAT by his FBI/CIA handlers for Polyakov's 1962 return to Moscow as an agent for the Americans. *(Courtesy of Edward Moody)*

There was one more thing the CIA wanted Polyakov to take with him, something much less run-of-the-mill: a special suit and shoes ensemble. The shoes had metal plates inserted in the soles, with another plate to be fitted across the chest, under the jacket. The suit had wires running up the inside of the pant legs and down the arms. Together, this contraption could transmit wireless information. The catch was that the wearer would need to find a high elevation to stand on, with arms outstretched, so that the transmission could go through unobstructed.

The FBI men looked at the wired shoes and suit and laughed. They called it the "Wizard of Oz" outfit, as it made them think of the Tin Man. When Polyakov heard of it, he laughed, too. Not surprisingly, the notion of bringing something like that through customs to Moscow, and then finding a hill to stand on with his arms outstretched, did nothing to improve Polyakov's assessment of CIA tradecraft.

Polyakov also rejected some of the CIA's proposed signal and dead drop sites. Instead, he named his own sites, and drew maps for the Americans, one of which was at the entrance to Gorky Park. It would be Polyakov, not the Agency, who would decide when communicating was safe. Operating in Moscow, with its smothering KGB presence, would require the most scrupulous attention to security.

Finally, Polyakov was given a special telephone number to call in an emergency, along with a password: the street address of their Madison Avenue safe house opposite Abercrombie and Fitch. The instructions were hidden underneath the leather covering of a key chain in case Polyakov needed a quick contact.

James Angleton sat in on one of the planning meetings the FBI had with the CIA. Moody and Mabey weren't surprised; Polyakov was a very big fish. Normally, having a GRU officer agree to spy for the Americans was cause to celebrate, but Angleton's demeanor and grilling about Polyakov's bona fides did not suggest celebration, or even respect. Angleton was dismissive of Polyakov's qualifications and suspicious of his motives. From the moment he first learned of Polyakov, Angleton had considered him a plant, a player in Angleton's master plan theory, and in his opinion, nothing had happened since then to change his mind.

★

In the Agency's Langley headquarters, Angleton had built a private fiefdom for himself that took up a good deal of the second floor, a fortress off-limits to most in the Agency. Within that fortress were various inner chambers and vault rooms, guarded by Angleton's secretaries, and the sanctum sanctorum, Angleton's own office. "When a visitor entered Angleton's office," the journalist Tom Mangold wrote in his book *Cold Warrior*, "it was almost impossible to see the head of the head of CI. His long, thin frame would be stoop-hunched behind a Berlin Wall of files. Since the blinds were firmly closed, the room was always dark, like a pool room at midday. The only lights came from the tip of Angleton's inevitable cigarette, glowing like a tiny star in the dark firmament of his private planet, and the dirty brown sun of his desk lamp, permanently wreathed by nicotine clouds." Here, Angleton insatiably gobbled up intelligence information from around the world, sharing his growing belief in vast Soviet schemes with only a few initiated loyalists.

If Angleton's obsessions had been set off by his friend Kim Philby's betrayal, they were propelled over the edge by a KGB officer who, in the fall of 1961, knocked on the door of the Helsinki CIA station chief's home and asked for asylum. Anatoliy Golitsyn was a KGB major, a midlevel analyst with an insider's knowledge of KGB structure and procedures. He was also a man driven by an inflamed sense of his own importance and a compulsive need for recognition.

Anatoliy Golitsyn defected to the United States with tales of the KGB's superhuman effectiveness at deceiving the Americans. He claimed he knew of an overarching KGB plan to destabilize the CIA by feeding it a series of phony volunteers and provocations, each of whom would be under KGB or GRU control while pretending to be genuine defectors. This, then, was the infamous master plan the Black Hats were persuaded by and that spurred the derision of SB Division officers such as Gus Hathaway and my father. The "Monster Plot," they nicknamed it.

Defectors often exaggerated their own importance and the importance of the information they brought with them, and many of the SB Division officers doubted Golitsyn and his stories, seeing him as self-aggrandizing and untrustworthy. Angleton, however, was all ears, looking for corroboration of his own deep-seated suspicions. Golitsyn reinforced Angleton's convictions about the reach and diabolical cunning of the enemy. In Anatoliy Golitsyn, he had found a soul mate.

In his debriefings, Golitsyn declared that anyone who came after him with claims to be a defector would of necessity be a Soviet plant. Golitsyn claimed he was the most valuable source ever to come out from Soviet intelligence, and this conviction struck perfectly with James Angleton's ever-more-paranoid psyche.

Angleton's obsession resulted in attacks on the bona fides of all the post-Golitsyn Soviet defectors and sources. The harm this did to American efforts to understand and counter Soviet power is incalculable.

"Angleton's destruction of the credibility of this squadron of defectors occurred during the years of the most crucial and potentially explosive relationship between great powers since World War II," Len McCoy, an officer with the CIA, later explained in *Cold Warrior.* "The West contained and confronted the USSR with great difficulty. There was the U-2 crisis, the Berlin crisis of 1961, the Cuban crisis a year later, the Middle East wars, the development of horrendously powerful new weaponry, missile gaps, missile superiority . . . My Lord, did we need information during the sixties! It was a time when the USSR and the U.S. were at each other's throats, with the future of the world at stake." Anatoliy Golitsyn brought the counterintelligence chief's deepest fears to life, and in the process, twisted the CIA into knots that would take a decade to untie. "Nearly everything the Soviet Division acquired from agents was poisoned by Angleton," McCoy recalled.

Dmitri Polyakov knew nothing about Golitsyn's declarations or Angleton's paranoia. Nor did he know that he'd had his first sit-down with John Mabey less than a month after Golitsyn defected, right on schedule with Golitsyn's warnings about others who would come after him. For this reason, James Angleton distrusted Polyakov, and made this clear to Mabey and Moody. Yet Angleton, in his position as head of counterintelligence, did not have formal authority over the SB Division, nor over the FBI's Mabey and Moody, both of whom believed that the Monster Plot was ludicrous. Ed Moody and John Mabey knew Dmitri Polyakov. They knew beyond any doubt how genuine the man was.

★

On June 6, 1962, Polyakov boarded Cunard's 83,000-ton flagship, RMS *Queen Elizabeth*, bound from New York to Cherbourg, France. Somewhere behind him in the line of passengers (traveling under the names John Mitchell and Edward Morris) were John Mabey and Ed Moody. Mabey would continue the contact on the voyage to France, and Moody would provide security.

Traveling on board the ship with Polyakov gave the FBI agents perfect cover as tourists to continue interviewing their new asset in the privacy of their cabins, and to spend time practicing the cipher system Polyakov had learned back in New York.

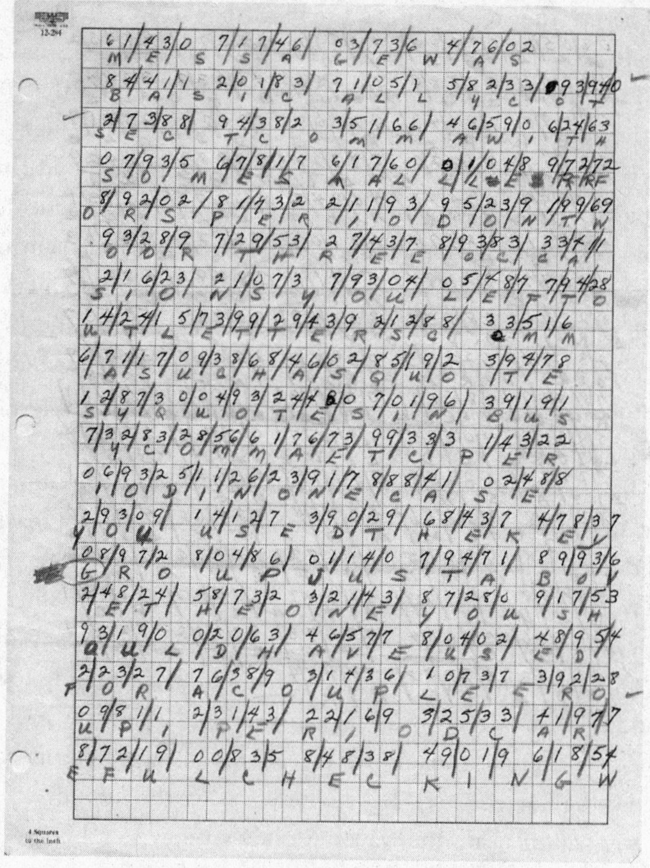

A cipher practice sheet in Polyakov's hand, April 1962. Letters were encoded to strings of numbers. The numbers were then translated back into letters for practice cipher grading. *(Courtesy of Edward Moody)*

Another item on the FBI's agenda was a stash of around three hundred pictures it had sent along of Soviets in the United States. Special Agent Mabey showed them to Polyakov to identify which might be intelligence officers and what their jobs were, and tape-recorded Polyakov's replies. Yet neither Mabey nor Moody had given any thought as to what to do with the photos after Polyakov finished identifying the people in them.

The crossing took five days, and as they approached France, Moody turned to the task of destroying the pictures. (He couldn't risk French customs finding them.) He tried first to rip them up, but they were stiff-backed, and the stock would not tear. Next, he put them in a bag, opened a porthole, and tossed them out. But a strong wind tore the bag open and blew the photos across the deck of the ship, causing Moody and Mabey to chase after them in a panic. Once the photos were collected, Moody tried flushing them down the toilet in his cabin, but it quickly stopped up and overflowed. In desperation, he set to burning them in his stateroom bathtub, but the cellophane-backed photos would not catch light.

Finally, a day out of Cherbourg, Moody took a plastic bag from the ship's laundry, put all the photos in it, filled it with water, and let it soak in his tub overnight. The next day, as they approached Cherbourg harbor, he tied the bag up, opened his porthole, and threw the sodden bag out. Watching it slowly begin to sink, his eye caught a submarine sitting a few hundred yards away from the *Queen Elizabeth*, sporting a large red star on its conning tower. Moody's heart began to sink along with the bag. There goes my career, he thought, imagining the photos of KGB spies floating around the Soviet vessel. But nobody was on the sub's deck, and the bag sank beneath the waves. Moody sat down on his bed and breathed a deep sigh of relief.

From Cherbourg, Moody and Mabey took the same train to Paris as Polyakov. They had arranged a final rendezvous with him in Paris, but when the two agents got to the meeting place, there was no signal and no Polyakov.

Their star Russian colonel was gone.

CHAPTER 6

HOME AND AWAY

Paul Leo Dillon, ID photo, c. 1970. *(Author's collection)*

Leaving Germany in early 1962 for Dad's posting back in Washington, Mom wrote to her sister, "As anxious as we were to get back to America, leaving Berlin turned out to be heartbreaking. It really has been home, with the children having been born and growing up there." She and Dad "were on the verge of tears," Mom wrote.

Our new house in Vienna, Virginia, a suburb of Washington, DC, was not as grand as our Berlin home with its fruit and nut trees and leafy surroundings, but we crowded in just in time for the arrival of another brother, Jacob, making a total of seven children. Mom and Dad had wanted a big family, but this was as far as my mother was willing to go, and she made that clear to Dad. Ever the conscientious Catholic, Dad talked to his priest about birth control. The priest told him he couldn't give him permission to use it, but he could absolve him of it when he came to confession.

★

Dad settled into the daily grind at Langley, work that focused on trying to scope out Soviet intentions and capabilities. The Cuban Missile Crisis was still fresh in America's memory, and the threat of nuclear annihilation was embedded in the country's psyche. Even at our school, Our Lady of Good Counsel, we were taught the drill: get into the hallway, away from the windows; sit with your head between your knees; and wait for the all-clear signal.

My father was making his career in the SB Division at a time when James Angleton's obsessions were tainting the Agency with suspicion and derision. Dad and his like-minded colleagues might have mocked Angleton's Monster Plot, but Angleton and his cohorts were grimly serious. Officers returning from overseas were told to read a briefing book Angleton's people had put together containing all the so-called evidence for the grand KGB conspiracy. The book purported to demonstrate how the Soviets were deceiving the Agency's field officers right across the board. Afterward, the returning officers were asked to sign off that they had "read and understood" the material, and were asked, "Do you believe the evidence in this book, yes or no?" Ed Juchniewicz, one of Dad's colleagues and the associate deputy director for operations, said, "We all just said no."

Angleton was the CIA's first chief of counterintelligence, and in the Agency's organizational chart, he was no higher than the chiefs of the other divisions. In reality, though, he exercised far greater power. Counterintelligence was responsible for protecting CIA operations from penetration by outside elements, which meant that Angleton needed to scrutinize all prospective recruitments and defections. To perform this task, he had the right to look over all the Agency's personnel, operational, and communications files.

SB Division field officers such as Gus Hathaway and Ben Pepper especially resented Angleton's intrusions and the implication that their judgment was questionable and their work incautious. Still, by the end of our first year back in Washington, Angleton's suspicions began to reach far deeper into the division's business. As the influence of the defector turned conspiracy theorist Anatoliy Golitsyn grew on him, Angleton became convinced that the CIA had been penetrated by a mole, a well-placed Agency employee who was selling his services to the Russians.

The result was the "Great Mole Hunt." The hunt homed in on SB Division case officers, the people who had developed contacts and relationships with KGB and GRU officers and other Soviets. These were the officers, Angleton believed, who were most vulnerable to being turned and who had ready-made pipelines back to Moscow Center via their assets. Yet the hunt wasn't confined to the SB Division. Officers in other divisions, and even outside the Agency, such as political appointees who had spent time in the USSR, came under scrutiny. (As just one example, Averell Harriman, the blue-blood former ambassador to the Soviet Union, was one such unlikely target.)

In order to ensure that the internal investigations were carried out secretly, Angleton created the Special Investigations Group, or SIG, a unit within the Counterintelligence Division so secret that most non-SIG counterintelligence officers weren't even aware of its existence. Its office, just around the corner from Angleton's own, was off-limits to all but his chosen few. "We non-Black Hats," Ed Juchniewicz later said, "were sectioned off from an area on the second floor. Only certain people could enter, people in the know.

It was ridiculous. They were like a bunch of monks going off to the priory."

"These guys were playing these silly games, selling us a bill of goods," Juchniewicz said. But the silly games had grave consequences. Through his close relationships with a succession of CIA directors, Angleton retained his position and influence into the early 1970s. During that time, his baleful impact fomented a creeping paralysis in the Soviet Bloc Division. Case officers came to realize that developing any Soviet asset would arouse suspicion about the asset and perhaps even them. The SIG was cloaked in secrecy, but a palpable air of a witch hunt hovered over the division. "The result," wrote Milt Bearden, a chief of the Soviet East European division, in his book *The Main Enemy*, "was that the Agency had probably missed out on a goldmine of secrets from citizens of the Soviet Empire who had sought to change sides."

From a national security perspective, Angleton's crusade was a disaster. The mole hunt ruined the careers of quite a few CIA officers on whom his suspicions fell, including some of Dad's colleagues from Berlin. Many of these people were never promoted, were assigned to dead-end jobs, or were simply dismissed for reasons they never did learn. In the SIG vaults, their personnel files were marked with an *H*, for HONETOL, the informal and closely held code name for the hunt. "Careers were destroyed, reputations smeared, and lasting enmities sown," wrote journalist Tom Mangold. Eventually, "between one and two hundred files stamped with black H's were stored in the secure area behind the yellow line," Mangold wrote, describing the cordoned-off SIG area. Yet among all those people investigated by SIG, not a single mole was ever discovered.

Ed Juchniewicz was one of the suspects. One day, he was called to Dave Murphy's office for a grilling. "Such was the paranoia within the division at the time," said Juchniewicz, "that Murphy actually turned up the volume of the radio in his own office to drown out any possible bugs."

Angleton continued to hold Anatoliy Golitsyn as a close and influential adviser, brushing off concerns from many around him who considered Golitsyn a highly questionable, unstable source of information. Dr. John Gittinger, the CIA's chief psychologist, had no doubt that Golitsyn was paranoid. "No question that he was mentally ill," Gittinger is quoted in *Cold Warrior.* "He showed a marked degree of paranoia . . . He suffered from a form of megalomania."

Gittinger made his diagnosis on the basis of an examination that was given to all defectors. His evaluation was circulated, and Angleton would almost certainly have read it. What should have rung alarm bells was apparently ignored or disregarded by the counterintelligence chief. Dr. Jerrold Post, a psychiatrist who founded the CIA's Center for the Analysis of Personality and Political Behavior and had significant contact with Angleton over the years, thought

James Jesus Angleton was the CIA's chief of counterintelligence from 1954 to 1975.

that Angleton and Golitsyn "shared the same delusional system and fed off each other, in a psychological *folie à deux*."

★

Of all the destructive consequences of Angleton's paranoia, none was uglier or left more soiled memories than the treatment of Yuri Nosenko, a KGB officer who defected to the Americans only a few months after Dmitri Polyakov's first meeting with John Mabey.

Yuri Nosenko worked in the KGB directorate responsible for internal security. Rising to the rank of lieutenant colonel, Nosenko targeted America's Moscow embassy, looking for spies and recruitment possibilities among foreign journalists and tourists visiting Russia. He came from Communist Party aristocracy—his father was the Soviet Union's minister of shipping—and was upwardly mobile, and trusted. Yet, like Polyakov, he had become dissatisfied with the hypocrisies of the Soviet system. Then, in 1964, on a mission to Geneva, he contacted an American diplomat and defected to the United States.

Also like Polyakov, Nosenko was unaware of the Golitsyn/Angleton conspiracy theories that were tainting the CIA's Soviet Bloc Division. He knew nothing about Golitsyn's declaration that fake KGB defectors were coming to the West to sow disinformation and confusion. Angleton's staunch belief in Golitsyn's warning sealed Nosenko's fate, however. To Angleton, Yuri Nosenko was without a doubt a KGB penetration agent.

The information Nosenko had to share with the Americans was explosive. He defected in February 1964, about ten weeks after Lee Harvey Oswald killed President Kennedy. The United States was still in shock, and the FBI and CIA were desperate to solve unanswered questions about the assassination.

One pressing question was about Oswald himself. Was he or was he not a Soviet agent? Oswald had spent three years in Moscow and married a Russian woman. He returned to the United States, and then went to Mexico, where he contacted the Soviet embassy and tried, unsuccessfully, to get a visa to Cuba. Piecing together this history after the assassination, the CIA hadn't been able to determine if Oswald worked for the Russians, or if Moscow might have ordered the murder of a U.S. president. Yuri Nosenko claimed that he knew, that he had seen the KGB's Oswald file.

The KGB, Nosenko reported, had never recruited Oswald. They had looked him over but concluded that he was mentally unstable and of no use. Oswald, Nosenko said, was *not* working for the KGB. The Russians had had nothing to do with the assassination.

Yet, if Nosenko was a plant sent to spread disinformation, as Angleton believed, what did that mean with regard to possible Soviet involvement in the president's murder?

The goal of the Black Hats was to get Nosenko to tell them what they regarded as the truth, that he was a penetration agent. Dave Murphy was now head of Eastern Europe operations and would shortly become chief of the SB Division. He shared his boss's certainty that Nosenko was a provocation. "The subject," Murphy wrote in a departmental memo referenced in David Martin's book *Wilderness of Mirrors*, "is here on a KGB-directed mission . . . Subject must be broken at some point if we are to learn something of the full scope of the KGB plan."

With Angleton's approval, Murphy and Pete Bagley, Nosenko's case officer, kept Nosenko in a small attic bedroom in a safe house under close guard and put him through extended hostile interrogations and several polygraphs. When Nosenko didn't break, they moved him to a ten-by-ten-foot windowless concrete cell specially constructed for him in a remote wooded area of the Farm, the nickname for Camp Peary, the CIA's training base near Williamsburg, Virginia. Here they imprisoned Nosenko for three years under extraordinarily harsh conditions. The bare light in his cell was never turned off; he had no blanket or pillow; he was given nothing to read, had no writing materials. He was fed scanty, unappetizing meals, and though he had smoked his entire adult life, he was denied cigarettes. He had no visitors. He claimed later that he had been drugged.

Despite the years of his illegal imprisonment, Nosenko continued to maintain that he was who he said he was, a defector, not a plant, someone who wanted nothing more than to live in the United States as an American citizen. With no mole in sight, the Nosenko case dragging on, and the Soviet Bloc Division virtually shut down, people who counted began to question Angleton's judgment. Nosenko's case was given a thorough review, then another. Ben Pepper, my father's good friend and colleague from Berlin, was a leading opponent of Angleton's serpentine theories, and participated in the CIA study that, in 1969, after four years of incarceration, exonerated and released Yuri Nosenko. To Angleton's dismay, Nosenko was later hired by the CIA as a consultant, and became a U.S. citizen.

★

Amid this environment of mistrust, suspicion, and plain immorality bred by Angleton and his cadre of Black Hat loyalists, why was it that Dad, who spoke Russian fluently and handled numerous Soviet cases, was not among the many whose careers were affected by the mole hunt? Sandy Grimes explained that "Paul managed to avoid scrutiny by the Black Hats in the division by packing up his expanding family and accepting overseas assignments far from their crosshairs."

Doing just that, Dad came home from work in the spring of 1965 and announced, "We're moving to Mexico!"

CHAPTER 7

TO THE MEXICO STATION

Julia, Leo, me, Paully, Mom, Maria, Jacob, and Clare at the Pyramid of the Sun, Teotihuacan, outside Mexico City, 1966. *(Author's collection)*

In the summer of 1965, Dad and Mom packed all nine of us into the Opel Kadett we'd brought back from Germany, and we headed out for the cross-country drive to Dad's new posting, in Mexico City.

When living in the United States or on home leave, we would alternate our summer vacations between Dad's brother's house in

Cape Cod and Mom's childhood home in Savannah, Georgia. Our visits to Savannah were magical. Our grandfather had personally built a simple two-story, four-bedroom brick house in the 1940s on the banks of a beautiful salt marsh that stretched for miles along the Vernon River, in a community called White Bluff. The dirt road leading to the house wound under a dense assemblage of live oak trees, lush with low-hanging Spanish moss.

Grandmother always had cold watermelon and chilled boiled peanuts ready when we arrived. We'd swim off the dock in the creek when the tide was high and slog through the fragrant pluff mud when it was low. We'd set traps to catch crabs by the dozens, and bring them to the kitchen door in a big tin tub, screaming in mock horror as Grandmother dropped them alive into a huge cookpot of boiling water. Dad would drive us all out to the beach on Tybee Island for the day, or we'd spend the afternoons reading on the dock, drinking iced tea that Grandmother always brewed fresh.

With the stop in Savannah, and visits to Mom's sister and brother in Memphis and Texas, it took us three weeks to get to Mexico. Our new house was a Colonial-style, cream-colored stucco castle—at least, it seemed like a castle to us kids—in the upscale neighborhood of Polanco. The windows, doors, and balconies were handsomely decorated with detailed wrought iron, and stone and hand-painted tiles covered the floors and staircase. An interior balcony from our parents' bedroom looked over a huge two-story entrance hall, with a banister sweeping down the staircase from the second-floor landing. (Mom and Dad could afford this grandeur because housing in Mexico cost a fraction of what it did in the United States.)

We took to the house immediately, using the balcony for performances of *Romeo and Juliet* and walking down the staircase only when our parents were present; when they weren't, we gleefully disobeyed them by sliding down the banister.

Shortly after we arrived, Mom wrote to her mother: "The first two days I was petrified to drive—the traffic is wild! Warm tortillas are delivered to the house every day. We have been out a few times in the evenings—once to the Ambassador's for cocktails—and once to dinner at Ben and Perky Pepper's."

Dad was reunited with Ben Pepper in the Mexico City station. It was wonderful when we overlapped with people we'd known in other postings. Our itinerant lifestyle meant that just as we were getting to know friends well, we or they would be off to another assignment. Dad and Ben were good friends, and Dad was always fond of the appropriately nicknamed Perky Pepper. We went on weekend outings with the Peppers and their children, and they'd come over for parties with others from the office.

We also made friends with kids in the neighborhood. Guillermo, Emilio, and Pepe lived on our block and were always running in and out of our house. On our birthdays, Mom would string up a piñata from the balcony.

To get us out of the house, Dad would take us to the ancient Mesoamerican ruins of Teotihuacan, about an hour outside the city, famous for its pyramids. We would scramble up to the top while Dad sat happily at the bottom, people-watching and smoking Pall Malls. Dad also loved attending bullfights. It was a little surprising that Mom did, too, though wherever we lived she was always drawn to local color. In a letter to her mother, she explained, "Tomorrow Paul is taking the day off and we're going to a 'Tienta'—a testing of the bulls for bravery." Sometimes my sisters and brothers and I would go along. When we did, I vividly remember the same very drunk man standing up among the seated spectators, swaying on his feet and yelling insults at the matador. We couldn't always hear what he was saying, but the crowds around him would erupt in laughter. "El Borracho," they called him. "The Drunk." He was a regular at the fights, a beloved part of the spectacle.

Not long after we'd settled in, we had a new member of the household, Angelina, a fifteen-year-old girl Mom hired to help out. Even though she was only a few years older than Maria, she seemed like an adult to us. Angelina was from a village a few hours from the city, had little experience with modern things, and would pick up the phone when it rang, ask callers in Spanish whom they wanted, and then hang up while she ran off to find the person. With her first payment in hand, she went to the market to get her ears pierced, and came back with gaudy, dangly fake diamond earrings. My sisters and I were mesmerized.

Angelina lived with us, and with her sweet disposition and guileless nature, we soon regarded her as one of the family. She had been working for us for a year or so when we began to spot a smartly dressed young man looking in from our front gate. Raul was tall, with green eyes, and Angelina was totally smitten with him. On weekends, he picked her up for dates, and we surreptitiously followed them to the park and spied on them kissing on the park bench. Mom, well attuned by experience to the signs of pregnancy, was the first to notice Angelina's expanding belly. When Mom and Dad confronted her, Angelina broke down in tears and unnecessarily begged them not to fire her. Raul had disappeared, she told them, and she was frantic. Mom helped her get ready for the baby, and Angelina gave birth to a little girl. Gloria became like a baby sister to us; we helped feed her and walked her in the stroller down to the park while Angelina worked. We were now a family of eight kids.

All the girls, along with Leo, attended a small American school called Lomas. Paully and Jacob were still too young. I soon became best friends with Liz, a girl in my third-grade class. Liz's parents, Jeanne and Frank, were from Boston, had the same accents as Dad, were Catholic, and had five young children. With so much in common, our two families quickly became fast friends.

Frank, Liz's dad, was head of Columbia Pictures in Latin America. The 1966 Acapulco Film Festival was coming up, and Dad knew that Frank was hosting a few tables at the opening-night gala. Could Frank make a seat available at the gala for his "man," and could that seat be at the table next to the one booked by the Russian filmmakers?

Frank agreed, without asking any questions. "We were pretty sure Paul didn't work for the State Department," Frank said years later. When the evening came, Jeanne made certain that she and Frank were sitting at the same table with Dad's "man," so she could watch the action up close. Jeanne remembered being so focused on the drama going on in front of her that she barely noticed the famous and glamorous stars seated at tables all around her: Gina Lollobrigida, Lynn Redgrave, Michael Caine, Dolores Del Rio, Bob Hope, and others.

As the dinner progressed, Dad's "man" proceeded to get "drunk," then even "drunker." Leaning over to the adjoining table, he cracked a joke with one of the Russians, and once a tipsy rapport had been established, he stumbled over their way, collapsing into an empty chair. Soon he was getting into sloppy but "heartfelt" conversations, slapping the Russians' backs and bursting into guffaws at shared jokes. After dinner, Jeanne noticed him hanging out with a few of the Russians at the bar, their arms around each other's shoulders, singing. What might have happened after that she didn't know, but it did leave her feeling that being an undercover agent might be more fun than she'd imagined.

A year later, Frank was offered a new job at Paramount Pictures, and he and his family moved to Rome. I was devastated at the loss of my best friend, Liz. Moving to new places and experiencing new cultures made for a rich and exciting childhood, but the downside was having the intense friendships of youth abruptly cut off.

Me holding Gloria, our housekeeper's daughter, Mexico City, 1967. *(Author's collection)*

★

Mexico City was one of the world's great spy capitals. Its proximity to the United States made it a natural center for Soviet operations. Mexico permitted the Soviets a large embassy and staff, more than half of whom were either KGB or GRU. Russian agents in the United States could easily cross into Mexico to meet with their handlers and plan their activities in less dangerous surroundings. Going the other way was just as easy: Soviet illegals could slip across the Mexican border with almost as little difficulty as they could coming in from Canada, as Kaarlo Tuomi had. Almost nowhere else in the world offered such opportunities for Soviet intelligence operations. Mexico City was "a labyrinth of espionage," wrote Jefferson Morley in *Our Man in Mexico*, "a city of intrigue like Vienna or Casablanca with spies of at least four powers angling for advantage: U.S., Soviet Union, Cuba and Mexico."

To counter this, the CIA base there was the Agency's largest and best equipped in the Western Hemisphere. Winston Scott, one of the CIA's most highly regarded and influential figures at the time, was the chief of station. When we arrived in Mexico City, Win Scott had already been station chief for nine years when the standard tour was four. (His tour would eventually last thirteen years.) Scott's task as CIA chief of station was to combat communism. Mexico's ruling elite, looking to protect their privileges, shared a deep interest in this agenda, and Scott was only too glad to collaborate in keeping a close eye on Communists, both homegrown and foreign.

Scott was an amiable man, with a talent for manipulation that made him a legend within the Agency, especially for those who knew about the remarkable net of influence he had woven around Mexico's top political leaders. He had recruited a succession of Mexican presidents and their chief deputies as paid agents of the CIA.

Scott's close relationships with the Mexican government heads gave him access and behind-the-scenes authority that made him, rather than the American ambassador, the de facto primary U.S. government representative in the country. During Win Scott's tenure, several ambassadors came and went. Fulton Freeman, the ambassador in place while we were in Mexico, insisted that he, and not the CIA chief, would exercise the full scope of an ambassador's traditional role vis-à-vis a foreign head of state. But he got nowhere with either Scott or Mexican president Gustavo Diáz Ordaz—nor with President Lyndon Johnson when the dispute made its way to the Oval Office.

Win Scott's diplomatic cover in Mexico City was under the title embassy first secretary. Dad's was second secretary, the title he provided to anyone who asked him what he did. In reality, though, Dad was head of the station's Soviet/Satellite section. And although he met with Win Scott regularly, Dave Murphy back at Langley, chief of the Agency's SB Division, was still Dad's boss.

The Soviet/Satellite section was the largest group within the Mexico City Base. Dad had eight case officers working for him, a support staff, and probably fifteen to twenty access agents, people recruited to cultivate friendly or casual contacts with Soviets and report what they were learning. With these assets, Dad kept tabs on the opposition and trolled for potential new sources who could provide him with inside knowledge of Soviet operations.

Occasionally, people came from headquarters to give lectures at the station. One was Pete Bagley, the Black Hat case officer involved in the imprisonment of Yuri Nosenko at Camp Peary. "Pete Bagley came to Mexico City and gave what became a famous lecture, full of Soviet provocation crap," Gus Hathaway said. "He was a mouthpiece of Angleton's. Ben Pepper and your Dad said it was full of shit."

Despite ongoing pressure from the Black Hats, Dad and his colleagues stayed focused on their mission of seeking information from the Soviets. They maintained three observation posts around the Soviet embassy, took photos and videos, and everyone going in and coming out was documented. From a section of row houses bought previously by Win Scott, Dad's people could see into the embassy's private garden and watch, if not overhear, activities there. They photographed license plates, ran traces on cars, identified people, and put tails on anyone of interest. In addition, they monitored Soviets entering and leaving the country, tapped Soviet phone lines, and tried to decipher electronic signals from Soviet cryptographic communications. Dad's section also kept personal files on all Soviets they thought might be significant, with information on their families, residences, interests, friends, work habits, drinking proclivities, and womanizing.

Through one of their access agents, Dad's section set a honey trap for the Soviet embassy's *zavhoz*, the chief administrative officer. The agent owned a little grocery store that was patronized by staff of the nearby Soviet Mission. The Mexican owner was friendly and talkative with the Russians, and the embassy's *zavhoz* liked to take breaks and chat with him. When the store owner learned that the *zavhoz* was eager for female companionship, before long a pretty Mexican girl began frequenting his store, gossiping with the owner and then with the *zavhoz*. A little flirtation with the Russian led to some backroom necking and then to visits to the girl's nearby apartment, rented by the Agency and equipped with recording devices. The intelligence results from that dalliance were closely held, but an officer who had seen the tapes later wrote that the Russian *zavhoz*'s "virility astonished both the girl and the station."

A more serious case involved another access agent working for my father, an American English teacher who was a devoted weekend fisherman. The Soviet KGB *rezident* was a fisherman as well, and eventually the two met and became friendly, taking weekend fishing trips together to mountain streams away from the city. The English teacher was reporting on the Soviet to Dad's section, which was preparing an attractive defection plan to offer the *rezident*. But an analysis of the teacher's reports by a KGB specialist from CIA headquarters indicated that the Soviets may have doubled the teacher, and ensuing investigations confirmed that he was likely reporting on my father to the KGB.

★

In July 1967, a young case officer named Philip Agee joined my father's staff in a special position. As a Mexico desk officer at Langley headquarters, Agee had gotten wind of an opening in Mexico for an "Embassy Olympic Attaché" to prepare for the upcoming Summer Olympics there in 1968. The opportunity was golden—

hundreds of Soviets were coming to Mexico to support their vast Olympic efforts. This huge international event provided significant opportunities for an American intelligence officer to interact with, befriend, and recruit Soviets (and Mexican officials) under the "deep cover" of an official member of the U.S. Olympic Committee. From Langley, Dave Murphy recommended Philip Agee for the "attaché" job.

What neither Murphy nor Dad (or anyone else) knew was that Philip Agee was arriving in Mexico City with a chip on his shoulder. As an operative in previous posts in other Latin American countries, he'd come to believe that American policies in South America supported only the ruling elites while most people remained in poverty, and that the CIA was a cog in the machine propping up the dictators and strongmen who were suppressing and exploiting the masses. Agee planned to quit, and he hoped that his Olympic assignment would lead him to another job outside the CIA. But that intention he kept strictly to himself.

All around Mexico City, Olympic preparations were going full steam. It was the first time the Olympics were to be held in a Spanish-speaking country, and the Mexicans were intensely proud. Yet the prominence of the upcoming Games and their public relations potential gave reform and antigovernment groups an irresistibly visible platform. In the lead-up to the Olympics, students demonstrated against government suppression of labor unions, and as the Games drew closer, the students gathered other grievances under their banner, in particular the huge sums that the government was spending on the Games. The money, the students declared, should have been used for education and social programs. The government, fearing that the image of Mexican progress and modernity the Games were meant to display was being compromised by the demonstrations, stepped up the repression. The police and military response to civil unrest became harsher and more brutal.

Ten days before the start of the Games, students gathered at the

Plaza de Tres Culturas in the Tlatelolco neighborhood, a major downtown demonstration site, shouting slogans: "No queremos olimpiadas, queremos revolucion!" ("We don't want Olympics, we want revolution!")

Without warning, the police and army units surrounding the square opened fire. Casualty reports of what became known as the Tlatelolco Massacre vary; it's probable hundreds died, with many more wounded. Amid the arrests and confusion, police quickly carted off the bodies, ensuring that the real number would never be known.

The CIA had provided the Mexican government with intelligence on the organizations taking part in the protests. After the massacre, Win Scott reported to CIA headquarters various theories, some put forth by Mexican leaders, on the cause of the shootings and whether outside organizations—Cuban? Chinese? Soviet Communists?—had played a part. A counselor at the American embassy in Mexico said later that "the CIA station had reported fifteen differing and sometimes flatly contradictory versions of what happened at Tlatelolco."

Despite his many high-level government sources, or because of them, Win Scott appeared to be in the dark as to how the Tlatelolco Massacre had happened and how many casualties there had been. "Win had become so dependent on his well-placed sources," wrote Jefferson Morley, "that he had no independent means of getting accurate information about a hugely important political event." About the relationship between Scott and the Mexican government, Morley concluded, "The puppet master had become a puppet."

★

That Olympic summer, Dad invited the special "embassy attaché," Philip Agee, out for a cup of coffee. According to Agee, Dad relayed an offer from Win Scott of a promotion and transfer to the political section. Agee turned it down, telling Dad he intended to resign in order to marry the girlfriend he'd met while in Mexico, and to look for a job outside the Agency.

Another version of the story circulated through the Agency: that Agee had not resigned, but that Dad had fired him for reckless and unprofessional conduct. Whatever the truth might have been, a saying went around the Agency in those days: "If Paul Dillon ever invites you for coffee, you'd better watch your ass."

Whether Agee left on his own or was fired, his leave-taking was to have the most serious consequences, for Dad and hundreds of others. No one then understood how much of a security problem Philip Agee had become, or foresaw the actions that would have such a grave impact on Dad, his colleagues, and the CIA as a whole.

CHAPTER 8

THE PERSONALS

Training photo of Gorky Park, Moscow, dead drop site "Bob," 1962. Polyakov placed a small container with classified information at C, a crevice between the bench and the wall. A CIA employee posing as a tourist was cut out by the CIA. *(Courtesy of Edward Moody)*

Dmitri Polyakov's son Alexander stared out the train window at the bleak Polish countryside. He and his brother Petr, along with their mother, Nina, had left New York a month before Dmitri, in May 1962. The devastation Alexander saw through the window shocked him, even at the age of nine. Many of the train stations they stopped at or sped through were in ruins, bare concrete platforms with wrecked main buildings, bombed during the war and still not repaired seventeen years later. The cities were still filled with rubble and the crumbled remnants of deserted buildings. At night in Poland, in Belarus, then in western Russia, the urban areas they chugged by loomed darkly—not enough electricity, Nina told the boys. In the daylight, cities were shrouded in smoke from smokestacks and coal-burning train engines.

Moscow was better. Grandpa Kiselev was waiting for them on the train station platform, and they all returned to the apartment on Kalininsky (now Arbat) Prospect, the same one the Polyakovs and Kiselevs had shared after Polyakov's first tour in New York. The apartment had been given to Colonel Kiselev as a reward for his wartime service—three small rooms in the huge and prestigious "Officers' House," in a desirable central location near the Moscow River. Alexander had been six when the family left Moscow in 1959 to return to the United States. Three years later, he had only vague memories of the big modern building that now looked to him like a huge white battleship. It featured a large statue of Lenin in a courtyard that, in summer, functioned as a basketball court; in the winter, it was flooded and turned into an ice-skating rink.

In stark contrast, surrounding the Officers' House was a large slum of wooden shanties and barracks, dwellings for the neighborhood's worker families. From the window of his apartment, Alexander could see people dressed in drab gray clothes, sometimes carrying pails of water to their homes or making their way to or from outhouses behind the buildings.

When Polyakov joined the family a month later, he brought with him the big TV set from their American apartment. He also brought a pull-out sofa, a piece of furniture unheard of in Moscow in the 1960s. With Grandpa and Grandma Kiselev in one bedroom and Alexander and Petr in the other, Dmitri and Nina had the pull-out for themselves in an alcove off the combination kitchen-living-dining room.

Polyakov also brought gifts with him—fountain pens, lighters, panty hose, small items of jewelry, a few American toys—for his superiors and their wives and children. Western items were a big hit in a country with limited access to consumer goods. Polyakov's major purchase was for himself, a Shopsmith all-purpose woodworking machine. Though he loved to hunt and fish, woodworking was his true passion. He took the machine to Shchelkovo, a town twenty minutes north of Moscow where his parents, Fyodor and Alexandra, had moved after being evacuated from Ukraine during the war and where they had built a little house for themselves using Polyakov's combat pay. Polyakov set up a woodworking shop in Shchelkovo and began spending weekends at his favorite hobby, building cabinets and furniture.

It was there, too, that he and Nina had settled Igor, chronically ill and progressively weakening from the polio virus in his system, before their return to New York in 1959. Igor's grandparents could provide full-time care for the sick child, and now Nina and Dmitri were able to visit easily and often.

In the fall, Alexander and Petr entered the local grade school. Most of their classmates were from the neighborhood that surrounded the Officers' House, kids whose parents worked in a nearby fabric factory or in one of the sector's smaller industrial plants. Among the proletarian kids, Alexander and Petr stood out with their American clothes and foreign manners. *Amerikanski*, the two began hearing. Where do you live? When they answered, "The Officers' House," it didn't help.

They might have been *Amerikanski*, but the toys they had brought back were irresistible to the other children. Alexander had three or four buddies who would come up to play with his Legos, the toy cars, and especially the Lionel train running down its own track blowing its whistle, all in front of the giant American television set.

From the day they arrived in school, the boys were immersed in Communist socialization. Lenin's portrait hung in every classroom and hallway. Lenin icons were displayed in the schools' *Krasnyi ugol*, or "red corners," shrines to the great leader that were also found in most public buildings and private dwellings. The children laid flowers around Lenin statues, and learned songs and wrote poems about him, "the best friend of children." Petr, like all the other kids his age, became a Little Octobrist (named for the month the Russian Revolution began), a Cub Scout–type organization that trained children in the virtues of patriotism and group togetherness and readied them at age nine to enter the Young Pioneers, the older children's Communist youth group.

Alexander went right into the Young Pioneers. Every day, he wore a red scarf to school over a gray shirt. Girls wore red scarves, too, over brown dresses with black aprons. While the civics lessons taught to the Little Octobrists were couched mostly in the form of fun and games, with the Young Pioneers, serious political indoctrination began. Pioneers learned about the Communist Party, its history and structure, its mission of bringing about pure communism—to Russia first, then to the rest of the world. They were taught to revere the Party's leaders, Khrushchev and then Leonid Brezhnev, who replaced Khrushchev as general secretary two years after the Polyakovs returned. And they learned about the constant malevolent plotting of the Main Enemy across the water, with its NATO confederates and underlings.

The Young Pioneers were taught that good Soviet citizens obeyed their leaders and always conducted themselves as cooperative members of their group, reinforcing the lessons they were absorbing in school, where all classes were divided into teams that trained students to act as part of a collective. The collectives competed against one another for grades, good attendance, and good behavior marks; they played games and sports, collective against collective. Thinking back on the experience as an adult, Alexander remembered, "Whatever you did, you did within a team. You belonged to this team, and your success was due not to your own abilities, but to the abilities of the team. Being too clever was not good. You were always under the eagle eyes of the teachers who kept the Party records."

In both school and the youth groups, the children were taught to be upstanding patriots and devoted Communists, to become New Soviet men and women. But Alexander also remembered an undercurrent of cynicism in the jokes the kids told each other. "He was an exceptionally good boy," went one. "He never smoked until second grade, and by fifth grade he had dropped his drinking habits."

Humor aside, the conditioning was as pervasive as it was serious. While American children read the Hardy Boys and Nancy Drew books, Soviet children were wild for the novels of Arkady Gaidar, which were filled with dramatic and romantic stories of young boys' derring-do in the face of evil spies and nefarious capitalists. (Some Gaidar titles were even assigned to the curriculum of Soviet schools.)

Gaidar's books filled Alexander's preteen imagination. One, *The Drummer's Fate*, was his favorite. In it, a young boy's father is sent to the gulag for the crime of embezzlement; then his stepmother gets a divorce and runs off with another man. The boy is left alone until, one day, a man knocks on the door, saying he's his uncle. But the uncle is a Western spy with an accomplice, and the two men take the boy on a spree around the USSR, stealing secrets. The boy wants to turn the men in, but they are dangerous and are watching him closely. Finally, he finds a pistol at his Young Pioneer camp. As the men seek to flee with their bagful of secrets, the boy blocks their way—there's a shoot-out; the boy is wounded and wakes up in the hospital. But the point is that he's stopped the spies and he's a hero. As he recuperates, his father comes home to be with him again, having just had his sentence in Siberia reduced for good behavior. As happy an ending as any Hardy Boys adventure ever had.

Alexander and Petr were holding their own in school, but Nina was never comfortable with the neighborhood's tough kids and the school's low standards, and began searching for something else. With no private schools in Soviet Russia, the only alternatives were those that specialized in disciplines such as mathematics, science, or languages. There were a number of these in Moscow, elite schools with strict admissions requirements. Eventually, Nina got permission to apply to the Twenty-Second Specialized English Language School which the boys attended, even though it was a long bus ride away. (Two years later Nina joined the staff as an English teacher.)

Throughout Moscow's dreary winters, red banners and flags gave color to the oppressive gray of the city and the ubiquitous lines of shoppers. With food shortages common, families stood outdoors for hours to buy flour and other basics. Nina would take Alexander and Petr along to hold places in one line or another, and when one of them got close to a store counter, she would rush to join that line, since allotments were often sold only to a designated household head. When the purchase was made, the two would rush again to check the other boy's progress in his line.

The years 1962 and 1963 were especially hard for food in Moscow. The collective farms were breaking down, and the weather was the worst it had been in years. Milk supplies ran out, leaving stores with only powdered milk—until that, too, ran out. Even bread was scarce, butter nonexistent. To prevent profiteering, the authorities went over to a direct-distribution system for flour: two kilos a month per person, distributed in the "red corners" of apartment buildings. Alexander watched food officers weighing out the flour in the Officers' House lobby: one thousand kilos for the building's five hundred residents.

The realities of food lines and the scarcity of consumer goods contrasted surrealistically with the fulsome agricultural and industrial reports issuing from the television. The propaganda couldn't be escaped. One day, there was a knock on the door of the Polyakovs' apartment: state workers had come to install a radio into the wall of their kitchen. All apartments were to have one. It, too, issued a barrage of propaganda. Cynicism flourished, to the extent people thought about what they were hearing. *Chto est', to est'.* "It is what it is."

Alexander didn't exactly miss their old life in New York—it just seemed to him that he had left one world and emerged into another, with its different rules and customs. But he knew that this second world was his motherland, his true home, not that other faraway place whose abundance was fading from his memory as he grew used to his new circumstances.

Sometimes the family would take in a movie together, often one of the war movies in which the Soviet film industry specialized. Polyakov rarely talked about the war, but the films irked him with their propagandized versions of what the conflict had been like. That's not the way it was, he told his family, Russians in freshly pressed uniforms killing Germans. We were wearing whatever we could possibly find to put on. We were under siege, running, sometimes without pants.

On weekends, the family often went to visit Igor and grandparents Fyodor and Alexandra in Shchelkovo. Igor's health was deteriorating. His grandparents made him as comfortable as they could, but there was nothing anyone could do to reverse the ravages of his polio. He died in the spring of 1965, at the age of seventeen. The family held a small, private ceremony and buried him near the home where his grandparents had cared for him through most of his years.

In Shchelkovo, Polyakov continued his woodworking hobby, building furniture and cabinets, which he took to the Kalininsky Prospect apartment. Usually a taciturn man, when Alexander showed an interest in woodworking, Polyakov became an enthusiastic instructor.

Nina and the boys spent most of their summers at Grandpa Kiselev's dacha, a simple cottage with no insulation and an outhouse in the backyard. The dacha, located in a small village called Chelyuskinskiy, seventeen miles northeast of Moscow, had been given to Petr Kiselev after the war as a reward, along with the Kalininsky apartment, for the battlefield courage that had won him an Order of Lenin. Polyakov came out on weekends, a fifty-minute train ride. With the bows and arrows they'd brought from the United States, he and the boys practiced archery, and occasionally he took them along on his hunting and fishing trips. The family was friendly with neighbors around the dacha, some of whom were GRU or KGB acquaintances of Polyakov's.

Back in Moscow, Polyakov immersed himself in another pastime, photography, setting up a darkroom in the apartment's bathroom and keeping the door locked so that no one would come in and ruin the exposures he was working on. The darkroom put a bit of a strain on the family, with six people sharing the one bathroom in the Kalininsky apartment. Alexander sometimes wondered why his father spent so much time in there, though he liked looking at the photos he snapped of the natural world. Neither Alexander nor anyone else in the family had any hint that Polyakov was developing a different kind of film in there as well, a specially sized film taken from an unusual miniature camera.

Just as my siblings and I thought Dad was a diplomat for the State Department, Alexander and Petr believed their father was a diplomat for the Soviet military. And like us, they didn't find out until years later that he was an intelligence officer. What he was doing in the bathroom/darkroom was a secret known only to him, and to those few Americans who were his handlers and the processors of his intelligence.

Polyakov's office was in the new glass-sheathed, nine-story GRU headquarters in Moscow, nicknamed the Aquarium. A senior officer with two tours in the United States under his belt, Polyakov was assigned to the American division, overseeing intelligence activities in Washington and New York. This position gave him access to a vast range of secret and top secret information, including the supersensitive identities of Americans working as spies for the Soviets.

One day, some months after his arrival, Polyakov sat on a bench at the Krasnopresnenskaya Metro station waiting for a train. Only a highly trained observer would have noticed the casual motion of his hand as it fell from his lap for the briefest moment to the underside of the bench. When the train arrived and he stood up to board, a small Band-Aid was attached to the bench bottom. On the inside of the Band-Aid was a piece of microfilm. Departing the train in another neighborhood, Polyakov drew a chalk mark at a predetermined site, in passing, quickly and unobtrusively. The mark signaled that his first dead drop had been filled and was ready to be picked up.

The information on the microfilm was a bonanza for American intelligence, the FBI in particular. Polyakov had given them the identities of four American military personnel working in the United States as spies for the GRU and KGB: Jack Dunlap, an army sergeant assigned to the NSA who copied top secret NSA deciphering codes and interception operations; Lt. Col. William Whalen, a Pentagon staff officer working for the Joint Chiefs of Staff whose intelligence position gave him access to war planning, atomic weaponry, missile strategy, and other classified documents; Nelson Drummond, a navy clerk with high-level clearances who was providing information on weapons systems, electronics, and training and operating manuals; and Herbert W. Boeckenhaupt, an air force sergeant radioman with top clearance who was giving over detailed cryptographic and other secret communications information.

Polyakov gave American and British intelligence a bonus gift as well: an Englishman in the employ of the Soviets. Polyakov didn't have the name, but he had photographed the photographs the Brit had sent to his GRU handlers. The photos led the CIA and MI6 to Frank Bossard, a technical officer in the British Ministry of Aviation. It was a spectacular haul.

Each of these spies was apprehended months or even years after Polyakov identified him, making it highly unlikely that the KGB would ever connect him with the arrests. All were sentenced to prison terms except Dunlap, who committed suicide by piping carbon monoxide into his car the day after the FBI called him in for questioning.

★

Before Polyakov left New York, he had suggested to Special Agent John Mabey a new way of communicating while he was in Moscow, via coded secret messages inserted into the *New York Times* personal ads. As a GRU colonel, Polyakov had access to the American newspaper, prohibited to ordinary Russians. Drop sites would be men's names (Art, Bob, Charles). Signal sites would be women's names (Betty, Clara). Meanwhile, Polyakov would check the GRU's copy of the newspaper regularly.

Several weeks after Polyakov left the Band-Aid under the Metro bench, a brief ad appeared as a public notice in the *Times*.

> MOODY, Donald F., late of N.Y. Letter from Art received. Everyone fine except Cousin Phil who has not been located for settlement of estate. Perhaps you can locate him. Uncle John sends his regards. Please get in touch with brothers Edward and John F., Closter, N.J.

"Donald F." was code for Dmitri Fedorovich. "Letter from Art was received" meant that the CIA had picked up the Band-Aid from the Metro drop code-named "Art." "MOODY" at the start and brother "Edward" toward the end identified the sender, and John F. was, of course, John Mabey. (The rest of the ad was filler.) Ed Moody, who had placed the ad, had to use his real name and address, Closter, New Jersey, because the newspaper, as the writer David Wise later characterized it, "required that individuals placing personal ads identify themselves and provide their correct, verifiable name and address. Even the FBI, engaged in a high-risk clandestine operation, had to bow to the rules of the *New York Times*."

The message ran for twelve days, from September 19 through September 30, 1962, against the chance that Polyakov's bureau might not receive the *Times* on any particular day. Yet all those consecutive days aroused the suspicions of the Gray Lady's ad editor, who decided to check on whether the ads were legitimate. Ed Moody was asked to come down to the *Times* and explain himself.

When he arrived for the appointment, he showed his ID and told the editor that he was a special agent for the FBI. The ad had to do with a case he was not authorized to discuss, though the *Times* was free to call his supervisor to confirm. The editor did call, and only then did he allow the ads to continue.

★

A few weeks after Moody's *New York Times* message, something happened that must surely have spooked Polyakov. Oleg Penkovsky was a fellow GRU colonel who had become an agent for both MI6 and the CIA. Penkovsky was attached to the Committee for Scientific Research, and had provided the Americans and British with reams of technical information on Soviet nuclear arms and missile systems. His information had allowed American intelligence to identify the type of missiles and warheads the USSR was placing in Cuba. But on October 22, less than a month after Moody's ad told Polyakov his dead drop had been retrieved, Penkovsky was arrested in Moscow. An American agent had been caught in Moscow clearing a drop Penkovsky had left, which told the CIA that Penkovsky himself was now in the hands of the KGB.

Penkovsky's arrest must have reverberated through the Aquarium's halls, surprising Polyakov along with the rest of the GRU. Oleg Penkovsky, a colonel, a personal friend of GRU chief Ivan Serov and other senior officers, and a man with access to the most secret nuclear and missile information, was now in the Lubyanka prison, and shortly afterward was executed in one of the prison's sub-basements.

With Penkovsky's arrest, Polyakov went dark. His CIA handlers in Moscow and the FBI back in New York were expecting to hear from him again, but months passed and there was still nothing. Despite Polyakov's strict instructions that the Americans not come looking for him if he went underground, Special Agent Moody was asked to place another ad, in April 1963:

> MOODY, Donald F. Everything O.K. with Brother Bob and Aunt Betty. Let them hear from you. Send addresses Charles and Don for future real estate closings. Phil's estate unsettled. We are confident our real estate position is secure and will grow. Regards, brothers Edward H. and John F., Closter, N.J.

The "Bob" drop site and the "Betty" signal site were secure, Moody was telling Polyakov. Please get in touch, make a drop. Send locations for the next drop sites, Charles and Don. Again the message ran for multiple days.

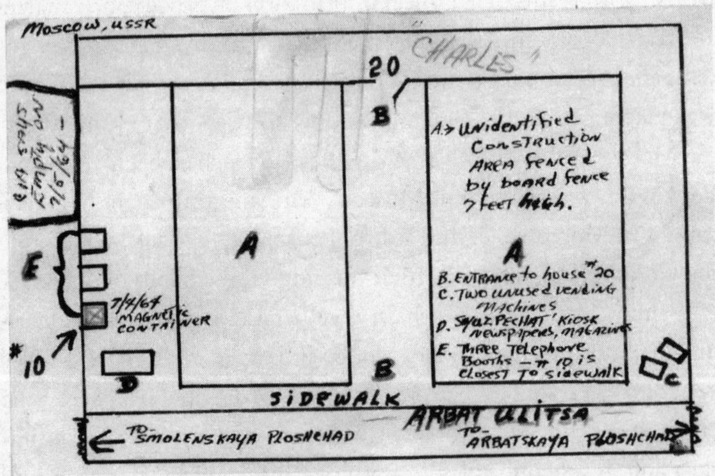

Drop site "Charles" was scheduled to be filled by Polyakov on July 4, 1964, using a magnetic container to be placed under a telephone booth's shelf. *(Courtesy of Edward Moody)*

Finally, two and a half months later, in early July 1963, Polyakov made his second dead drop and left a signal at "Betty," indicating it had been filled and was ready to be serviced.

Polyakov had filled "Bob," a drop site in Gorky Park, again passing over miniaturized photos of secret documents, including the names of the entire Soviet General Staff command. This time he had placed the film inside a small, hollowed-out rock, plastered the rock with tar, sat down on a stone bench in front of the park, and surreptitiously inserted the little rock into a narrow crevice between the stone seat and the abutting wall. Then he got up and strolled away.

When the Americans cleared one of his drops, they were supposed to mark a signal site acknowledging that they had received his information. But days passed, then weeks, and no signal came. Now Polyakov was worried. What had happened? Good tradecraft would never allow for a missed signal. If the Americans had not cleared the dead drop, it could mean that the ever-suspicious KGB watchdogs had found Polyakov's message. Polyakov had checked carefully for surveillance before he made the drop and hadn't seen any, but they still might have been following him. Perhaps the KGB was waiting to see who might come to check the site, the spy who filled it (him) or a CIA case officer coming to clear it.

There was another possible explanation. He wondered if the Americans could have been so careless as to simply miss his signal that the drop had been loaded. Bad tradecraft, but a possibility nonetheless. He didn't yet have enough experience with the American spymasters to judge their skills.

Polyakov was a master of controlling his emotions, so his family didn't detect any special signs of stress. Neither did his demeanor arouse any suspicions in the Aquarium. But he must have been in considerable inner turmoil. "It can only be suggested," said Special Agent Moody, "as to the thoughts which took place in his mind during this period."

Had Polyakov known why the dead drop wasn't serviced, he would have been not just astonished but also angry. James Angleton had never abandoned his conviction that Polyakov was a plant. Given the level and quality of intelligence Polyakov had provided, Angleton's judgment was no longer simply improbable; it was absurd. Yet, lost in his wilderness of mirrors, Angleton wasn't operating on the basis of reason: Polyakov could have signaled that the drop had been filled in order to lure a CIA officer there to clear it, setting up an ambush; or perhaps he was giving the Soviets an up-close opportunity to observe the Agency's modus operandi regarding agent communication; or maybe he was up to something even more nefarious.

Ed Moody, ever protective of his ward (the man he'd followed, documented, and believed in for over ten years) didn't like the suspicions the CIA was casting on Polyakov. In a long memo to his supervisor, Moody wrote, "It is noted in [the] referenced CIA memorandum that CIA makes the statement to the effect that the TOPHAT subject was under KGB control at the time he placed a message in a dead drop in Moscow in 1963." Not true, Moody insisted. "TOPHAT ranks with the best informants, having the greatest potential of any informant in the history of the Bureau." "His security," Moody declared, "is of paramount importance." Moody's voice echoes here through the stilted style of his official report, straining to convey the truth of his assessment, almost pleading with his superiors to believe him—and to protect the life of this unique individual to whom they owed so much.

Eight weeks passed before the Agency retrieved Polyakov's intelligence. To cover themselves, they claimed Polyakov had neglected to signal that he had filled the drop. Moody questioned their sincerity. "CIA makes a great deal of the fact that they say the signal was not left, however, CIA has not clarified how, when or how many times the signal site was checked."

In mid-September 1963, two and a half months after he filled the drop, Polyakov read in the *Times* personals:

> MOODY, Donald F. Letter from brother Bob received in August. However, Aunt Betty never heard from you. In April his daughter passed away and her child decided to stay with us. Our address is the same. Uncle Charles and sister Clara are in excellent health. Please write. Regards, Brothers Edward H. and John F., Closter, N.J.

The "Bob" site was cleared in August. We have your package. But "Aunt Betty never heard from you"—i.e., how come you didn't signal that you'd filled it? The next drop and signal sites, Charles and Clara, are secure. "Please write"—we're waiting for more information.

But Polyakov wasn't about to send more information. He must have wondered why the Americans were claiming he hadn't signaled. Of course he had signaled. He prided himself on his tradecraft. But what was going on with the CIA's?

On top of that, the day after he'd made the drop in Gorky Park, the Egorovs and Sokolovs, the two illegal couples he had identified to Mabey a year and a half earlier, were finally arrested in New York. The FBI had taken its time, delaying the arrests in order not to cast suspicion on Polyakov. Now, though, the New York newspapers were having a field day, splashing sensational headlines on their front pages about the "Reds" who had been caught as spies. When the Egorovs were traded for two Americans the Soviets had imprisoned, a headline screamed, "U.S. Frees Red Spy Couple." But the *New York Times* reported that a grand jury had indicted the Sokolovs, which meant they would be going to trial. Polyakov wondered who was going to testify against them—anything could come out.

With too much going on and too many risks, Polyakov decided to again lie low. With any luck, the CIA would adhere to its agreement and not come looking for him to reestablish contact, with all the attendant dangers that would bring.

Yet, in the *Times*, one personal ad after another appeared, imploring Polyakov to communicate.

> MOODY, Donald F. Our business will re-open August 28. You should see Brother Bob before then and advise him in detail on your position in this matter. Write Aunt Betty. We will visit Bob after August 28. All is well. Best regards, Edward H. and John F., Closter, N.J.
>
> ~
>
> Donald F., please write as promised. Uncle Charles and sister Clara are well and would like to hear from you.
>
> ~
>
> Traveling? When? Where? We hope for family reunion soon.

Polyakov ignored them all.

★

The Sokolovs' trial occurred in the fall of 1964. "The top drama of all is expected to come from the government's key witness," an article in the *New York Sunday News* reported, "a mystery man described as a former Moscow ace spy . . . Presumably, Russia still does not know of his defection." Then, on September 28, 1964, an article appeared in the *New York Times*: "Finn Disclosed as Double Agent at Spy Trial Here." The "Finn" was Kaarlo Tuomi, the illegal whom Polyakov had trained and who'd been doubled by the

FBI. Tuomi was about to take the stand as the government's star witness against Alexandr Sokolov and his wife.

Polyakov must have been amazed that the Americans would identify Tuomi, their agent, in public. Such a thing could not possibly have happened in the USSR. Farther into the article, he read, "Other Russians mentioned as members of the spy ring were Dmitri Fedorovich Polyakov . . ." The Americans had allowed his name to be revealed! Not as their agent, thank God, but as a Russian spying on America.

If Polyakov was mystified by a court system that would identify Tuomi and allow a newspaper to print his own name and lay bare his activities, several days later he read something equally astonishing. The Sokolovs' trial had been called off, just as it was about to begin. Citing an arcane 1795 law, the Sokolovs' defense attorney had demanded the names and home addresses of all the potential witnesses against the Sokolovs, a list that included seventy-five FBI agents and, of course, Kaarlo Tuomi. The FBI, Polyakov read, had refused to furnish that information, which meant that the prosecutor could not pursue his prosecution. With the jury already empaneled, the trial was canceled and the Sokolovs were whisked off by federal agents to be deported. The New York *Daily News* featured pictures of the Sokolovs on the front page with a huge headline, "SPIES FREED: Why U.S. Stopped the Trial."

More crucially, Polyakov's own cover was blown. During his entire intelligence career, he had been engaged with the United States, the Main Enemy, most of it on America's home soil. That wasn't going to be possible any longer. What would happen now, he wasn't at all sure. Having his identity publicized like this was almost certainly going to be disastrous for his career. He had trained and run Tuomi, and now Tuomi had been publicly revealed as an FBI source working against Moscow. For Polyakov, exile to Vladivostok or another distant outpost was not out of the question.

CHAPTER 9

HANDOVER

Nina and Col. Dmitri Polyakov at a diplomatic reception, Rangoon, Burma, c. 1967. Nina is being greeted by Burma's military dictator, Prime Minister Ne Win.

To Polyakov's relief, Vladivostok turned out not to be in his future. Instead of banishment, he found himself transferred from the American department to the Asian, and appointed station chief, *rezident*, in Rangoon, Burma. This was a strong signal that the GRU's leaders retained their trust and confidence in him, despite the Tuomi debacle. In Rangoon, he would be operating again under diplomatic cover as military attaché to the Soviet embassy.

As a foreign service post, Rangoon might have seemed like

a backwater to most. In terms of the Soviet intelligence effort, it was anything but. The Burmese *rezidentura* handled much of the important Soviet intelligence on China. Then there was Vietnam. In 1965 the United States had begun pouring ground troops into South Vietnam to counter the Vietcong insurgency. Meanwhile, North Vietnam was infiltrating its own regular army units. In Indochina, a major war was shaping up, and Burma was the nearest Soviet listening post.

Through a special agreement with the Burmese military regime, the GRU installed a huge electronic eavesdropping facility in its Rangoon station. In return for a generous supply of Russian military equipment, the Burmese permitted this outsize listening post to be manned by a large number of Soviet intelligence officers and technical experts. Polyakov was now the new chief of this operation, a responsibility that reaffirmed the trust his military and party superiors had in him. His new position gave him access to troves of highly secretive information.

★

Polyakov arrived in Rangoon in November 1965 with Nina and Petr. The Soviet Mission's school in Burma went up to only the fourth grade, so Alexander, entering sixth now, stayed behind in Moscow with his Kiselev grandparents in the Kalininsky Officers' House apartment.

The information to which Polyakov was now privy was, naturally enough, equally valuable to his American handlers—except that his links to them had been broken. He hadn't been in touch with them for more than a year.

That was about to change. A month after Polyakov arrived in Burma, Dave Murphy also found himself there on a stopover visit as part of a station tour of the SB Division's Asian operations. The Rangoon CIA chief of station told Murphy of a new Soviet military attaché who, during the usual introductory round of diplomatic cocktail parties, seemed curiously comfortable with Americans. The new attaché had even come by the American embassy once, on a visit to an air force colonel—ostensibly to ask about acquiring a car from a departing American diplomat. When Murphy saw the new military attaché's photo, he recognized him instantly. It was TOPHAT.

Murphy's cable to Langley set in motion an unusual pas de deux between the CIA and the FBI. Before Polyakov returned from New York to Moscow in 1962, the two agencies had decided that the CIA would handle his dead drops and signals in Moscow, but his intelligence would be shared, and the FBI would be responsible for communications, which was why Ed Moody had been placing the *New York Times* ads. But Rangoon was a new ball game. The connection needed to be reestablished, and the only American intelligence officer to have had a significant relationship with Polyakov was the FBI's John Mabey. The decision was made to send Mabey to Rangoon to reconnect. It was the first time ever that the FBI would be case-managing a spy outside the United States. The FBI and CIA jointly gave Polyakov a new code name (or cryptonym, in the Agency's parlance): BOURBON. (For reasons of security, it was customary to change an asset's code name/cryptonym regularly.)

Burma's postindependence parliamentary government fell under military control in a coup d'état in 1962, after which it became one of the world's most isolated places, closed to all foreigners except those connected with national embassies or on official business. In January 1966, Mabey traveled there under a false name and under military cover, purportedly a member of a U.S. military assistance team.

The American embassy's air force colonel called the Soviet embassy to invite Polyakov to discuss the car he was "interested" in, and when Polyakov arrived, Mabey was in the colonel's office, sitting off to the side. It took a moment for Polyakov to notice him, and as he did, the Russian's face broke out in a smile, a rare show of emotion on his part.

For the next four months, Mabey and Polyakov met twice a week in safe houses Mabey had arranged. Again the information flowed—on Russian intelligence personnel, Soviet missile systems, Russia's military assistance to North Vietnam, and other Soviet activities relating to Indochina and China. Still, there were limitations: Polyakov's English had deteriorated since his time in New York, and Mabey spoke no Russian. As a result, highly significant technical information was fuzzed in translation, or missed entirely. Another handler was going to have to take over. "I was there four months," Mabey later reported. "All this time I was supposed to be CIA, not FBI." Both agencies understood that a handover was required.

When John Mabey returned to the United States he got an up-close taste of James Angleton's preoccupation with Polyakov. Summoned to Langley to be debriefed, he found himself sitting opposite the counterintelligence chief in a CIA conference room. It was, Mabey said later, a cold, almost hostile debriefing with "the inquisitor," as Mabey called Angleton, who framed his questions to extract the "truth" about Polyakov. Mabey maintained that Polyakov was genuine, insisting to Angleton that the intelligence gleaned from his source had always been of the highest value. Angleton doodled incessantly during the entire interrogation. To everything Mabey claimed about Polyakov, Angleton had a consistent answer: it was "all bullshit."

★

In June 1966, a chalk mark appeared near the doorway of the bathhouse at Inya Lake, a popular resort area outside Rangoon, announcing to Polyakov that his new CIA handler had arrived and was ready to meet with him. When Polyakov showed up at the designated rendezvous he found not one but two CIA men, one of whom he recognized: Paul Dillon.

Dmitri Polyakov, 1962. *(Courtesy of Edward Moody)*

Dave Murphy had sent my father to Rangoon to introduce Polyakov to Jim Flint, his newly arrived handler, since Dad "had been the guy in touch with Polyakov from the very beginning." Murphy stopped short of revealing in what capacity my father would have interacted with Polyakov earlier in the case. The most probable scenario would have been in 1962, when Dad was working at Langley—he likely traveled up to New York to help the FBI coordinate Polyakov's communication plan with the CIA prior to his return to Moscow. When Dad went to Rangoon to smooth the way for the continued flow of information, our family had only recently arrived in Mexico City. For us children, Dad's leaving suddenly for a couple of weeks was nothing out of the ordinary.

Jim Flint was an odd choice to be Polyakov's new handler, however. He was an idiosyncratic Yale graduate who peered at the world through thick glasses and won few friends with his tendency to look down on those he considered beneath his intellectual level. Flint owned three suits, all black, each with holes burned by ashes falling from the cigarettes that constantly dangled from his lips. His Agency colleagues nicknamed him "Digger O'Dell," after the mortician on the popular TV show *The Life of Riley.*

With his tobacco-stained teeth and unkempt appearance, Flint most likely did not make a good first impression on the neat and meticulous Polyakov. There was little warmth in their handshake, or in the relationship as it progressed. But Flint was smart and knowledgeable, and spoke excellent Russian. Most purposefully, Dave Murphy had appointed Flint as Polyakov's handler for a reason: like Murphy, Flint was a hard-core Black Hat, a true believer in Angleton's Monster Plot theory. Flint was on a dual mission: to handle Polyakov and his material, but also to prove that Polyakov was a provocation, as James Angleton believed, and not to be trusted. It was a bizarre, conflicted role, not one conducive to developing a warm rapport between handler and spy. The Monster Plot paranoia was so intense among the Black Hats that they believed the KGB might try to kidnap Flint in Burma, so he was authorized to carry a gun for protection.

Polyakov might have found Jim Flint distasteful, but he handed over prodigious volumes of information. The flow grew to such proportions that the SB Division at Langley set up a special branch wholly dedicated to processing Polyakov's material.

Polyakov/BOURBON regularly provided photographed copies of the contents of GRU pouches coming from and going out to Moscow, as well as cable traffic, information on GRU operations and spies throughout the world, secret technical data with specifications for the newest rocket systems, military and foreign policy directives, and information on the Chinese and North Vietnamese militaries, along with their strategic and tactical doctrines.

The value of Polyakov's intelligence was evident in the strata of the people and organizations that consumed it: the White House, the Pentagon, and the State Department. Dmitri Polyakov was a gold mine, and in Mabey's view, thousands of pages of reports and documents attested to his legitimacy. Most in the FBI, including J. Edgar Hoover, were equally convinced. But Angleton's obsession had turned the CIA schizophrenic; his power and influence and the fear he inspired pervaded the Agency, and officers resisted his convoluted reasoning at their peril. As Walt Lomac, an Angleton disbeliever at the CIA who would head up the special Polyakov-dedicated branch, put it, the counterintelligence chief and his Black Hats "turned every fact around to fit their premise."

Angleton's determination to unmask Polyakov was further provoked when Polyakov reported that the GRU hierarchy had been shocked and appalled by Yuri Nosenko's defection. This information contradicted Angleton's belief that Nosenko, locked away in solitary confinement deep in the woods at the Farm, was a provocation and not a genuine defector. Anatoliy Golitsyn had also convinced Angleton that the so-called China-Soviet split was a sham, that it was engineered by the two Communist powers to deceive the gullible Americans, and that Polyakov's intelligence to the contrary should not be trusted.

The Black Hats' efforts to prove Polyakov's duplicity also centered on the networks of illegals that Polyakov had given away when he first volunteered in New York. Polyakov had personally trained many of those illegals and dispatched them to their assignments in America. For most, the jumping-off point between East and West had been East Germany, where a GRU officer handled their transit. This officer, Petr Popov, had also volunteered to the Americans and had provided information on the illegals. Popov's bona fides as an informant were brutally established: he had later been caught by the KGB and executed. So, if Polyakov's information on the illegals conflicted with Popov's in any way, that, in Angleton's opinion, would prove that the Russian was lying and that he was indeed a Soviet plant.

In Rangoon, Polyakov found Jim Flint's persistent interest in the details of the illegals operations strange. The illegals were ancient history; the intelligence Polyakov was providing now was urgent, often actionable. Why, he wondered, was his handler so obsessed by those old cases? It was an aggravating waste of the limited time they had together in the safe houses and darkened movie theaters where they met. (The BOURBON analysts back at Langley could tell that Flint was dangerously annoying Polyakov with his interminable questioning about the obsolete illegals cases.)

Eventually, though, after two years Flint's tour was over, and his successor was Al Kapusta, yet again another Black Hat. Polyakov told Kapusta he considered the West weak, American leaders irresolute and, worse, "bound by civilized rules of behavior," wrote Sandy Grimes, handling the case back at headquarters. His leaders, Polyakov believed, were not. After the 1968 USS *Pueblo* incident, in which North Korea captured the American vessel without its having fired a shot, Kapusta got a lecture from Polyakov on the cowardice of the American commander. "A Soviet naval commander would have fought to the death before surrendering his ship to the enemy," Grimes paraphrased Polyakov as saying.

Polyakov took "special delight" in supplying the Americans with technical documentation on spy equipment, but he was never reckless. He did it carefully, never requesting manuals and design plans except where there might seem good reason for him to have them.

So, when one of his assets in Rangoon was scheduled to receive training on a long-range agent communications device, Polyakov asked GRU headquarters to send him, along with the training pamphlets, the top secret, one-hundred-page design manual. Moscow denied the request, saying the manual was of use only to the engineers at headquarters. Determined, Polyakov argued that it would be helpful for repairs in the hot, humid climate of Burma, and Moscow relented. He used the same argument to obtain documents on other devices the Soviets had developed (rollover cameras, copying gadgets, miniature recorders), all of which he turned over to the Americans. "Over time he had developed a distrust of CIA spy gear, opining that it was neither user-friendly nor reliable," wrote Grimes. He preferred the Soviet-made equipment: simple, rugged, dependable. Polyakov believed that CIA engineers would gain from the technical documents he was providing.

Al Kapusta handled Polyakov until August 1969, when Polyakov was rotated back to Moscow after finishing a four-year tour. In preparation for his return, Kapusta furnished him with an elaborate communication plan, including dead drop and signal sites, onetime pads, secret writing materials, and instructions for using a one-way radio voice link.

Polyakov reiterated to Kapusta that it would be too dangerous for the CIA to initiate contact with him in Moscow. He'd had his experience with the CIA's Moscow operation. He himself, he emphasized again, would initiate contact when necessary.

By the time he left Rangoon, Dmitri Polyakov had become one of the most productive spies in America's Cold War history. But he was still under the gimlet eye of James Jesus Angleton, and that was not a healthy place to be.

CHAPTER 10

EXIT THE MOLE HUNTER

Sandy Grimes, 1971. Grimes supported the Polyakov case at CIA headquarters for more than twenty years.
(Courtesy of Sandy Grimes)

One evening in Mexico City, in the spring of 1969, Dad came home from work and gathered us all together. We're moving to Rome, he said. For a thirteen-year-old, the thrill of going to live in such a magnificent and historic city was overridden by the realization that I'd be reunited with my best friend, Liz, who'd moved to Rome one year earlier.

We were all excited about going, but what about Gloria? We begged Mom and Dad to adopt Gloria and bring her and Angelina with us. They were part of our family. Gloria, almost three, was our baby sister now. But it was not to be: Mom and Dad found Angelina a job with another family from the embassy. We cried for hours on our last day together, taking turns holding Gloria for the last time.

When we got to Rome and saw our new accommodation, we understood better why Mom and Dad said that keeping Gloria and Angelina wouldn't be practical. In Rome we couldn't afford anything like our huge house in Mexico City. Instead, we moved into a small apartment on the top two floors of a building near the Ponte Milvio, an ancient bridge over the Tiber. On the bottom floor, the three boys shared a bedroom with a triple-decker bunk bed. Up a narrow spiral staircase, all four of us girls slept in one room with double bunk beds, next to a second little room that we turned into a dressing room/study.

Upstairs in our private little suite, we pretended we were in a college dormitory; we felt sophisticated, grown up. We were all tweens or teenagers by then—Julia, the youngest of the girls, was twelve; and Maria, the eldest, was sixteen. And we were in Rome, the Eternal City!

A letter from Mom to her mother, a few days after we arrived, was typical of her making the best of every situation: "The apartment was at first glance a disappointment. But I decided that it will work out very well. Our terrace is magnificent, with a nice view of the city. So far we are delighted with being here. The Italians are friendly, and don't seem to be bothered at all by the fact that we scarcely understand them. They still babble away at us a mile a minute, and are very patient with our bewilderment."

Liz and I were in heaven in Rome. We went shopping, watched pickup soccer games in the streets, and ate gelato in the Piazza Farnese or the Campo dei Fiori. We sat on the Spanish Steps and made bead necklaces. Liz even convinced me to jump into the Trevi Fountain with her to reenact the famous fountain scene from *La Dolce Vita*. (The carabinieri were not amused.)

Frank, Liz's father, now worked for Paramount. We were again invited to private screenings, which we thought were the epitome of chic, but the glamor didn't end there—the American Overseas School of Rome was bigger than Lomas in Mexico, and more sophisticated, filled as it was with the children of diplomats and those of the rich and famous. Maria was friendly with Sighle Lancaster, Burt's daughter, who pronounced her name Sheila, but whom the kids nicknamed "Sigley," after the spelling. Even though a chauffeured town car dropped her off and picked her up every day, she was considered down-to-earth if very stylish, coming to school in casual dress-down jeans and fur jackets. Sammy Davis Jr.'s daughter, Tracey, was a student there, too.

Despite the fashions, the school was liberal, and the atmosphere thick with the revolutionary feel of the times. There were anti-Vietnam War protests and sit-ins on the campus. Some of the kids at school referred to themselves as "Communists," and they joined "cells," which was considered a very cool thing to do in the late 1960s. The American embassy was on Via Veneto, and one day Maria was walking by with her friends when she saw a cute and popular senior boy handing out Communist leaflets in front of the embassy. Wanting to impress him, Maria helped with the handout, but it was all being watched, and the participants were quickly identified. When Dad got home that evening he was angry. "Are you out of your mind?" he said. "Now I have to explain why my daughter was handing out Communist propaganda in front of the American embassy!"

On weekends, Dad took us to see the Catacombs, the Forum,

and the *Pietà* at St. Peter's Basilica in Vatican City. At the Pantheon, we were amazed that the rain fell right through the roof and all over the beautiful marble floor. At the Bocca della Verità (Mouth of Truth), a first-century Roman sculpture of a god's face, Dad explained that if you put your hand in the sculpture's mouth, it would bite it off if you'd told a lie. The boys wouldn't put their hands in there, at least not in front of Dad.

At the famous Baths of Caracalla, Mom and Dad took us to see Verdi's opera *Aida*, performed in the open-air amphitheater. The boys were bored and fidgeting, and Mom constantly shushed them. In the grandiose climactic scene, elaborately decorated horses were led onto the stage, and one of them lifted its tail and pooped. Having held back hours of suppressed energy, the boys burst into a loud laughing fit they just couldn't contain. It was days before Mom would speak to them again.

With the Vatican at its center, Rome was filled with beautiful old churches, and Dad would take us to Masses around the city. Once, we went to St. Peter's Square for Easter Mass, where Pope Paul VI, a speck up on the distant balcony, intoned in Latin to a huge gathering of the faithful. Although we were at the majestic center of the Holy Mother Church, with the Bishop of Rome and Vicar of Christ presiding, in the middle of the service a man standing next to Maria pinched her butt repeatedly. She brought it to the attention of Dad, who angrily shooed the man off. "Scusi, scusi, Signore," the man said to Dad, bowing apologetically and backing away.

★

Dad worked in the Palazzo Margherita, the magnificent nineteenth-century palace that housed the American embassy. He was heading the CIA's Soviet section again, but as a haven for espionage activity, Italy was not as active as Mexico or Germany had been. In Rome, he was supervising four or five case officers, trying to develop contacts with Soviets or potential targets from Soviet Bloc countries. He directed his officers, read their contact reports, developed new avenues of approach, and personally handled any significant cases that came along.

Italy had one of the largest Communist Parties in the capitalist world, propped up with Soviet assistance. Italian intelligence efforts were focused mainly on scientific or technical information, the stealing of which was something of a sport in Italy. As a result, the Soviet embassy concentrated on either the Italians who were stealing information from the Americans or the American scientists or businessmen from whom they were stealing it. GRU and KGB officers had little interest in meeting American diplomats (or people masquerading as diplomats, such as Dad and his colleages). Because a primary channel for developing contacts was through social interaction, opportunities for Dad's section were limited.

This meant that he was operating in a relatively relaxed setting, a pleasant contrast to the hornet's nests of Mexico City and Berlin. Italian intelligence wasn't even particularly interested in keeping track of American agents. Unlike French security, which never quite trusted the Americans, the Italian security teams were not likely to place surveillance on Dad and his colleagues.

A typical overseas tour for a CIA officer was four years—we had been in Berlin for six years and Mexico City for four. Still, we had lived in Rome for only a year when Dad was suddenly posted back to the United States. Mom told us it was because Dad didn't get along with someone in the office, but even to us that was transparently improbable. Dad got along with everybody. It was more likely, a senior Agency official told me, that he had been compromised, that his cover was blown.

It's unlikely that he was under any imminent threat, though, because as a final good-bye to the country, we took Dad's accumulated vacation time to go on a five-week camping trip. We went to Naples, Sorrento, Capri, Pompeii, Siena, Florence, Perugia, Pisa,

Verona, and Venice in the Ford station wagon we'd had shipped from the United States, nine of us packed in tight with three Wenzel tents (which leaked in the rain), folding chairs and tables, a Coleman stove, coolers, sleeping bags, suitcases, and other paraphernalia, all ordered out of the Sears catalog.

On that vacation Dad took delight in going with us to Sunday Mass in the greatest cathedrals in Italy: St. Mark's in Venice, the Basilica of Saint Mary of the Flower in Florence, the Duomo of Pisa. In Venice, we took a gondola tour and begged Dad to give us money for birdseed to feed the pigeons in St. Mark's Square. They had enough to eat, he said. In Florence, we giggled at Michelangelo's anatomically correct *David*, to Mom's annoyance. We dove for sea urchins off the Amalfi coast and took a hydrofoil ride in Capri, where we also went into the Blue Grotto, lying flat in the bottom of a rowboat in order to get through the low cave opening.

Just before we left Rome, Mom wrote to her mother, "Paul has been reassigned to Washington. The only regrets we have are for the girls, who have loved Rome and the school and their friends. Nonetheless, they are not too downcast."

The truth was that we were heartbroken to be leaving Italy.

★

On our way back to the States we stopped in Paris to visit Dave Murphy, now the station chief in Paris. The prestige of the Paris job, actually a demotion, helped mask the staggeringly Machiavellian motive for his transfer out of headquarters.

With Nosenko having been cleared, and resentment building within the SB Division, Angleton could sense that his star was fading. In desperation, he employed a new strategy to prove his longstanding belief in a master plot and a mole within the Agency: turning the spotlight on his own people, his cadre of loyal Black Hats.

From within his super-secret Special Investigation Group, he selected a protégé, Clare Edward (Ed) Petty, to lead the newly directed search for a mole, and one of Petty's first targets was Dave Murphy. Murphy had not only overseen a number of failed Eastern European efforts, but he was married to a Russian woman and spoke the language fluently—more than sufficient prima facie evidence to cast a pall of suspicion over him.

Visiting David Murphy in Paris in 1970 after he was secretly banished from CIA headquarters by CIA counterintelligence chief James Angleton. *Left to right:* Julia, Maria, Dad, Murphy's wife, David Murphy, their daughter, me. Leo is above, on the statue. *(Author's collection)*

Angleton's conviction that Murphy was a mole still astonished the few retired officers left from that period. "Jim Angleton went over to Paris," a colleague of Dad's, Walt Lomac, remembered. "Dave Murphy was chief of station at that point, and Jim called on the chief of French intelligence and said, 'Listen, be careful with Dave because we suspect him of being a Soviet agent,'" Gus Hathaway said. "He called on the equivalent of the French FBI and said Murphy was a KGB spy. Can you imagine that? Our own counterintelligence director! Angleton was mad as a hatter by then, in my opinion."

Hathaway, who at the time was stationed at headquarters, went on: "Two French internal security officers came over here to follow up on the story that Angleton told them Murphy was a spy. The French guys said, 'We know it's bullshit, but we got a free trip out of it.'"

Had Dad known that his former boss was under suspicion of being a mole, it would have given him a foretaste of the atmosphere he would be returning to at Langley, where Angleton still had the ear of the CIA director, Richard Helms by this point, but where his obsessions were failing him and his authority beginning to slip away. The SB Division was stanching the losses it had suffered from Angleton's divisive and demoralizing pursuits at a time when Dad was climbing in rank and stature within the division.

★

We were back in the Vienna, Virginia, house. That September, we all enrolled in public schools, but it wasn't an easy transition. Most of our new classmates had grown up together, and we stood out, newcomers with slight European accents and cultural backgrounds that were suspiciously esoteric. There were anger and protests about the Vietnam War, too, and a growing conviction that "Government is the problem!" For the first time, we became a little self-conscious about Dad's job, working as he did for the "State Department."

At Langley, Dad took over as head of the SB Division's counterintelligence branch. His return to headquarters was fortunately timed, just as the division was regaining some control over its operations. A high-level review was beginning to reveal the devastating effect of Angleton's paranoia on the division, and a new division chief was brought in to steady the ship's course and reignite operations. This included establishing the special branch to process the voluminous Polyakov intelligence flow from Burma. Unfortunately, although Angleton's star was beginning to fall, lingering doubts remained about Polyakov's credibility.

While still chief of the SB Division, Dave Murphy had named a seasoned case officer, Walt Lomac, to head the GRU/Polyakov branch. "Murphy thought I'd be one of the Black Hats," Lomac said years later, "but it didn't end up that way. Ed Juchniewicz told me, 'It's like St. Elizabeth's [a Washington, DC, psychiatric hospital] up there.'"

As the new branch head, Lomac attended a meeting in Angleton's offices. "They were all talking about a big plot going on. I suggested there was a less lurid explanation for all this. Pete Bagley [Nosenko's case officer] practically lunged across the table. I thought he was going to strangle me. That was the last time I was invited to one of those meetings."

For Walt Lomac, there were only two questions to ask about Polyakov's bona fides: Was he providing information that someone in his position would have access to, and did the consumers of that information (State, Defense, and the White House) believe it was accurate and valuable? The answer to both these questions was yes, so for Lomac, Polyakov was who he said he was.

Lomac continued to assert his belief in Polyakov's bona fides against relentless pressure from his superiors. Dave Murphy eventually cast Lomac out into the farthest reaches, exiling him to Africa and stifling his career. (A decade later the CIA awarded Lomac the Intelligence Medal of Merit in recognition of his courageous stand on Polyakov's behalf.)

★

One of Lomac's employees in the Polyakov support branch was a junior analyst—Sandy Grimes, in fact. Grimes had majored in Russian at the University of Washington, applied for employment with the CIA, and was hired as an "intelligence assistant." She was called to Washington for training, where she and six other young women aspiring to professional careers instead found themselves grouped with one hundred new secretarial hires being tested in typing and shorthand skills, which neither Grimes nor the six others possessed. No one in charge seemed to know why the women had been grouped with the secretaries. It was 1967, though, and the Agency was still largely blind to the stereotyping of females in the workplace—even professional agents.

Grimes's first assignment was to Walt Lomac's GRU branch in the SB Division, which she was told was supporting GRU officers worldwide. She spent a couple of months filing, making copies, and entering information on three-by-five index cards before Lomac confided to her that the team's ostensible purpose for overseeing GRU operations in general was actually cover for providing support for one GRU asset in particular: Col. Dmitri Polyakov. As Grimes copied and filed report after report, she wondered who this man was, the sole object of her entire work life, eight hours a day, five days a week.

While several of her young female coapplicants quit, frustrated by their relegation to menial work, Grimes made the best of it, reading deeply in the Agency's internal publications on the operations and structure of Soviet intelligence. Finally, she was sent to the Farm for training in tradecraft and operational procedures.

Grimes loved it. Returning to her branch, she understood better that in processing the thousands of pages of Polyakov material, she had in fact "struck gold," as she put it. "Polyakov had become my first teacher on the Soviet Union and its intelligence services," she later wrote. "I was learning about the enemy from one of its senior officers." When Dad arrived to take over the SB Division's counterintelligence branch, Grimes had just been promoted to full professional status. She was now reporting directly to him.

The vetting for Grimes's promotion had gone well, all except the interview. She had recently married, and the senior officer interviewing her asked when she planned to get pregnant. She didn't have to read too far between the lines. Motherhood would put an end to her career, he was inferring, since she'd have to stay at home to take care of the child.

Grimes wasn't happy that the Agency had taken so long to upgrade her in the first place, and the motherhood question didn't sit well. Do you have children? she asked the officer. Tell me, what are *your* plans for any additional ones? That ended the interview. He walked out without saying another word. Worried that her abrasive response had sunk her chances, she was relieved to hear several days later that she had met all the requirements and was now officially an SB Division professional officer.

With her strong work ethic and outgoing, optimistic personality, Sandy Grimes fit in with Dad's branch, and with Dad personally. Dad and Ben Pepper, who was also back at headquarters now, would take her out to lunch, regaling her with stories about their spy adventures in Berlin and Mexico City. Many years later, Grimes wrote about Dad in her book, *Circle of Treason*, praising his operational skills and his human qualities. "He never demanded the respect and loyalty of those he led," she wrote, "he unknowingly commanded it with his wit, charm, and unassuming way." He was also, she wrote, "a devout Catholic, and when he was out of earshot, his subordinates respectfully and affectionately called him Father Paul."

Two years later, Grimes did get pregnant, exactly what her interviewer had asked her about. She was afraid that my dad might have the same attitude the interviewer had. (Even worse, getting pregnant meant she'd had sex, an embarrassing admission to make to Father Paul.) When she got up the courage and told him, Dad hugged her. "I am so happy for you," said the father of seven children.

Sandy Grimes and a few other exceptional women were challenging the Agency's stereotypes. When we returned to Washington in the fall of 1970, the women's rights movement was in full swing, and at some point we noticed that a copy of Betty Friedan's *The Feminine Mystique* appeared in the house. Mom had been an editorial assistant at the *Middle East Journal* when she met Dad. She had enjoyed working in an office, but with marriage, her life had been children and housework and supporting Dad in every way she could, including hosting scores of cocktail parties and dinners for his work. At times it was overwhelming for her, maybe a little stifling. Looking back, we think the women's liberation movement came as a wash of relief for her. With newfound confidence, Mom began to let go of her pent-up guilt for not wanting to be June Cleaver. Testing a new sense of freedom, she told Dad that the government wasn't paying her to host all those cocktail parties, and she wasn't going to do them anymore. She found a part-time job at the local library, and when Dad came home from work, he would walk the two miles into town, have a beer at the Vienna Inn bar (a CIA hangout), and drive home with Mom when she got off from work. Mom wrote to her mother, "I'm enjoying the job tremendously."

Dad was a man of his time and place in many ways. He grew up in the thirties and forties, in Catholic Boston, attended a Jesuit high school and Jesuit Boston College, and joined the Marines. His convictions and values were rock solid, above all his Catholicism and patriotism. But he was never straitlaced or sanctimonious. His generous nature and love of a good joke saved him from that. And as deeply devoted as he was to his religion, even that wasn't immune to his sense of humor. Later on, the boys were besotted with the British comedy troupe Monty Python. They memorized whole Python routines and would reenact their favorite sketches for Dad, who would howl with laughter.

The most pointed skit for Dad might have been the one featuring the conspiratorial Judean People's Front and its competitors, the People's Front of Judea, and the Judean Popular People's Front, all of whom spent their energy fighting one another rather than their common enemy, the Romans. (The boys perfected the slapstick performance.) That must have seemed amusingly reminiscent of what had been happening at Langley when Dad was there in the early '70s. The boys entertained Dad for years with those skits, a welcome respite from the stress he often carried home from the office.

★

When we arrived back from Italy, Ed Petty, the man Angleton had empowered to conduct the mole search among his own Black Hat loyalists, was fast at work trying to solve the mystery. And in perhaps the most ironic turn of events, reflective of the desperate and cannibalistic suspicions within Angleton's fiefdom, Petty asserted that the mole was James Jesus Angleton himself!

Petty had collected at least twenty-five questionable cases in which Angleton was involved. Ironically, Petty's argument was based on the same kind of circumstantial evidence Angleton himself had used in his own witch hunts. As one journalist wrote later, "The sorcerer would have been proud of his apprentice."

Petty's findings were reviewed at the highest levels of the Agency, but the new CIA director, William Colby, called them "baloney." Almost no one believed that Angleton had ever been anything but devoted to his country, no matter the twisted and paranoid nature of his logic. But Colby was no friend of Angleton's, and after hearing from a succession of insiders of the havoc that Angleton had wreaked on the SB Division over the years, he fired him on Christmas Eve 1974.

News of Angleton's "retirement" was received in shocked silence by those who attended his farewell meeting. He had run counterintelligence for two decades, through the reigns of six directors, seven counting Colby. One senior official who saw him in the parking lot afterward and exchanged a few words with him said, "I had never seen a man who looked so infinitely tired and sad." Angleton stood there in the lot by his car, his head lowered, looking up once in a while at the building, "a tall, gaunt figure growing smaller and smaller" in the official's rearview mirror as he drove away. "He was still standing by his car looking up at the building when I turned a corner."

CHAPTER 11

BACK IN THE USSR

Signal site "Betty" was on this pillar outside a Gorky Park gate along Krimskiy Val. Polyakov was to signal he'd filled a dead drop by making a dark mark eighteen inches below the "rk38" painted on the pillar. An American embassy employee was posing as a tourist. *(Courtesy of Edward Moody)*

In August 1969, just as we were arriving for our yearlong stay in Rome, the Polyakovs returned to Moscow from Burma, reuniting with Alexander, who had stayed behind in Moscow with his Kiselev grandparents to attend the Twenty-Second Specialized English Language School.

Living alone with Grandma and Grandpa Kiselev, Alexander had found their three-room apartment spacious; he even had his own bedroom. Then the rest of his family returned, and things crowded up again. He and Petr bunked together, and Dmitri and Nina went back to the old pullout sofa in the kitchen alcove.

In those days, the Soviet standard for living space was six square meters per person, about sixty-four square feet. The Kiselevs' apartment, at four hundred square feet, or sixty-eight square feet per person, was slightly over the limit. By Soviet standards, the family was doing well with their living space, and to be assigned a bigger apartment was a forlorn hope: waiting lists for new apartments were ten years long.

There was an alternative, though. During the late 1950s and early '60s, Nikita Khrushchev instituted a massive building effort to alleviate the cramped quarters of the communal apartment system that had characterized urban living conditions under Stalin. His goal was to provide city dwellers with single-family apartments, a rarity in Russia. Thousands of low-cost prefabricated five-story buildings were built in cities across the country. They were called *khrushchevki.*

As awareness of this option in communal living increased, so did demand. The government responded by offering alternatives to state housing that required people to invest their own labor, money, or both. In 1958, "cooperatives" became available, and Polyakov's salary as chief of the *rezidentura* in Burma allowed him to invest in a one-bedroom cooperative apartment not far from Kalininsky Prospect. Alexander and Petr's grandparents moved into the new flat, and the Polyakovs spread out in the Officers' House. Dmitri and Nina finally had a real bed in their own bedroom.

At the Twenty-Second School, Alexander, now sixteen, was improving his grades so that he had a chance for admission to a good university. Every evening while his parents were in Burma, Alexander and Grandpa Kiselev had watched a half-hour news show together called *Vremya* (Time), viewing required by his school. *Vremya* was the Kremlin's official newscast, featuring worker and peasant heroism, the latest agricultural successes, and the most up-to-date anti-American propaganda. After the show, Alexander and his grandfather discussed what they'd seen. It was an opportunity for the old World War II hero to teach his grandson some essential life lessons. "Grandfather Petr was a man who managed to live under the radar," Alexander recalled years later. "He had survived the purges; he knew how to survive in difficult situations. 'Watch this, listen,' he was saying, 'you're hearing all this madness about steel production, about the Vietnam War, Soviet heroes fighting American aggression. Don't make waves, but understand the propaganda.'" At school, when students were called on to report what they'd seen on *Vremya* the night before, Alexander was well prepared, perhaps more so than he let on to his approving teachers.

Earlier, when Alexander turned fourteen, his Party conditioning had begun in earnest via his membership in Komsomol, the Communist Youth League—"a one hundred percent photocopy of the Communist Party of the Soviet Union," as he put it. He was issued his red Komsomol membership book, a document he would keep with him until he turned twenty-eight and was inducted into full Party membership.

Like every other Soviet high school, Alexander's had a Komsomol trainer who selected a student leader—"a guy with a brain, but also very steerable," as Alexander put it. Under this school leader, each class had its own student cell leader. At Komsomol meetings, cell members gave anti-American speeches: how America exploited and oppressed Native Americans and blacks; how American Communist Party leader Angela Davis was jailed and threatened by the FBI; about young people protesting against the war in Vietnam, living in tents in front of the White House. The enemy, they were told, was planning nuclear war against Soviet children, and they had to be prepared. The boys marched, drilled, and learned to use weapons; girls were given basic medical training. Pure communism, they were told, would be achieved in the 1980s—not that far in the future. They were inheritors of the bright socialist future, growing into New Soviet men and women.

Aside from the propaganda and training in party politics, Komsomol provided a sifting mechanism, one that identified and held back headstrong or recalcitrant tendencies. Voting on policy matters at meetings was open, which meant that those not voting "yes" were isolated and shamed, labeled an antisocial "White" as opposed to a loyal, patriotic "Red." Results of the votes were recorded in the meetings' minutes, brought to Komsomol regional headquarters, and entered into members' permanent records. Since Komsomol approval was a requirement for application to a university, the consequences of voting "no" could be thorny. Later on, housing, too, could be a problem for those with unfavorable records.

Komsomol membership required exemplary behavior. Troublemakers of any kind weren't tolerated, and members were lectured about smoking and drinking. But a streak of adolescent defiance was inevitable, and Russians of Alexander's and Petr's age groups fastened onto the deliciously forbidden music of the Beatles. ("Back in the USSR" came out in 1968, when Alexander was fifteen.) Alexander and Petr were huge fans, part of a generation that found an outlet in the Beatles' irrepressible, antiestablishment energy. Polyakov brought back tapes from Burma (probably provided by his American handlers), and Alexander copied them for his friends. As a Komsomol member, he had to be careful, but a whole generation of Soviets was surreptitiously listening to one of the world's most popular bands.

Polyakov wanted Alexander to go to one of the military academies, but his nearsightedness disqualified him from the army. With his good grades and recommendations from Komsomol, he was instead admitted, in the fall of 1970, to the Moscow State Institute of International Relations, considered one of the most prestigious and elite schools in Russia. His father suggested he get a "real profession" and enroll in the law faculty curriculum. (It was good advice, as Alexander would find out later.)

His studies were rigorous, and Komsomol requirements were more onerous than they had been in high school. Classes filled the weekdays; Saturdays were devoted to military training, field exercises, and studies. Since America was the main enemy, all the weekend student soldiers studied American English along with American army organization, American armaments, American tactics, American commands, and American communications. "We were considered to be reserve military interpreters in case of war," Alexander said. "After five years of it, we had to pass the state exam to get our diploma."

There was also no diploma without passing grades in Marxist-Leninist theory. The students studied the history of the CPSU (Communist Party Soviet Union), scientific communism, critiques of Western scientific theories, and critiques of capitalism with all its fatal flaws—topics for their required classroom speeches.

A couple of times a year the students were sent to the countryside to help with the harvests. Such trips were designed to remind them of their proletarian roots and to stimulate their feelings of solidarity with workers and peasants, but those feelings were lost on Alexander when he witnessed the true state of the harvest. Inefficiencies in the Soviet food supply led to some harvests going unshipped, left to rot in depots around Moscow, and labor was sent in to sort through huge piles of beets, potatoes, or cabbages, to pick out the least rotten produce. The stench was awful. "We'd have to do it all day, for a weekend, sometimes a week," Alexander recalled, "working with a doctor of science on the left, with a military officer on the right, for you not to forget how to work with your hands. Be a good worker. Remember your roots."

With all the political studies and "volunteering," only about 50 percent of Alexander's time was left to spend on his professional studies, putting immense pressure on the students to keep their grades up. It was the same for students in engineering, science, medicine, and other fields. His instructors, he recalled, put more emphasis on the importance of communism than on the students' professional studies. "You might turn out to be an incompetent lawyer," Alexander joked, "but it was imperative that you be a good Communist."

The CIA provided Polyakov with items to take back to Moscow as gifts for his Soviet colleagues and superiors, such as these sterling silver pieces.

When the family moved back to Moscow in 1969, Polyakov brought with him the CIA communications plan given to him by Al Kapusta, his final handler in Rangoon. It was a two-way plan that set procedures for him to communicate with the CIA's Moscow Station, and vice versa.

Polyakov's caution about contact with the CIA was empirical—he knew the fate of too many others who spied for the West. And he was still mistrustful of the inexplicable probing into extinct illegals cases he had been subjected to in Burma. But he meant to maintain his relationship with the Americans on his terms—he didn't owe the CIA anything. Unlike the common run of spies, he wasn't trading intelligence for money. Polyakov wasn't beholden, which meant that he was in charge, exactly where he wanted to be.

Not long after he arrived back in Moscow, Polyakov loitered for a few minutes at a tram stop. This was by arrangement; he was being observed by a CIA operative walking down the other side of the street. His presence at the tram stop announced to the Americans that he was back and ready to start. Polyakov's superiors had been pleased with his performance in Rangoon, but there was more the CIA was yet to know: Polyakov had been promoted to a more timely and critical position, chief of the China Direction, responsible for GRU operations against the People's Republic of China.

The Soviet Union's relationship with China had been under stress for some time. Beijing had long been Moscow's junior partner, but ideological differences caused the two Communist giants to break relations in 1962. In the following years, Mao Zedong challenged the Soviets' leadership of the international Communist movement, attacking what he saw as Russia's softening stance on the United States. The Soviet Politburo watched angrily as Mao aggrandized himself at their expense, calling the Russians "revisionists," a dirty word in the Communist lexicon. "The Americans are bastards," said Mao. "But they're honest bastards. The Russians are liars, too."

Running the USSR's eavesdropping operation in Burma, Polyakov had swept the Chinese airwaves and reported his findings swiftly and accurately. The Soviet-China rivalry had extended to Vietnam, where the two countries were vying for influence. Polyakov's intelligence had been significant on that front as well. Then, just before Polyakov returned to Moscow, a Chinese ambush on a disputed island in the frozen Ussuri River killed sixty Soviet soldiers and wounded almost one hundred. As a result, the Soviets began moving theater nuclear weapons into the region, and the makings of a border war were in place. The top brass of the GRU looked on Polyakov, a seasoned military man and a diplomat, as the ideal choice to head their China desk during this delicate period.

For First Secretary Leonid Brezhnev, the Cold War balance between the Communist and capitalist blocs was threatening to come apart, and China was the key. With China in line behind Moscow, the Kremlin had led a united front against the decadent West. Without this unity, Washington had an opening to play Moscow and Beijing against each other and reset the world's geopolitics to its advantage. But what actually was going on behind the walls of the Forbidden City? What was Mao Zedong's endgame? To understand his strategy, the Kremlin needed informed intelligence, and Dmitri Polyakov became a central player in that effort.

Beijing's intentions were of essential interest to the White House, where in January 1969 Richard Nixon assumed the presidency. Nixon instinctively understood that after twenty years of hostility, a historic opportunity might be at hand to upend the China/Russia equation. Like the Soviets, he required the best intelligence to inform his decisions. And in this, too, Dmitri Polyakov became a key player.

From his Rangoon station, Polyakov had been feeding reports to the CIA's Soviet Bloc Division, reports that highlighted a real and profound schism taking place between the two Communist states. Now, in the power center of the GRU's China desk, his reporting was even more authoritative, nuanced, and definitive. Counterintelligence chief James Angleton had always believed (influenced as he was by his informant Golitsyn) that the apparent China/Soviet split was a sham engineered by Beijing and Moscow to deceive the gullible West into hearing what it wanted to hear and letting its collective guard down. Polyakov's continuing intelligence flow provided concrete and credible evidence that the split was very real.

To get the information to the CIA's Moscow Station, Polyakov used the prearranged communication plan of dead drops and signal sites. He photographed the intelligence he thought significant, and wrote messages using the Agency's secret writing techniques. These laborious procedures were a challenge, not in terms of difficulty—Polyakov was an expert operative with a talent for devices and technology—but in terms of finding the necessary seclusion. At work in the GRU's Aquarium headquarters, he had none, and home was a crowded apartment where there was virtually no privacy.

Nonetheless, Polyakov spirited documents out of his office to photograph at home, in the only place available to him where no one would barge in: the family bathroom. The Minox Model III subminiature camera that Kapusta had given him in Burma wasn't specifically designed for covert work. It was noisy—the shutter was slow and made a loud click; film had to be advanced by hand; and it needed a special stand and a light source. Polyakov found his basic Soviet camera easier to use, so he took full sets of pictures with both cameras, photographing page after page while keeping an ear out for family members wanting to use the bathroom.

If that wasn't enough, on occasion he also used his bathroom's privacy to listen to the Panasonic RF-3000 shortwave radio the CIA had provided him. At the time, this was the Agency's favored means of communication with its agents in "denied areas." Along with the radio, Polyakov was given a schedule of dates and times when the Agency would send messages. Headquarters would encrypt the messages using a onetime pad and send them by cable to a communications unit in Frankfurt for transmission to Moscow, a system called a "one-way voicelink," or OWVL. Polyakov was supposed to tune in to his frequency at the prearranged time to hear a synthesized woman's voice counting in German: *eins, zwei, drei, vier, fünf . . . zehn*, one to ten repeated for a full ten minutes. This would give him time to tune in as accurately as possible, as the atmospherics between Frankfurt and Moscow were not always clear. Once he was on the right frequency, the woman's voice would begin to read five-digit groups of numbers, the first group coinciding with a particular five-digit group on his own onetime pad. Polyakov would write down the recited number groups, along with the subsequent groups the voice intoned. Once all the groups were read out, and Polyakov had transcribed them—in all, about a twenty-minute process—the woman's voice would say *Ich wiederhole* ("I repeat") and run through the sequence all over again. For another twenty minutes, Polyakov would double-check the numbers. Then, using his onetime pad, Polyakov would decode the numbers, a complicated formula in and of itself—all in order to reveal a message in Russian, and all while behind the locked door of his apartment bathroom.

Once the coded messages were delivered and deciphered, the handler and Polyakov were to discard their onetime pads. Russian cryptographers knew that by using the pads the Americans' codes were unbreakable, but they monitored the transmissions anyway, trying to determine the vectors—toward Kiev, or Moscow, or Leningrad—attempting to discover at least where the spies were located and possibly how many there might be. But the Americans knew this, too, and filled the air with dummy traffic in order to confuse them. Thus, in the skies over Europe and Russia, a constant arcane warfare raged, spy versus spy.

At Langley, the SB Division generated messages that told Polyakov about drop sites and signaling and content requests. But Polyakov tuned in to the broadcasts rarely, if at all. "Although he was issued a two-way plan," Sandy Grimes wrote years later, "he simply chose to ignore any CIA-initiated communication, which he considered too dangerous given the omnipotence of the local KGB and, by extension, the CIA's inability to operate securely in that environment." And as an astute chess master on the intersecting fields of military secrets, political secrets, and intelligence gathering, Polyakov understood what the Americans needed without being told.

For the first year and a half after his return to Moscow, Polyakov's intelligence flowed to the CIA's Moscow Station through a string of dead drops, and from there to Langley. Then, early in 1971, he went dark. No one knew why; he simply stopped communicating.

Also in 1971, David Blee became the new Soviet Bloc Division director. His background was in the Near East Division, with little or no Soviet operational experience, but as an outsider he was in a position to bring clarity and independence to his new job. CIA director William Colby had laid down Blee's mission to jump-start the fettered SB Division. "Let's go, let's go," Colby said. "Let's recruit all over the world!" Blee brought a laser-like focus to rooting out the Black Hats, making it crystal clear to the division's officers that their job was to go after the Soviets aggressively.

Sandy Grimes appreciated the orientation, though she was wary of Blee's single-mindedness and felt that with his lack of Soviet experience he didn't have a good feel for the target he was going after. In particular, he had no operational experience facing the KGB on its home turf.

Grimes wrote about Blee's impact on the division. "Aggressiveness and risk-taking would be the norm. No longer would the security of an operation determine its pace, whether that operation was abroad or inside the Soviet Union." She was especially unhappy that "Polyakov became the centerpiece of Blee's dictum."

By early 1972, Polyakov, the SB Division's most prolific source, had been silent for over a year, and Blee thought that the GRU colonel needed a kick-start. He demanded to know Polyakov's status, and ordered the team to make personal contact.

Grimes was horrified. Years of working on Polyakov's case had made her protective of him, and she valued him not just as a penetration of the GRU, but as a human being. Grimes had come to personally admire her asset's courage and determination, his motivations and values, not to mention his astonishing ingenuity. He was one of the greatest sources the Agency had ever had, and he deserved every protection that could be afforded him.

Besides, Polyakov had specifically told the CIA not to come looking for him.

Blee's demands, Grimes wrote later, constituted a reckless endangerment of the agent. The KGB had tens of thousands of officers operating in its homeland, and if the Agency tried to contact Polyakov directly and made even the smallest mistake, it would be putting his life in grave danger.

Grimes and her colleagues tried hard to dissuade Blee from pushing for a personal contact plan in Moscow. They pointed out that standard staffing procedures in the GRU meant that after two years at home, Polyakov would almost certainly be posted overseas soon, and their analysis predicted that New Delhi, India, would be his next posting. Outside the Soviet Union's borders, personal contact would be much easier and safer. Making an effort to contact him in Moscow was not just dangerous, but pointless.

Grimes believed they had made their case, but Blee listened to their analysis and dismissed it. Their predictions, Blee said, were "witchcraft." He wanted a personal contact plan, and he wanted it soon.

After generating and discarding various ideas, headquarters settled on a potentially workable and safe approach. Polyakov was professionally acquainted with an American diplomat in Rangoon, and their meetings there, sanctioned by his GRU superior, would have been recorded in the GRU files. That diplomat was now retiring, and the Agency hatched a plan whereby he and his wife would stop in Moscow as part of a retirement tour. The embassy would hold a cocktail party in the retiree's honor, and as a former diplomatic acquaintance, Polyakov would be among those invited. Then, an undercover CIA officer would make contact with him at the reception.

The plan had its risks. An unsolicited invitation from the U.S. embassy would automatically trigger suspicion and attention from both GRU security and the KGB. At home in Moscow, GRU officers didn't normally attend embassy functions. Overseas, with diplomatic cover, it was expected, but not in Moscow, where only KGB officers pretended to be diplomats and attended diplomatic functions.

Since Polyakov's previous sanctioned relationship with the American diplomat would lend legitimacy to the invitation, this plan seemed the safest available option to Grimes and her colleagues, given that they would have preferred no contact in Moscow at all. But when Polyakov received the invitation—and he wasn't pleased by it—his GRU bosses weren't able to find the files that documented the approved relationship with the American diplomat. As a result, Polyakov was subjected to an unpleasant and potentially dangerous interrogation by the KGB, who wanted to know who this American was and what his interest was in Polyakov. It was only after some of Polyakov's coworkers vouched for his claims that the relationship had been approved and properly reported that the KGB backed off, and Polyakov was allowed to attend—actually, he was ordered to go, whether he wanted to or not.

Alexander recalls his father preparing to leave for the affair. "I remember this reception because he was not happy to be going. He said he was busy, and this reception with the Americans was wasting his time."

In the course of small talk at the party, Polyakov told the undercover CIA "diplomat" that he would soon be posted to North Vietnam, and in preparation, he would first be visiting Hanoi with a Soviet military delegation. A little while later, some embassy people inconspicuously stood around him, briefly screening him off from the other Russian invitees. One of the Americans pressed a small metallic cylinder into his palm. Polyakov pocketed it, then calmly moved on to talk with other partygoers.

Behind his usual impassive mask, however, Polyakov was boiling with anger that the CIA would try something like this. The reception itself was bad enough, but to attempt a handoff in a room filled with KGB was extraordinarily reckless. Not only was it unplanned, but he had expressly told the Americans to leave him alone if he went dark. Had anyone observed the handoff, and had Polyakov been found with the incriminating evidence, the consequences would have been dire. Walking home after the party, he tossed the tiny cylinder into the Moscow River without even looking at it. If the Americans weren't going to follow agreed-upon procedures and so blatantly risk his security, he wasn't going to give their information the time of day.

After that, Polyakov went underground again. Six months later, the Soviet military delegation arrived in Hanoi, but without him. At Langley, this no-show created a spasm of panic. Had their plan been compromised? Had the KGB noticed the handoff? It was months before Polyakov came out of the dark, with a chalk mark on one of his signal sites. Moscow Station unloaded the drop and read Polyakov's brief message. Instead of going to Hanoi, he was being posted to New Delhi.

The "witchcraft" analysis of Sandy Grimes and her team had been right after all.

★

One evening, a few weeks later, Dad gathered us for an exciting announcement. We were leaving Virginia again. This time we were headed to India.

CHAPTER 12

ENTER THE MOLE

CIA officer Aldrich Ames would become the Agency's most destructive mole, selling secrets to the KGB for nine years.

When Polyakov filled the drop in Moscow in early 1973, Sandy Grimes was immensely relieved to know he was safe. Working in the branch devoted solely to Polyakov and his prolific flow of information, she had done everything she could to protect the GRU colonel to whom she felt so close.

Grimes and her husband, Gary, had, by this point, settled into a home in the Washington suburb of Reston. There, she had become friendly with a new case officer in the Soviet Bloc Division who lived nearby. His name was Aldrich Ames.

Rick, which is what everyone called him, was smart and easygoing, but not someone to take too seriously. His dress was unkempt and messy: he wore bargain-basement suits with rumpled shirts, and his hair was disheveled and didn't look clean. His eyeglasses were of an outmoded style, and his teeth were stained from tobacco use. (Grimes even noted that his socks rarely matched.) Rick Ames was "a gentle sort," she wrote later, "whose company his fellow officers enjoyed while silently laughing at his goofy physical appearance."

Before his assignment to the SB Division in Langley, Ames had served his first overseas assignment in Ankara, Turkey. He didn't flourish there. At the usual busy round of Agency parties, his wife worried about his excessive drinking, and his boss, in a performance review, noted that he was not good at recruiting, as he did not have the character or charisma necessary to get foreigners to trust and confide in him. The report recommended he be reassigned as an analyst, a job that required intelligence but not necessarily interpersonal skills.

Instead, when Ames returned to Langley, he was sent to a yearlong course in a foreign language school to study Russian. Logically, and in his eyes, that meant he "was being groomed for another promotion," Ames recalled years later. After completing the course, he was assigned to the SB Division, where he met Sandy Grimes.

Ames had a habit of procrastination and was rarely on time. When he, Grimes, and some others began carpooling, Ames was often late, keeping everyone waiting whether he was a passenger or the driver. Also, his drinking continued to be a problem. At two consecutive office Christmas parties during those years, he was cited for drunken and unseemly behavior by the CIA's Office of Security.

Ames spent those first years at Langley as a desk officer handling a modest workload of Soviet cases. He did a passable job, and received some standard-issue promotions. At one point he was temporarily assigned to New York City, a tour Grimes later described as well suited to him because, unlike in Ankara, he was not required to spot and develop Soviets. Rather, he was handling two assets who were already in place.

Then he bungled a job delivering a briefcase of photos of Russians to a safe house by leaving it behind on the subway. It was a monumentally careless and dangerous gaffe for a case officer, one that could have ended his career and imperiled those identified in the pictures. Despite this screwup, though, he was promoted to a full-time position in New York City and given an even bigger case to work on.

Aldrich Ames was the classic product of a well-intentioned but fallible bureaucracy. He rose through the ranks despite an unimpressive career, behavior problems, and operational mistakes. It's possible that had it not been for the Vietnam War and its demand on the CIA for additional personnel, he might not have made the cut in the first place. Given his subsequent activities, the CIA would have good reason to regret that he did.

Dmitri Polyakov, America's most highly placed asset, would, too.

CHAPTER 13

YOU DON'T SEE ONE OF THOSE EVERY DAY

Left to right: Leo, our neighbors Dimple and Kittu, Paully, and Jacob at our home in New Delhi, 1974. *(Author's collection)*

The drive in from the airport was like nothing we'd ever experienced. Even in 1973, Delhi was one of the world's most populated cities, and the streets were swarming: bicycles, tricycles, motorized rickshaws, taxis, and motor scooters—some with mountainous loads of produce or wood or dry goods tied precariously onto the backs. Drivers stopped for cows wandering through the chaos, and a cacophony of horns and backfiring engines and the sputtering and roaring of motors was incessant. The smell of burning dung hung in the air. And everywhere you looked were people and more people, going about their daily routines out in the open: washing their hair, cooking, squatting in semicircles with their neighbors for a chat and a smoke, all on the side of the road.

We arrived in August, and Mom was instantly dazzled by the rich and exotic life of her new home. "Just on our little neighborhood street, typical traffic almost any time during the day might include a donkey cart, a banana or grape vendor, rickshaws, the knife sharpener or rag man, a few white cows and maybe a pig," she wrote to her mother. "Sometimes one sees monkeys clambering wild from rooftop to rooftop, and I saw a mongoose in our back yard a few mornings ago."

We had moved into a house on the outskirts of Delhi. As usual, Mom and Dad wanted to live among the locals, rather than in an American enclave. "We moved in on a Friday afternoon, and on Saturday there was a soccer game (or was it rugby?) going on in our back yard, with four or five boys from the neighborhood," Mom wrote home.

There were other reasons for living outside the diplomatic enclaves. Indian intelligence monitored U.S. embassy officials, and Dad wanted to make that as impractical as possible. In the neighborhoods where most Americans lived, such as Vasant Vihar or Golf Links, it was easy for a team from the IB, India's Intelligence Bureau, to keep track of the comings and goings of American embassy employees. One or two watchers—*fielders* was the Agency's term for them—could plant themselves at an intersection and keep track of the numerous diplomats who lived in the enclave. But our new home was in South Extension II, a neighborhood outside the Ring Road. The fielders could still watch Dad there, but they'd have to devote men, and sometimes a car, exclusively to him. My siblings and I occasionally noticed men strolling by the house or standing around, seemingly without a purpose. The boys liked to have fun with them, waving or going over to say hi, so they could watch them scuttle away.

Mom was probably happier in India than in any other foreign posting. She loved the local color, the exotic flowers and spicy foods. An avid gardener, she knew her flora and fauna, too. "There is little vegetation that is totally unfamiliar, after Savannah and Mexico," she wrote to her mother. "Royal poinciana, jacaranda, eucalyptus, chinaberry and palm trees, and bougainvillea, crepe myrtle, oleander, plumbago, lantana, hibiscus, banyan, mimosa and coral vine—everything I've ever seen before in the tropics. But the birds! I have never, never seen so many unfamiliar and exotic birds. Paul and I spend half our time with the bird book trying to identify the common types. It will be a long time before we get around to the less common varieties."

The neighborhood we lived in was decidedly upscale by Indian standards. Our house was designed to allow plenty of air to flow through, with French doors opening onto a large patio covered by awnings. A wide staircase swept up to the third floor, and the stone and marble floors always stayed cool. Like all the other houses in the neighborhood, ours was protected by a surrounding wall and a *chowkidar*, or night watchman, who invariably fell asleep at his post not long after the sun went down. All the *chowkidars* did, and we didn't like to wake them—they all had day jobs, too.

As is common in Delhi, with so many people needing employment, Mom had servants to help out—a small staff, in fact. They were like a cross section of Indian society: Gupta, the "bearer," who served meals and did light cleaning, was Hindu, from one of the midlevel castes, but well above Ram, the bathroom cleaner and floor sweeper from the Dalit, or "untouchable," caste. Wilson, the fastidiously dressed driver, was Christian. Prashad, the cook, was a higher-caste Hindu who had worked for other Americans and wanted to show off his American cooking skills to my (uninterested) mom.

In the back of the driveway, across from our garden lawn, was a small separate building, servants' quarters, with two rooms, one bath, and a tiny kitchen. Ram, the Dalit, lived there with his wife and three children. But they were soon joined by his brother and an uncle and their families. Then we noticed that another family of relatives had moved in. Then another one. Within a few weeks of our arrival, there were at least twenty-five people living there. They did their cooking in the driveway, played with and fed their babies in the garden, drank chai and laid their laundry out to dry across the bushes that formed the garden hedge. Mom loved watching these activities in our impromptu village, the women in their saris, with their dark eyes, the men in their white shirts, or dhotis, walking down the driveway past our house to get to their quarters, deferential and unassuming in their greetings to Mom, "Namaste, memsahib."

Still, eventually the situation became insupportable. Our higher-caste servants, appalled at Mom and Dad's egalitarian permissiveness, complained of the noise and clutter, and there were probably a few raised eyebrows among our well-to-do neighbors. Mom had to tell Ram that only his immediate family could live there, and the others melted away as quickly as they'd arrived.

★

Dmitri and Nina Polyakov had arrived in Delhi a few weeks before us. His office was at the Soviet embassy, within a compound whose parks and landscaped boulevards were a tranquil green oasis set improbably in the throbbing center of a third world megalopolis. As chief of the GRU *rezidentura*, Polyakov was assigned a two-story apartment inside the compound, along with a private driver and cipher clerk whose apartments each had their own entrances.

New Delhi was home to a large GRU contingent, which Polyakov ran while operating under diplomatic cover as military attaché.

A colonel at the time of his arrival in New Delhi, Polyakov was in line for promotion to major general, which would place him among the elite in the world of Soviet intelligence, with access to a much higher level of military and political secrets. He had been told privately that this upcoming promotion would be formally announced in the near future, but First Secretary Leonid Brezhnev's state visit to India in November 1973 hurried the promotion process along. Polyakov's duties would require him to formally greet and host the visiting Soviet leader, and for this, a mere colonel wouldn't do.

Alexander and Petr had stayed behind in Moscow. Petr had graduated from the Twenty-Second Specialized English Language School and been admitted to the Military Institute for Foreign Languages. Alexander was in his second year at Moscow State Institute of International Relations, living with his grandparents in the Kalininsky apartment.

One night at around eleven, shortly before Brezhnev's India trip, Alexander was at home studying Hindi verb conjugations (he'd been assigned the language by the State) when he was startled by a loud knocking at the door. In earlier times, a knock on the door at such an hour would have set off waves of panic; late night and early morning were the KGB's favorite times to swoop in and make arrests. Alexander opened the door to find a GRU officer standing there.

"Where's his uniform?" the officer demanded.

"What uniform?" Alexander said.

"Where is Dmitri Fedorovich's uniform? We need it."

"Why?" Alexander asked.

"Later," said the officer. "You'll know everything later."

Alexander did find out later: the GRU urgently needed to make a general's uniform for his father so he could properly greet the first secretary, and they needed an old one for sizing. It took the GRU tailors three days to make the new one and rush it to New Delhi in a diplomatic pouch just in time for Brezhnev's arrival.

★

Two years before Brezhnev's 1973 visit, the Soviet Union and India had signed a treaty assuring each other of strategic mutual cooperation. India had needed this because Pakistan, India's prime enemy, had the support of both the United States and China. India had fought three wars with Pakistan, including the 1971 war, when the United States moved a carrier task force into the Indian Ocean and threatened to intervene on the Pakistani side. India had also fought a war with China, over disputed territory on its thousand-mile-long Himalayan border. For India, the Soviet alliance was a global counterbalance to American pressure and, locally and more important, to a potentially aggressive China. Brezhnev's visit was an opportunity to focus international attention on the strength of India's Russian ties.

For the USSR, Brezhnev's visit was equally important. Nineteen seventy-three had not been a good year for Soviet foreign policy. Salvador Allende's Soviet-supported Marxist experiment in Chile had ended disastrously. The prodigious Soviet investment of arms and money in Egypt and Syria had crashed and burned when Israel, with American support, broke the Arab armies in the Yom Kippur War. The year before saw Nixon's surprise trip to China, which heralded a potential Sino-American front working against the USSR's interests. Amid these setbacks, the Soviets needed to demonstrate their continued geopolitical strength.

Polyakov's new uniform was a rush job, but nothing was rushed about the promotion itself. All general-rank promotions were vetted with extreme thoroughness. Any flaws in the candidate's background (military, political, or personal) could result in rejection. Approval, on the other hand, indicated the highest level of trust.

Polyakov was not only cleared for the promotion, but also awarded his second Order of the Red Star for courage and exemplary service. He had passed all the tests for trustworthiness and outstanding performance.

In the Delhi Soviet embassy's intelligence departments, Polyakov was seen as reserved, meticulous, and ultimately serious. He handled his work and kept his own counsel. He didn't mingle much or join in the embassy sports competitions. He also kept his distance from the compound's KGB operatives, and he warned his deputy to do the same. He wasn't fond of the KGB in the first place, but he had other reasons none of his colleagues guessed at. "I attributed his attitude to his natural demeanor," said one of them many years later. "Little did I know he had concrete reasons for being careful."

★

Dad took up his cover position as first secretary at the American embassy, an imposing wedding cake of a building only two blocks from the Soviet compound. The front of the huge embassy building boasted golden columns, and a broad marble stairway faced a large reflecting pool with a waterspout fountain. Behind the main building was a large complex—a guesthouse, facilities for the U.S. Marines contingent, a baseball diamond, a swimming pool, a snack bar, a commissary, a bar, an auditorium and movie theater, and the Roosevelt House, the ambassador's own impressive residence.

When we arrived, Daniel Patrick Moynihan was the U.S. ambassador, a larger-than-life man who later became ambassador to the United Nations and long-term senator from New York. Dad and Moynihan developed a close relationship, and Leo and Moynihan's son John became good friends.

Moynihan was outgoing and friendly to everyone, including the diplomats' children, and we all liked him. While we were there, a new bowling alley opened in the embassy compound, and Moynihan hosted a dedication ceremony. John Moynihan told the boys that his father was a terrible bowler and would probably gutter the inaugural bowl. The boys challenged the ambassador to a bet: 10 rupees ($1.25) each that he would miss all the pins. The ambassador took them up on it, and at the end of his introductory remarks he playfully told the gathering about the bet with the kids. Moynihan's first ball knocked over several pins, and he rakishly made the boys pay up on the spot, to the delight of his audience.

One evening, John Moynihan invited my brother Leo to the Roosevelt House for a sleepover. Mrs. Moynihan told the boys to stay in their room upstairs because there was a reception for the Indian interior minister going on in the hall below. The reception was a bigger deal than usual because the then-secretary of state, Henry Kissinger, visiting India at the time, was one of the guests. Nonetheless, the boys sneaked out of their room to watch the proceedings from the balcony overhead. As the interior minister took his turn addressing the company, the boys saw Mr. Dooley, the Moynihans' unruly Irish terrier, dart past a servant coming out a kitchen door and into the hall. Mr. Dooley made a beeline for the Indian interior minister and began energetically humping his leg. It took the mortified house staff some effort to remove the determined dog from his mission. The boys, on the balcony above, couldn't contain their laughter, and Mrs. Moynihan had a hard time keeping a straight face herself when she admonished them later.

★

More than fifteen hundred people worked in the embassy complex, one thousand Indians and five hundred Americans. On the embassy roster, Dad was first secretary, ostensibly an economics expert. On the CIA roster, he was head of the Soviet branch and chief of operations. In fact, he was in India for one job only: to handle Dmitri Polyakov.

General Polyakov and Nina, New Delhi, India, c. 1974.
(Courtesy of Sandy Grimes)

Dad met with the CIA station chief once a week, and took part in high-level meetings inside the "bubble," the Plexiglas-enclosed room-within-a-room that was proofed against electronic eavesdropping and guaranteed total security. Yet even within the station he was very much under cover. "Paul's case was extraordinary," explained Richard Allocca, a CIA officer who served with my father in New Delhi, "because he was handling an existing source, and *only* that source. That meant he was not circulating, he was not looking to develop assets. He was keeping his head down so as not to attract attention."

"I knew it was very discreet," said Terry Douglas, another Delhi colleague. "It wasn't something that you'd ask questions about. Nobody reported to him, and he didn't report to anyone but the chief of station, but even there it was only in name, because he was not part of general operations. He was a senior guy buried in the economic section, on special assignment."

Shortly after we arrived in New Delhi, the American military attaché, Col. William King, spoke with his Soviet counterpart, Dmitri Polyakov, at a diplomatic reception. In a moment away from others, King told Polyakov that Paul Dillon had just come in as first secretary to work with him. Not long afterward, King invited Polyakov to his house, where Dad was waiting for him. In that first meeting at Colonel King's house, Polyakov needed to get something off his chest: he was still fuming over the Agency's clumsy and dangerous personal contact ploy at the reception he'd been forced to attend at the U.S. embassy in Moscow. "Don't ever do that again!" Polyakov told Dad, intending the message for Langley headquarters.

Polyakov was impressed with my father. "He carried himself confidently . . . and there was nothing contrived about him," he later reported. My father and Polyakov began a relationship that was warm and productive. Something clicked between the two of them, and the volume of intelligence that started flowing back to Langley demonstrated the effectiveness of the new partnership. At her desk eight thousand miles away, Sandy Grimes sensed the change. "Paul D[illon] and Polyakov were the perfect match," she wrote in *Circle of Treason*. "The GRU general came to understand that he had a trustworthy co-conspirator in Paul and it was time to discard his belief that he was merely an agent whose only value was the information he provided."

Grimes knew Dad felt the same protectiveness toward Polyakov that she did. By appointing him to handle Polyakov, the Agency had now put Angleton's suspicions in the past and could accept the Russian for the trustworthy and reliable agent of inestimable value he had always been.

Grimes thought she could feel Polyakov's relief. His new partner was relaxed and unpretentious, serious but not forbidding, and approached the job at hand with plainspoken intelligence. He had none of the suspicion and wariness of his previous Black Hat handlers. In working with Dad, she thought, Polyakov had found "sanctuary." "The CIA," she concluded, "had finally gotten it right."

Grimes later wrote that with Polyakov's promotion to general and his trusting relationship with my father, his time in India "was the pinnacle of our long and productive association." The intelligence he provided was astonishing in its importance and detail, and came, she said, from the fact that Polyakov, by dint of his rank, his years of service, and his war heroism, was now a member of the GRU's elite inner circle. As such, he had access to the highest level of Soviet war planning, strategy, and military philosophy. He knew the specifics of worldwide GRU operations. He knew the identities of GRU agents and their modi operandi. As a senior party activist, he was trusted with secret Ministry of Foreign Affairs materials and party directives. He was a member of the "old boy" network, noted Grimes, "which gave him access to state secrets that he otherwise would have been denied solely by his rank and position title."

To facilitate their meetings and to make Polyakov look good, the CIA developed a useful ruse: offering my father up as a fake developmental contact. Polyakov reported to Moscow that he was attempting to engage an American embassy official, the first secretary in the economics section, whom he'd met at a number of diplomatic functions. They both enjoyed hunting and fishing, activities that would give Polyakov the privacy and leisure to develop this asset for undercover work. Back at the Aquarium, the GRU chiefs were encouraged, and sanctioned the relationship, giving their new potential American contact a code name: PLAID.

Polyakov's meetings with my father now had official Soviet approval. This meant they could meet relatively out in the open. KGB minders would be informed that Moscow Center knew about and had approved of Polyakov's meetings with the American Paul Dillon. Dad and Polyakov thereafter had regular meetings at two favored hotels, the Oberoi and the Ashok, and they saw each other at the frequent receptions hosted by different countries' embassies. They also went on fishing and hunting trips together.

Polyakov had lied to his superiors; Dad was neither a fisherman nor a hunter, but he knew how to play a role. Soon, we noticed fancy shotguns arriving at the house, and Dad joined a local fishing and hunting club (even getting himself elected vice president). My father and Polyakov fished the upper reaches of the Yamuna River, where the water from the Himalayas was still pure, my father tape-recording Polyakov's information while they cast their lines. In that rugged wilderness, it would have been difficult for someone to watch them undetected, but if this were possible, all anyone would have seen was two anglers enjoying their sport. On one of their outings, Dad gave Polyakov a combination gift/concealment device: a spinner for his fishing rod that had been reconstructed to function as a chamber for hiding clandestine information.

They hunted, too—an expert outdoorsman, Polyakov was as good with a rifle or shotgun as he was with a fishing rod. The remote and wild forests and riverbanks of India must have been tonic to him, a sanctuary from the dangers of his double life. Dad likely never fired a shot—on those expeditions his quarry was information, not animals.

The volume of intelligence Polyakov passed to my father swelled to such proportions that Langley sent an analyst, Diana Worthen, to New Delhi to help handle it. She had been in the SB Division (which around this time changed its name to the Soviet East European [SE] Division) working with Sandy Grimes on the Polyakov take, so she had an insider's familiarity with the case.

An organized, no-nonsense individual, Worthen was exactly what Dad needed to efficiently handle and transmit the mass of information he was receiving. Worthen managed the information flow via cables and pouches between Delhi and Langley and occasionally sent requests to headquarters for the gifts Polyakov wanted for his superiors and their wives. Polyakov also asked for a few things for himself, such as "fishhooks, sinkers, fly rods, shotguns, ammunition, bows and arrows, wading boots, hand warmers, drills, and sandpaper." Once, Worthen ordered the wrong size fishhooks from a catalog. "I mistakenly ordered some that were twenty times larger than what he wanted," Diana was quoted in Pete Earley's *Confessions of a Spy*, "and he told his handler [my father] to tell me that he wasn't trying to catch whales. He had a good sense of humor."

★

While Dad was engaged with his one-man caseload, his family was reveling in their life in India. Mom loved the local food, but our cook, Prashad, was disappointed that she showed little interest in his mastery of Western cooking. We all loved the Indian dishes Prashad cooked for us, too, but for a special birthday treat we might get a frozen pizza from the commissary.

Then there were the itinerant wallahs, the practitioners of different specialties: the *aam* wallah, who peddled mangoes; the "bottley wallah," who collected empty bottles; the *chhuri* knife-sharpening wallah, with his bicycle-powered whetstone. We would hear them coming down the street, each with his own distinctive singsong cry: "Bottley wallaaaaah" or "Chhuri wallaaaaaaah," and Mom or Ram would run outside and engage their various skills.

We lived next door to a Sikh family with two boys who were

the same age as my brothers. Mom wrote to her mother, "Dimple (he *says* that's his name—he spelled it for me) and Kittu (whom the children first called K-2) are the two Sikh boys next door. Ours won't learn any Hindi playing with them. Their English is better than ours."

With Dimple and Kittu and other neighborhood kids, my brothers especially began to immerse themselves in the city's street culture. The boys were now entering their teens. Leo, the oldest, was thirteen when we arrived and sixteen when we left, with Paully and Jacob a year and two years behind him, respectively. Mom and Dad gave all of us plenty of latitude, and the boys could be a wild trio. Every spring, India would celebrate Holi, the Hindu festival of color and water. Stalls all over Delhi sold brightly hued powders, and people spent the day in a free-for-all, throwing water balloons and colored powders all over one another. Anyone was fair game: young and old, rich and poor, adults and children. The madcap celebrations went on everywhere around the city, in the streets, alleys, and parks, or from one passing rickshaw to another.

This, of course, was open season for the impish boys, who got Kittu and Dimple and the other neighborhood kids and servants involved in water balloon fights in the gardens and from the upstairs balconies of the houses along our street. (The boys discovered that the cheap, state-subsidized condoms sold at every street shop in Delhi made highly effective water balloons that could hold a full gallon of water.) The servants, Ram and Gupta, would get into it with ferocious gusto. The taciturn Prashad didn't much approve, and Wilson, the well-dressed driver, locked himself in the car. Mom, always wishing to embrace local customs, didn't object, and watched the mêlée from behind closed windows.

Mom and Dad always gave us a lot of leeway. They were easygoing, liberal minded, and trusting, and believed we'd learn by experience. We wore kurta shirts and chappal sandals and ran around the city on our own, taking advantage of their trust by going to lots of parties where hash and bongs were smoked liberally.

It was at one of these parties that I met an English Burmese boy who did not go to our school. He was a little older, slick, and not too trustworthy a character. But I was seventeen, with little experience and a lot of naïveté, and I thought he was cool. My parents were as polite to him as they were with all our friends and boyfriends, but I knew they were wary of him. Many evenings after Mom and Dad went to bed, he and I would go into the den, sneak booze from the bar, and "fool around." My trusting parents never once came down and checked on us. (But, I would find out one day, that was the least of my worries.)

★

In 1974, my sisters Maria and Clare took the spring semester off from college for a four-month stay in Delhi, Clare bringing along her boyfriend, Paul Finn. Paul was of Irish-Catholic stock, and like Dad, his father had gone to Boston College High School. Dad and Paul hit it off and spent time playing tennis at the embassy compound, going on sightseeing trips, and taking after-dinner walks around the neighborhood. Later Dad told Clare that the IB fielders, and hence the KGB who paid the IB for information, thought Paul Finn was a new agent trainee, and kept a close eye on what he and Dad were up to.

Paul slept on a cot in the open-air *basarti* room on the roof. One night, at around 3:00 a.m., he got up for a glass of water. Coming down the circular stairway, he stopped when he heard my father talking in the foyer at the foot of the stairs, where our one phone was located. Dad was speaking to someone animatedly in some other language. Paul didn't show himself, but he listened. Dad was speaking Russian.

The next morning, Paul told Clare, "I heard your Dad speaking Russian on the phone last night. Fluently."

Dad was speaking Russian? This was news to us. We knew he spoke German, Spanish, and some Italian, but how could it be that in all these years we hadn't known he spoke Russian?

Then, one evening, Mom and Dad told us that a Russian general was coming over to talk with Dad, and the two were not to be disturbed. Intrigued, the boys made sure they were in the foyer when the Russian came in, resplendent in his uniform, with shoulder boards and a big military hat. The Russian looked down at them, amused by their bold approach, their long hair, tie-dyed T-shirts, and scruffy sandals. The man smiled and handed them each a candy from his coat pocket, then went into the den with my father. Dad locked the door behind them, something he'd never done before.

"Wow," my brother Leo said later. "A Russian general. You don't see one of those every day."

CHAPTER 14

THREE STAR

General Polyakov at the Soviet embassy in New Delhi, c. 1978. *(Courtesy of Alexander Polyakov)*

Polyakov's relationship with my father had been sanctioned by GRU leadership, so his visit to our house was probably known and wouldn't have set off any alarms. When Dad and Polyakov went into the study and locked the door, Mom told the boys the men were talking about hunting, but the boys didn't think so.

Dad had his own obligations as a fake developmental contact for the GRU. Moscow Center wanted specific information from

PLAID, their new American friend. What could he tell them about China's strategy toward the Soviet Union, now that the United States under Nixon was opening up to Beijing? What details could he provide on the Americans' understanding of Japan's posture vis-à-vis the USSR? Could he find out anything about the Pentagon's plans for any possible nuclear first strike against the USSR?

Many of the requests were beyond what an embassy economic official would know, but significant inside information on the Japanese and Chinese economies was not—PLAID would also have access to sensitive cables coming into the American embassy on strategic developments in Asia. In order to generate credible feedback to the Russians, the Langley support team went to the State and Defense Departments to help decide what genuine material to release, or what to doctor or simply fabricate. My father passed on this vetted information to Polyakov, who in turn relayed it to Moscow Center, making Polyakov look ever more valuable to his GRU bosses. Another promotion in his future would open up additional levels of sensitive and productive intelligence for the Americans.

Back at headquarters, as impressed as Sandy Grimes was by Polyakov's tradecraft, and by the careful security measures he took to protect himself, she could be equally struck by his daring. When Soviet deputy foreign minister Mikhail Kapitsa was visiting New Delhi on a tour of southeast Asian capitals, a cable arrived for him at the Soviet embassy classified TOP SECRET OF SPECIAL IMPORTANCE. The cable spelled out Soviet plans and objectives for every country in the world. "Immediately recognizing the significance and importance of the information, and that this was a one-time bonanza," Grimes wrote, Polyakov decided it was worth the risk to copy the document in its entirety, a blatant violation of the *rezidentura*'s security regimen.

He wasn't alone in the *rezidentura*; his code clerk sat next to him; others were at their desks nearby. Polyakov took the cable to a little curtained space off to the side and photographed it with a T-100 subminiature camera provided to him by the Americans. The T-100 was an improvement on the Minox that Polyakov had used in Moscow; for a start, it was small enough to be concealed inside a specially made pen; it didn't need a tripod or a light source; and it had a silent shutter. The full-page pictures it took were crystal clear, too. That said, the T-100 was extremely tricky to load, and it was finicky.

Polyakov photographed the entire document with the CIA's new camera, but he didn't fully trust the Agency's fancy gear. Despite the danger of being discovered, he took a full second set of pictures of the document with his simpler, more basic 35-millimeter camera. His caution paid off; when the film was developed back at Langley, the T-100 roll was blank except for the first frame. The 35mm pictures, however, were perfect. As a result, the United States had the Soviets' global foreign policy plans for the next few years.

The Kapitsa cable was only one of several documents Polyakov photographed, sometimes in his own residence, when he could spirit them out, sometimes in the danger-laden *rezidentura*, under the eyes of other GRU officers and the occasional KGB snoop. *Military Thought*, a monthly journal issued by the Soviet Ministry of Defense, contained frank commentaries and studies on tactics and strategy by leading Russian military figures and war planners. The publication came in two versions, one generally available and the other top secret. Polyakov photographed the secret version each month and gave it to my father, and thus to its ultimate consumer, the U.S. Defense Department. To American military analysts, it was an invaluable resource—they came to expect it, said Grimes, as one would a "subscription to a favorite magazine."

The full effect of Polyakov's intelligence output in helping the

United States manage the Cold War is, in retrospect, astonishing. By reading the candid thinking of the Soviet high command in *Military Thought* and other documents that Polyakov slipped to the Americans, U.S. military experts came to understand that the Russians' assessment of nuclear war was not much different from their own. This was not the Pentagon's judgment prior to the clarity provided by Polyakov's intelligence. "Many believed," wrote Adm. William Crowe, who was leading the yearly American political/military special war games at the time, "that the Soviets would use [nuclear weapons]—that was the American defense establishment's best judgment."

The documents Polyakov passed to the Americans "gave us insights into how they talked to each other about these issues, whether they thought that victory in a nuclear war was possible," said Robert Gates, director of the CIA under George W. Bush. They did not. Polyakov's intelligence showed that Soviet military leaders were as worried as their American counterparts, that they were not, in fact, "crazy warmongers." This was a revelation that "may have prevented U.S. miscalculations that would have touched off a shooting war," said Gates, and helped change American political-military doctrine in the latter years of the Cold War.

★

Polyakov also photographed hundreds of pages of secret documents from the GRU and KGB detailing the American military technology their agents were directed to steal. These orders, issued annually by the Soviet Military-Industrial Commission, startled American analysts with their detailed knowledge of classified American systems. The directives, for example, might require a particular part of a component for a missile engine, indicating that the Soviets had already stolen the other elements of the component. The most significant Soviet requirements (regarding nuclear delivery systems, advanced equipment for nuclear bomb production, specialized radar systems, and other technologies) were passed on by Polyakov and became an especially invaluable resource for the Americans.

The Soviet technology-gathering effort revealed by Polyakov was "breathtaking," according to Richard Perle, assistant secretary of defense for international security. "We found there were 5,000 separate Soviet programs that were utilizing Western technology to build up their military capabilities." The documentation Polyakov provided spurred the United States to severely tighten controls on Western military technology.

Polyakov's production, including data on strategic missiles, nuclear strategy, antitank missiles, chemical and biological warfare, and Soviet war planning, filled up more and more dedicated space at Langley. "Christmas came early and often for everyone involved in the Polyakov operation during the New Delhi phase," Grimes wrote, "and we waited anxiously for the highlights cable from Paul D[illon] after each meeting."

When Polyakov went to Moscow for home leave, he spent time with his sons. Alexander was now twenty years old, well along in his studies at the Moscow State Institute of International Relations. He had a girlfriend, Larisa Bourov, an economics student also at the Moscow State Institute. He had known Larisa from when they were summer playmates at the beach in Rye, New York. Back then, her father, Nicolai, had been the editor of a magazine called *Soviet Life*, part of a U.S.-Soviet cross-cultural agreement to foster knowledge and trust between the peoples of the two countries. (In turn, the Americans published *Amerika* for the Soviets. Both magazines were unabashed propaganda vehicles, but while American interest in *Soviet Life* was tepid, *Amerika* was hugely popular in the Soviet Union and sold out quickly.) The two young people hadn't been in touch since, but when Alexander called, Larisa remembered him, and even had some photos of them as children. They had begun dating, and now their relationship was growing serious.

Petr was still enrolled as a cadet in the Military Institute of Foreign Languages. As with every other higher education institution, the curriculum included heavy doses of Marxist theory, Communist Party history, and anti-Western propaganda. And since it was a military school, he and the other cadets were subject to military discipline and restricted to their barracks, with little home leave allowed.

Among the austere conditions of barracks life, Petr and his colleagues found the food situation especially depressing. The monotonous, tasteless cafeteria rations left them longing for food parcels from home. But those weren't permitted; nor were visitors, which left Petr and the other cadets scheming about ways to get parcels smuggled in to them. In this endeavor, Alexander was Petr's outside coconspirator.

Alexander bought a narrow suitcase that could fit through the fence posts and filled it with sausage, breads, jams, juices, and other tasty items. Then he and Larisa hid near the school, waited until the security guard had passed, and shoved the suitcase through the fence. Petr quickly retrieved it and shared the booty with his comrades.

Petr managed to get the empty suitcase back to Alexander through one of his friends who had a weekend pass. With their first venture a success, Alexander and Larisa made the clandestine run on a weekly basis.

In 1974, Alexander and Larisa married. He was twenty-one, she nineteen. His mother, Nina, came back from India for the brief official ceremony at the registration office, followed by a reception and dinner for the families and their friends at Moscow's legendary Praga restaurant.

A year later, Alexander graduated with an MA in law, with language specialties in English and Hindi. One of only two in his class to be assigned to the Ministry of Foreign Affairs, he was posted immediately to Kathmandu, Nepal.

Nepal was hardly Alexander's first choice—jammed between China, Russia's number two enemy, and India, Russia's number one friend, the country was of negligible interest to the Soviets, so the legation there had little to do. The saving grace was that Larisa was able to join him, doing her postgraduate work with the Soviet trade mission there.

In Kathmandu, the newlywed Polyakovs lived in a nineteenth-century "palace" owned by the royal family, which was actually a dilapidated log building with no central heating and only sporadic electricity. Kathmandu, Alexander thought, would be an interesting place to visit for a week or two, but living there was another matter. With no cinemas or restaurants worth going to, there was little to do outside work hours. The social life for Foreign Service or trade personnel was limited mainly to inter-embassy meet-and-greets and the occasional sports competition. Alexander and Larisa would sometimes go to the American or French diplomatic clubs to see movies and have a beer, but invitations were dependent on the geopolitical situation. When relations with the Americans or other Western diplomats were strained, the invitations dried up; when they eased, people would start seeing each other again. Life became more boisterous for the Polyakovs, though, when Larisa gave birth to a baby girl, whom they named Marina.

With his parents in New Delhi, Alexander was able to stop off and visit them whenever he traveled to and from Moscow. As a new Foreign Service officer, he enjoyed talking to his father about diplomatic issues and current events. Polyakov would occasionally caution his son to keep conversations private. Alexander was astonished when his father told him that Soviet military leaders didn't believe they could win a nuclear war against the United States and would do anything to avoid actions that might trigger direct hostilities. (The younger Polyakov had grown up deeply conditioned to believe that the Soviet Union, the stalwart leader of the progressive world, would always be able to overcome its enemies.) The general also described the mistakes he felt Russia was making in India, where the Soviets were providing massive arms assistance for India's ongoing tensions with Pakistan. We should be helping to grow India's economy, he told his son, instead of building their military with our World War II–era equipment while the Pakistanis are getting advanced American models. Polyakov had observed Indian military exercises. The Pakistanis are watching their foes through American radar screens, while the Indians are looking back with Russian binoculars, he told his son facetiously. It wasn't really a joke. In ten years, the older Polyakov said, India isn't going to forgive us for selling them second-grade armaments for these billions of rupees.

★

Once a year or so, my father would fly back to Washington, DC, for a week or two of meetings at Langley. On one trip from Delhi, he flew through London to visit with Frank and Jeanne, my best friend Liz's parents and our friends from Mexico and Rome, who were now living in a flat in Knightsbridge, across the street from Harrods department store. Years later, Jeanne told me a story about that visit.

Dad came to their apartment from the airport and left his bags there while they all went out to lunch. When they returned to the flat a couple of hours later, Dad immediately noticed that his suitcase and briefcase were gone. Nothing else was missing from the apartment, and the door hadn't been forced open; the lock had been expertly picked. Frank moved toward the phone. "I'm calling the police," he said. "No, please don't," Dad said, waving him off. Although shocked and worried, Frank and Jeanne knew enough about my father's line of work not to ask questions. As is typical of the few stories my father's friends and colleagues have relayed about odd or suspicious things they observed over the years, what became of the stolen belongings or how my father was affected by the incident is unknown to me. But Dad came back from that trip bearing the items from home we'd requested: a stash of albums for the boys, books and makeup for the girls. To us kids, nothing seemed amiss.

But then, a few weeks later, Gupta, our bearer, disappeared. He had been with us since we arrived, and with the best command of English among the servants, he had helped run the household for Mom. We were fond of him, even though he could be a pest, always wanting to hang out with us and tell us terrible jokes. He flew kites with the boys, did errands for Mom, and took care of the little emergencies. When a cobra was discovered in the backyard, he was the one who called for the mongoose wallah, who tied the animal on a long rope in our backyard and then came back a couple of days later to collect his mongoose. We saw no more cobras.

The day before Gupta disappeared, Dad had come home from work and asked Mom to go for a walk before dinner. The conversation around the table that night was strangely subdued. Dad, who loved our entertaining stories of the day, seemed distracted. Even Gupta wasn't his usual chatty, nosy self, quietly bringing in the food.

The next day, when we came home from school and Gupta wasn't around, we asked Ram where he was.

"I don't know," Ram said, looking away. "Please, ask memsahib."

"I had to let Gupta go," Mom said. "He talked more than he got work done."

We sensed that there was something specious about Mom's explanation. We found out years later, after Dad's death (during a rare conversation with Mom about anything having to do with Dad's job) that they'd found out Gupta was spying on Dad. (Had he informed on Dad's plans to travel through London, and hence the stolen luggage?) He'd even bugged the den, Mom told us.

A hot wash of embarrassment came over me when I heard that. All those late nights in the den with my boyfriend! Who had been listening? The IB? The KGB? The servants? It was certainly not a line of questioning I was going to put to my mother.

★

On May 28, 1975, the following news article appeared in the international English-language newspaper *Times of India.*

MYSTERY DOCUMENT
IDENTIFIES CIA MEN IN INDIA

A two-page material, copied by the Xerox process and identifying three United States diplomatic personnel in India as U.S Central Intelligence Agency officials, was received in several news organizations today. The material arrived by post in dark brown manila envelopes . . . The two-page material named Paul L. Dillon, first secretary and consul in the US Embassy in New Delhi, and identified him as the Paul Dillon mentioned in Philip Agee's book as the person who headed the CIA's Soviet/Satellite operations in Mexico.

This news was more illuminating to us than surprising. There'd been so many hints along the way, building up to the more recent ones: Dad spoke Russian; he met with Soviet generals to discuss "hunting"; strangers were watching us.

So now we knew for sure: Dad was in the CIA. This knowledge

put our past lives into a different perspective. In all those places we'd lived (Berlin, Mexico City, Rome, and now in Delhi), our father had been recruiting and running spies. Yet, we were still not inclined to confront him with this news, or ask him to confirm it. If he'd never brought it up in all these years, there must have been a reason, and we loved and respected him too much to put him in an uncomfortable spot. As for the "mystery documents" that had arrived at the newspaper in "dark brown manila envelopes," those, no doubt, had been sent by the KGB, making trouble. The article also said that Dad had been outed in a book by former CIA agent Philip Agee. We hadn't heard of him, but the Agency certainly had.

Agee was the "Olympic attaché" who had worked for Dad in Mexico City, the one Dad had fired, or not, if you believed the story Agee told in his book, *Inside the Company: CIA Diary*, which was just hitting stores when the *Times of India* article came out.

In his book, Agee claimed to have told my father that he wished to leave the Agency in order to marry his Mexican girlfriend and start his own business. But there was much worse: Agee's book exposed every CIA officer and contact he had ever worked with, as well as Agency operations and methods, code names and targets. Calling his book an act of moral dissidence in the American tradition, Agee sought to do as much damage to the CIA as he could. His book was a huge blow—hundreds of agents and operations around the world had their covers blown, including Dad's. Agee's revelations ended many overseas undercover careers.

Still, at the time, nothing much changed for my siblings and me. My younger siblings continued in school, where their friends briefly teased them and then moved on. Dad was universally popular and respected in our expatriate community, so other than Gupta's sudden departure earlier, nothing changed in the household.

General Polyakov with his daughter-in-law, Alexander's wife, Larisa, in Agra, India. Polyakov was an avid photographer and used his hobby as an excuse to spend hours alone in the Moscow apartment's converted bathroom photo lab to process documents for dead drops.
(Courtesy of Alexander Polyakov)

But the revelation forced Dad's life to take a more clandestine turn. As his relationship with Polyakov had been sanctioned by Moscow Center, he had been able to meet Polyakov somewhat openly. Now Polyakov was ordered to cut the contact. That didn't stop them from meeting—they were both expert operators, and the work they were conducting was too important and valuable to cease. Instead, they went underground, getting together surreptitiously in safe houses or out in the wilderness of the Yamuna. Sandy Grimes noticed little if any decrease in the flow of intelligence to headquarters.

★

Before long, that situation would change, though. Polyakov's tour in New Delhi would be ending in the fall of 1976, and once he was back in KGB-infested Moscow, communication with him utilizing the usual risky methods of dead drops and signal sites would again be limited, painstaking, and dangerous. Anticipating long months of silence, as was Polyakov's habit while in Moscow, the CIA determined that a more efficient and secure method of communication was critical.

So, the SE Division in Langley made a request to its technical support component: develop an innovative communication device, one that would lower Polyakov's chance of compromise as much as possible by reducing personal contacts and dead drops. In fact, they wanted something quite revolutionary for the times: a "short-range, high-speed, two-way communications device that encrypted the transmitted information, was small in size to allow for concealment, was portable, and would function for years." The explanation for this request was direct: "We were currently handling the highest ranking Soviet Intelligence officer in the history of the U.S. government . . ." Sandy Grimes wrote. "Time-critical intelligence would be available to this source [in Moscow] and we were obligated to provide him with the most secure, current, and reliable means possible to report that information." Most important, they had to have it ready before Polyakov left India in two years.

The Agency's Office of Technical Service balked, pointing out that the technology the SE Division had in mind didn't exist. (It would be twenty years before instant text-messaging devices were introduced to the public.) Undeterred, the SE Division went to the Agency's research and development branch, and together they enlisted an outside scientific contractor. Working against the clock, the Agency's research people and the contractor built on cutting-edge communication technology to produce a prototype transceiver that had no precedent in either the espionage or civilian ds. Suitably code-named UNIQUE, it was "a technical leap in covert communications equivalent to the telephone in public communications."

UNIQUE was a transmitter and receiver, a two-way system small enough to put in a coat or jacket pocket. It had a tiny Cyrillic-script keyboard that automatically encrypted messages entered on the pad with a stylus. Its sending radius was a thousand feet, and it transmitted messages in bursts of 2.6 seconds, fast enough so that electronic monitoring would have an extremely hard time picking them up. A message sent from the device would be received by a base unit, which would automatically send back a preloaded message and turn on a small red light on the device, signaling that the message had been received and a new one sent.

UNIQUE, developed specifically for Polyakov, was a stunning breakthrough in communications technology. "It was the first of its kind in U.S. spy equipment annals," wrote Grimes. "The cryptography in the equipment was revolutionary . . . Although [it was] built only for Polyakov on an accelerated basis, many of the lessons learned from its development were incorporated in successor systems."

"In a primitive form," wrote Robert Wallace, a former CIA director of the Office of Technical Service, UNIQUE "possibly represented the world's first text message exchanges."

When my father told Polyakov what the Agency's technical gurus were building for him, Polyakov was, for once, deeply impressed. As a technology connoisseur, he understood the leap in capability UNIQUE represented. When they later did a test run in an outdoor Delhi market, with the agent unit in Polyakov's coat pocket and one of Dad's colleagues walking nearby with the base unit in a shopping bag, it worked perfectly.

With input from Polyakov, the Agency's technical team then worked out a way to ship the device back to Moscow without any fear it might be noticed by a customs inspector. They took the innards out of a Panasonic three-in-one (turntable, radio, cassette) portable stereo player, and rebuilt it with UNIQUE nestled inside the mechanics, undetectable yet removable by someone with Polyakov's technical expertise.

★

During the summers in India, our family would leave the oppressive heat and miasma of Delhi for the clear, cool air of Mussoorie, an old British station in the Himalayan foothills. Traveling to a rented bungalow there in 1974, we noticed that Dad, who loved to go on long walks, was getting easily winded walking up and down the hills. We'd noticed a few times before that he would exert easily, usually when going up staircases. We weren't too concerned at the time—he had long since quit smoking Pall Malls. Still, it was obvious his breathing was becoming more and more labored.

In the summer of 1976, instead of going to Mussoorie, the family decided to take their vacation in Kashmir. (I had returned to the States for college.) Mom and my siblings planned to go ahead for the first week, and Dad would join them for the second. Wilson, our driver, drove the family ten hours straight from New Delhi to Srinagar, Kashmir's summer capital. This 2,500-year-old city lies on either side of the Jhelum River, next to the glass-smooth Dal Lake, with its famous houseboats and floating markets. At an elevation of 5,200 feet, the mountain air was heavenly, my siblings told me. Fields of tulips overlooked the lake, running in stripes of yellow, red, and violet on the outskirts of the city.

For the first few days, the family stayed in a houseboat on the lake. In the afternoon, vendors paddled their canoes up to where the boat was moored, calling out their wares for dinner: vegetables, freshly caught fish, eggs, spices, ghee, breads, and teas.

Then they took a bus up to Sonamarg, an ancient stone village near the great Himalayan glaciers of the Kashmir Valley. With porters and pack mules carrying the bags, they hiked uphill from Sonamarg to a campsite that catered to expat families like ours. Wooden platforms supported dozens of tents equipped with cots, and a kitchen tent where cooks served up traditional Indian meals. The campsite was near the huge and pristine Thajiwas Glacier, where the family hiked and fished the streams during the day and, in the evenings, sat around campfires talking with American and British tent neighbors. The site was also within a few miles of the 1972 Line of Control, the de facto military boundary with Pakistani Kashmir, where Indian and Pakistani troops faced each other in a stand-off over disputed territory that occasionally erupted in exchanges of gunfire. But the stunning beauty of the mountains and valley, with its crisp air and pristine waters, belied the nearby hostilities.

At the end of the week, Mom and the kids were looking forward to Dad joining them. On the expected day, though, he didn't arrive. Instead, a porter came up the path.

"Memsahib Dillon?" the man said to my mother, handing her a note.

"Don't worry," my father's note read. "The elevation is a little too much for my lungs, so I'm heading back to Delhi."

Dad had made it from Delhi to Srinagar to Sonamarg, but he had gotten no farther. My mother left with the porter, and my siblings tried to enjoy themselves for the rest of their visit in that magical place, but worries cast a pall. When they returned to Delhi, they got distressing news. Dad, who at the time was forty-nine years old, had just gotten back from Frankfurt, where he'd been evacuated from Kashmir for medical treatment. Given a diagnosis of primary pulmonary hypertension (a lung disease that was always fatal in those days, a fact my parents did not share with us), he was returning to the States in a couple of days and wouldn't be coming back. The rest of the family would be joining him in a month, in time to start the new school year in Virginia.

Dad met with Polyakov to say good-bye. "The last meeting

between Paul and Polyakov was bittersweet," wrote Grimes. "The atmosphere and banter was simply that of two old friends relaxing and enjoying one another's company . . . Neither discussed the future difficulties each might face, although each understood that Paul's had more clarity than Polyakov's."

Dad had given Polyakov a variety of gifts since the two of them arrived in India: fishing gear, a couple of American shotguns, some woodworking equipment. Now Polyakov had a gift for Dad, the first he'd ever given to one of his handlers: a bottle of Three Star Armenian cognac. It was a token of respect, of a bond between spy and handler, of the trust built between two men who had gone some way toward shaping the events of their time. Neither of them would come to know quite how far.

CHAPTER 15

ENDGAME

УДОСТОВЕРЕНИЕ ЛИЧНОСТИ
СМ № 070808
Беленко
(фамилия)
Виктор Иванович
(имя и отчество)
состоит на действительной военной службе в Вооруженных Силах СССР.
1. Личный №
2. Число, месяц и год рождения 15 февраля 1947 года
М. П.
3. Личная подпись

СМ № 070808
4. Место рождения г. Нальчик, Кабардино-Балкарская АССР
5. Национальность Русский
6. Кем выдано удостоверение
(выдавшего удостоверение личности)
7. Подпись должностного лица, выдавшего удостоверение
М. П.
8. Дата выдачи „28" октября 1971 г.

Lt. Viktor Belenko's military ID was one of the few items he carried with him when he defected from Siberia to Japan in a MiG-25 Foxbat in September 1976.

By the summer of 1976, Alexander Polyakov had been in Kathmandu for two years in his post as diplomat for the Ministry of Foreign Affairs. One American whom he ran into at diplomatic functions from time to time was Scotty Skotzko, a second secretary at the American embassy. Skotzko seemed like a nice guy, and Alexander enjoyed their chats. Skotzko once visited Alexander in his office for a brief discussion between diplomats. As innocuous as one might be, any meeting with an American had to be reported immediately to the ministry chief, and because Alexander was the chief's aide, he reported it to himself, entering the meeting in his logbook.

What he did not know at the time was that Skotzko was, in reality, a CIA officer trolling for prospective targets. He had marked Alexander, a personable young diplomat who spoke far better English than the average Russian Foreign Service officer, as a potential recruit. Langley's response, however, was that Alexander Polyakov was not to be considered a target, and under no circumstances was he to be approached again. It wasn't until later that Skotzko would understand why.

One September morning, not long after Skotzko and Alexander had met, Alexander's offices in the Kathmandu Soviet embassy were abuzz with a major news story: a MiG-25 pilot had defected from Russia, flying his jet below radar across the Sea of Japan to the northern Japanese island of Hokkaido, where he was now in the custody of the Japanese police.

The Soviet MiG-25 Foxbat was considered to be the most advanced fighter jet in the world. As a diplomat with access to Western news sources, Alexander knew that its capabilities gave the American defense establishment considerable worry. No Westerner had ever seen the legendary technology and mechanics of the super-secret jet, which flew faster than any American planes could. The fact that a MiG-25 was now in the custody of a U.S. ally was headline news around the world. So was the revelation that its pilot, Viktor Belenko, had asked for asylum in the United States.

Reading both the Soviet and Western accounts of the incident, Alexander noted the propagandized version of his motherland's reporting. TASS, Russia's official news agency, published that Belenko had strayed off course on a training flight and had run out of fuel, which had forced him to land at an airport in Hakodate, a city on Hokkaido. The Japanese authorities had arrested him and were holding him in isolation, refusing to let Soviet representatives see him. It was known that American president Gerald Ford was offering the pilot political asylum, although the facts showed that Belenko was not a defector but had been illegally detained by the Japanese, who were acting in collaboration with their American allies.

As the days passed, Russian news agencies reported that official remonstrations and international pressure had forced the Japanese to make Pilot Belenko available for an interview with Soviet officials. But the Soviet newspapers reported that Belenko was kept at a distance from his Russian compatriots and that no doctor had been permitted to examine him. His few responses to the officials' questions had been brief and incoherent—in fact, according to TASS, he seemed drugged. Shortly afterward, Belenko was flown to the United States under armed guard.

Later, when it became obvious that Belenko had defected intentionally and was cooperating fully with the Americans, the Soviet accounts changed. They were now saying that Belenko was not a hero who had made a daring forced landing and was then abducted. Instead, it was now learned that he had been recruited by the CIA years back as a young trainee. Since then, he had been receiving CIA instructions to appear as a devoted Communist Party member and loyal Soviet pilot over the years, until he could rise through the ranks and defect to the Main Enemy, taking with him the world's most valuable secret aviation information.

Alexander knew better.

★

After the family returned from India to Virginia at the end of the summer of 1976, I went back to college, and the boys went to high school. After a full evaluation from his doctors at Georgetown Hospital, and under strict orders not to exert himself, Dad settled in at Langley headquarters.

While Mom and Dad didn't let us know this, further tests had revealed that Dad's condition was acute, an incurable narrowing and atrophying of the lungs' veins and capillaries. Pulmonary hypertension inevitably progressed until the patient could no longer breathe. (Now it's treated with Viagra.) But its course was often slow, and at the time of Dad's diagnosis, it wasn't well understood, making it hard to judge the deterioration. "I'm fine," Dad often told us. "Some days better, some days worse, but generally speaking, I'm getting better."

★

One day early that fall of 1976, my father brought home someone associated with work, a young man named Viktor Schmidt. Dad occasionally had friends or associates home for dinner, foreigners from one place or another, but Viktor Schmidt was younger than most of Dad's dinner guests. He looked to be in his late twenties, and Dad said he was from East Germany. His English wasn't very good, but he had a sense of humor about it.

For a while, Viktor was a regular visitor to our house, coming over for dinner or for outings with Dad. We girls saw him on weekends when we were home from college, or on holiday breaks—he even spent Thanksgiving and Christmas dinners with us. Viktor was exotic and handsome, with blond hair, bright blue eyes, and broad, athletic-looking shoulders. Once in a while, he'd go running with Clare or ice-skating with Maria, and I will admit that I had a little crush on him, which he didn't seem to notice. Instead, he began to flirt with Maria. Then, with a couple of curt comments, Dad put an end to that.

At the time, Washington was buzzing with the story of the Soviet pilot who had defected with the super-secret MiG-25 Foxbat and had been granted asylum in the United States: Viktor Belenko. In school, wrapped up in our busy lives, we didn't put two and two together. Viktor "Schmidt" was just Viktor, a new family friend who came and went. Viktor Belenko's true identity was a matter of great secrecy, known only among government officials cleared for access.

Viktor Belenko was a rich mine of information on the Soviet Air Defense Command: its organization, command-and-control systems, training methods, strategy, tactics, equipment, and everything else a Russian top-gun pilot would be expected to know. He had an intimate understanding of both the strengths and weaknesses of the USSR's air defenses. My father was responsible for managing who, among the many government agency officials clamoring to debrief Viktor, would get a piece of his time.

Handling Viktor was the perfect job for my father at this stage in his life. Over the years, Dad had developed an intimate understanding of Soviet life. He wasn't just fluent in the language; he knew the culture, the history, the politics. He was attuned to the Russian mentality and had exactly the background, temperament, and sensitivity to deal with a valuable but emotional young defector looking for trust and needing guidance. And with Dad's lungs slowly worsening, the physically undemanding nature of the job was ideal.

Back in Japan, American and Japanese experts took Belenko's MiG-25 jet apart piece by piece to analyze it. Viktor Belenko and his unexpected gift were an invaluable treasure for the West. Analysis of the plane laid bare the true state of Soviet aeronautical and manufacturing technologies, and more valuable still was Viktor's knowledge of the MiG's operational characteristics and purpose. Together this information revolutionized the Pentagon's tactical and strategic planning.

Before Belenko's debriefings, American military planners believed the MiG-25 was a fighter jet far superior to its American counterparts. (One MiG streaking across Israel during the 1973 Yom Kippur War had been clocked at Mach 3.2.) The United States was facing the need to develop a new generation of fighters in order not to lose air superiority to the Soviets. But Belenko's defection shocked Western military analysts when it revealed that the MiG-25 was in actuality a short-range, high-speed interceptor with limited maneuverability, incapable of classic air-to-air combat against other fighter aircraft. It had, in fact, a single purpose: to shoot down high-flying bombers. As a fighter plane, it was next to useless. The result was a reorientation of America's air force priorities and, as a consequence, of the allocation of major segments of military funding.

Belenko opened up a panorama of priceless intelligence. He was forthcoming, articulate (in Russian), and immensely knowledgeable. He fought with and against American top-gun pilots in simulated combats on all current models of American and Soviet aircraft. "The value of what he gave us, what he showed us, is so great that it can never be measured in dollars," said an air force general involved in Belenko's many months of debriefing. An asset of this sort called for an extraordinary level of support, care, and nurturing.

This is where my father came in. In addition to overseeing Belenko's months-long debriefings, Dad was to help Viktor integrate into the fabric of American life. For Soviet defectors, assimilating into a new culture was almost always rough. While they were generally driven by a powerful desire to escape from the hardships and hypocrisy of life in Russia, defectors often carried an unrealistic idea of what they would find in the United States. And being abruptly separated from their own culture was an unexpected psychological shock that took time to process.

Viktor had been conditioned to think of America, the capitalist enemy, as "the Dark Forces." He'd had a grim, deprived childhood, with a largely absent father, and as a pilot he'd found the disrespectful and callous treatment of Soviet military officers and rank-and-file men intolerable. He understood the deceptive nature of propaganda, and he suspected that the picture of America he had always been fed was a distortion.

But Viktor didn't really have any idea what he was going to find in America once he got there. Spending time with his debriefers and American jet pilots who treated him like a hero and sought out his knowledge and opinions was uplifting and massaged his ego, but he also faced the daunting challenge of fitting into his new country's strange and unfamiliar society. It was Dad's job to assimilate him, to help him feel at home in America.

To help him relax, Dad told Viktor jokes.

"What is the difference between capitalism and socialism? In a capitalist society man exploits man, and in a socialist one, the other way around."

Viktor replied with his own jokes.

"Why is our government not in a hurry to land our men on the moon? Because what if they refuse to return?"

When Dad first took him out for a ride in the Virginia countryside, Viktor was amazed by the neatness and lushness of the farms they passed. Barns and fences were well maintained, cows in the pastures were stout and healthy, fields were high with corn and hay. In the Soviet Union, he had spent time at a Siberian collective farm. He knew the destitution and neglect in those places.

One day, Dad was taking Viktor shopping for some new clothes when, at Viktor's request, they stopped at a supermarket. If Viktor was amazed by the farms he had seen, the supermarket was simply beyond his concept of reality—the full bins of fresh fruit and vegetables, the meat counters stocked with chicken and beef, the frozen foods, the coffee aisle, refrigerated cases full of cold beer, shelves of wine. And the shoppers were freely taking anything they wanted and piling it into specially designed carts. There were no lines out the door.

Viktor's initial shock gave way to skepticism. This was not a real store, and these were not real shoppers. Surely the entire shopping center was a Potemkin village, created by the CIA to deceive him and other defectors or to impress Soviet dignitaries—just like the model kolkhozes used to show off Soviet agriculture for visiting VIPs. Dad's insistence that it was quite an ordinary supermarket, that there were tens of thousands just like it all around the country, wasn't convincing. Dad had to drive Viktor to five other supermarkets in the surrounding suburbs before he was persuaded that these marvels were actual stores, for ordinary people.

When they finally made it to the clothing store, this, too, seemed to Viktor an obvious fake—the racks of suits, slacks, sport jackets, overcoats; the piles of shirts, underwear; the rows of shoes, and all of it lying there, with no guards around. Dad helped Viktor pick out a couple of suits, pants, shirts, a warm-up outfit, and an overcoat. The experience left Viktor impressed with the vast power of the CIA, which could execute deceptions like these so realistically.

Decades later, Viktor described to me how surreal those early days in America were. "I was much worse than Mork from the *Mork & Mindy* show," he told me, referring to an American television sitcom of the time and its protagonist, an extraterrestrial alien comically trying to understand his new environment. "I didn't know anything about the stores or anything else. Your dad had to instruct me how to use an American bathroom. I used the toilet brush to scratch my back. I was like a dry sponge soaking up new experiences."

"Sometimes I felt lost," he said. "It's hard to leave your country. I was homesick. Your father understood, he calmed me. He was my friend, my mentor. I felt like he was *my* father, too."

To help convince Viktor that the things he was showing him represented real American life, Dad told him he could ask to see or do anything, within reason. Viktor asked Dad to take him to a workingman's bar, to see how the ordinary people of America relaxed after work. Dad also took him to the zoo in Washington, DC; an amusement park near Richmond, Virginia; and an X-rated movie. (Dad *had* said "anything.") Viktor asked for a tour of an air force fighter base and to go aboard an aircraft carrier, and both requests were granted.

He also taught Viktor how to drive—few people in Russia owned cars—and Viktor relished the challenge. He learned quickly, but he was a hot shot, too, often speeding and weaving through traffic. Driving with Dad one day along a Virginia highway, they found themselves the target of a state trooper, who flipped on his siren behind them.

Damn it, Viktor, you're driving too fast, Dad said, and then told him to pull slowly off to the shoulder, roll down the window, and wait for the trooper to come up and ask for his license. Viktor should not say or do anything, Dad told him, other than hand over his license, receive the ticket, and thank the officer.

But Viktor wanted to show Dad he knew the drill. He handed the trooper two twenty-dollar bills. In Russia, every traffic stop was a small shakedown; enough rubles exchanged, and you were on your way.

Nyet! Nyet! Dad yelled at him, telling him to take the money back. Forestalling a serious arrest, my father identified himself to the trooper as a CIA officer and asked if he could have a private talk with him. Outside the car, Dad explained the situation. The trooper returned to Viktor, sitting nervously in the driver's seat, and shook his hand. He, like so many others, had heard of the daring MiG pilot who had defected to the United States.

"Your father never talked down to me," Viktor told me. "Even when he was angry, like after the cop stopped me, he was patient with me. He explained things. He told me you don't bribe a cop in this country."

Dad also helped him settle in to his first personal residence, a CIA safe house. One day, when my father was in the process of moving a portable television set from one room to another, he had to stop after only a few steps. Viktor noticed for the first time that there was something wrong with him—even the slightest exertion caused him trouble breathing. "Your father downplayed it," Viktor told me, "but I could see he was not well, that he was really struggling."

While Dad protected Viktor by honing his American interpersonal skills, a whole other team of people was working to protect his person and home. Guards were posted around the perimeter of his house, and when he later moved into an apartment, he still had a Marine bodyguard. The threat of kidnapping couldn't be ruled out.

Through diplomatic channels, the Soviets continued to demand Viktor's return, applying every form of pressure they could. My father told Viktor that there wasn't anything the Russians could do to force him to return, but they were insisting on another meeting with him. They claimed that they needed to be sure he hadn't been forced into handing over the plane and staying in the United States. Viktor didn't have to meet with them if he didn't want to, Dad told him, but the pressure wasn't going to go away. His defection was a huge blow to the Soviets, a blow not just in terms of intelligence but also to their international prestige. They had no real leverage with the United States in this affair—Brezhnev and Kissinger had committed themselves to détente, and nobody wanted to upset that. Still, the Soviets kept up the pressure by harassing the Japanese, seizing their fishing boats and blatantly violating their airspace. They wanted their plane, and their pilot, back.

In the end, Viktor agreed to see the Soviet representatives. He wanted to tell them to their faces that he had defected willingly and that he intended to stay in America.

The meeting took place at the State Department. Yuli Vorontsov, the Russian chargé d'affaires, did most of the talking. He had a physician with him and another representative, a KGB man posing as a Soviet diplomat.

Vorontsov told Viktor he knew he had been coerced, that Viktor really wanted to be back in his homeland, with his wife and child, who missed him terribly and were pleading with him to come back. (At the time of his defection, Viktor and his wife had been in the process of an angry divorce. It had been wrenching to leave his three-year-old son, but his wife had told him she was taking the child with her to her parents, a thousand miles away.) Vorontsov placed pictures and letters from his family on the table in front of Viktor. Viktor ignored them. Vorontsov assured him that if he returned, all would be forgiven—Viktor could walk out of there with his Soviet compatriots and be back in their beloved country tomorrow, where he would be honored. He told Viktor they did not believe his decision to stay with the Americans was voluntary.

Viktor stood up and declared that he had not been coerced. He was here of his own free will. He'd made his decision and was staying in the United States. There was nothing more to discuss.

The State Department representative announced that the meeting was over. Vorontsov, dropping the veneer of a supportive and sympathetic fellow countryman, gave Viktor a hard look and said, "We *will* get you back," making Viktor slightly uncomfortable.

After the meeting, Dad commended Viktor on his composure and bravery. He knew how difficult a face-to-face encounter with his former government was.

Knowing they weren't getting their pilot back, the Soviets concentrated on securing the return of their precious plane. Their threats and posturing to the Japanese and Americans turned into cajoling, and then begging. Meanwhile, Western engineers and specialists continued to take the plane apart for analysis. Finally, nine weeks after Viktor landed in Japan, the Soviets got their plane back . . . in pieces. Eight Japanese tractor trailers delivered the plane in crates to a dock at the port in Hitachi, where a Soviet freighter loaded them on board and sailed away.

Thanksgiving dinner with Viktor Belenko, Vienna, Virginia, 1976, two months after his defection in a MiG-25 Foxbat. *Clockwise from bottom left:* Jacob, me, Maria, Clare, our cousin, Mom, Dad, Viktor Belenko, Julia, a friend, Paully, and Leo. *(Author's collection)*

★

Viktor's debriefings took many months, after which he faced the inevitable fate of the defector: his Agency debriefers, air force analysts, and technical specialists had elicited all the information they needed from him, and there were no more questions.

That was a break point, a precipice Viktor knew he would have to face but for which he wasn't fully prepared. The relationships he had built during his interrogation period constituted his social world. Now those people would be moving on, leaving him more or less on his own, to carve out a life for himself like any other immigrant or refugee with little command of English. For months, Viktor had been treated like a celebrity and a hero, so transitioning to some kind of normal life was bound to be a challenge, and that normal life, a psychological letdown.

The Agency had been taking steps to alleviate the hard times Viktor was going to face, with English classes and my father's patient instructions in cultural assimilation. It had covered all his expenses and given him a regular stipend while he was being debriefed. Now that he would be on his own, a trust fund was created for him. Viktor had never asked for anything; this was a grateful payment for the literally priceless information he had provided to the United States.

But it wasn't in Viktor's nature to live off a trust fund. He thought about his future, and it seemed to him that he needed to get to know his new country better. He was still processing the propaganda and distortions he had been fed in Russia, and his excursions with Dad, and experiences with our family, had revealed a way of life he hadn't imagined. He was being looked after and cared for, but that wasn't the life he wanted to lead in his new country.

His Agency managers understood, and encouraged Viktor's need to explore, but they drilled him in procedures for communicating secretly with the CIA, if necessary. The threat to his new freedom was unknown. "We *will* get you back," Vorontsov had threatened.

For a time, Viktor audited courses at a university, looked into medical school, and even considered becoming a commercial pilot flying 747s. He eventually asked the Agency to arrange a job for him in agriculture, and he spent months as a hand on a family-run midwestern farm, working with the livestock and riding a combine.

Later, in Florida, at an intensive English-language training school, he met a beautiful and gregarious young South American woman. Their relationship developed into a full-blown love affair, but within a few months, she needed to return to her country. Viktor wanted to stay with her, but he couldn't bear to uproot himself again, starting over in another new country.

While outwardly Viktor seemed in control after the breakup,

he was actually in deep turmoil, and the end of the relationship set off a cascade of doubt and confusion. Had he made a mistake to defect? He felt himself overcome by waves of homesickness more powerful than anything he had experienced before. He was overcome by a belief that, whatever the hardships of life in Russia, it was his motherland. That was where he belonged.

"I simply lost my senses," Viktor told me those decades later. "I absolutely needed to go back to the USSR." He decided to leave Florida and drive to Washington and the Soviet embassy, but he had one last stop to make before turning himself over. "I drove like a madman," Viktor later said. "Twelve hours straight to your house in Virginia, pounding on the door in the middle of the night. I had to tell your father that I could not live in America. That I had to go home."

The boys remember that night; the banging woke them up. They followed Dad down the stairs to the front door, but when Dad saw who our night visitor was, he sent the boys back to bed and brought Viktor inside.

"I was a mess," Viktor told me. "It was four o'clock in the morning and your dad listened to me for hours. He was calm. He convinced me that it was a bad idea to go to the Soviet embassy. He saved my life. Your father saved my life."

★

My siblings and I lost track of Viktor after that. Thirty-two years later, looking to interview him for this book, I found no trace of a Viktor Belenko or a Viktor Schmidt in any database I searched. So many years later, he was still, it turned out, taking security precautions.

My husband, James, had read somewhere that Chuck Yeager, the famous American test pilot who was the first man to fly faster than the speed of sound, had become friends with Viktor. When I contacted General Yeager, he was kind enough to connect Viktor and me, and it was a wonderful, emotional reunion for us both. Viktor had been married and divorced; he had made a career as a consultant to major aircraft manufacturers. He was retired now, living in the Midwest. When I asked if he was happy, he quoted Robert Tew: "You are not what happened to you in the past. You are now, you are this moment. What will you do with it? Who will you choose to become?"

Intrigued by the quote, I researched Robert Tew, and found dozens of sayings attributed to him but no credible record of the man who wrote them. How appropriate, I thought—a man living secretly in the shadows, inspired by a phantom author.

★

In 1977, as Viktor set off to make his own life in America, the CIA posted Dad to Camp Peary, the Farm—where Dave Murphy and Pete Bagley had illegally imprisoned Yuri Nosenko in the 1960s—to head an operational training course. Near Williamsburg, Virginia, this ten-thousand-acre semisecret training base for clandestine agents had living facilities for administrators and staff, and my parents and the boys moved there from Vienna to a small one-story house on the banks of the York River. Most of the buildings on "Base," as we called it, were one story, with no staircases, which suited Dad's tightening lungs.

Soon after they arrived, Dad told us—with the exception of Maria and Clare, who were away at college, though Julia and I, also in college, were home for break—that we all needed to go to a meeting at the Administration Center. It turns out that there is an Agency policy requiring families and children living on Camp Peary to know who their parents work for, since the site's existence as a CIA training facility is an open secret. So, sure enough, a camp administrator got straight to the point:

"Does anybody here in the room know what your father does for a living?"

A little embarrassed because Dad had never said anything to us directly, even after his cover was publicly blown in India, we all admitted that we did—and the administrator confirmed to us that he worked for the CIA. Dad remained silent.

The moment was awkward. Sitting in this stark, utilitarian room, we were being forced to confront a lifetime of unspoken, brokered deception, of never being told the truth on my father's part, of willful ignorance on ours. The warm and loving father who would deal directly and honestly with us regarding any personal issue we wanted to discuss or any problem we ever faced was himself, I believe, embarrassed to have an official inform us that he worked for the CIA. Yet the situation was telling: it was an example of my father's need to compartmentalize and yet stay true to those two institutions, work and family, to which he'd faithfully committed himself.

Still, even after Dad's real job was made official to us, we rarely had conversations with him about what he did. We just knew he wasn't going to want to talk about it. He wasn't all of a sudden going to tell us his secrets.

Security at Camp Peary was tight. We had to show IDs to get on the grounds, and visitors had to be prescreened, with a two-day notice. The Base administration tried to make life as normal as possible for the kids who lived there, including my brothers, but there were still moments when the boys were irrepressible. Despite the restrictions, they actually had a lot of fun at Camp Peary, which led to trouble on occasion.

There were a number of "off-limits" roads on Base, and anyone caught on an off-limits road would be in serious trouble with the Military Police, whom the boys called "the serious enforcers."

One night at the Base's teen club, Leo and a girl decided to take his car and find a lonely road for a little necking. It was a dark night, and Leo drove down one of the off-limits roads by mistake, a narrow asphalt strip slicing through a densely wooded area. The two were making out on the side of the road when suddenly gunfire and explosions erupted in front of them. Armed men ran across the road firing weapons and throwing grenades and flares that illuminated the little VW Bug and its startled occupants. A man in camouflage carrying an M-16 approached the VW, rapped on the window, and demanded the kids' IDs. Leo and the girl handed them over and held their breaths while the "serious enforcer" studied them. Thrusting them back, the man said, "Get the hell out of here now, and I'll pretend this never happened." Leo did a fast three-point turn and fled. This was a major security breach, one with significant consequences, Leo thought; getting kicked off Base was a very real possibility. He dropped the girl off at her house and went home, scared to death that Dad would find out.

★

Dad was never much of a disciplinarian, and by then, with his declining health, he didn't have much energy or spirit for chastising his teenage boys. He walked slowly those days, and looked haggard, and he often used a portable oxygen tank. But Dad was stoically selfless, deflecting concern over his illness, and he and Mom did all they could to shield us from how grave his situation was. But we knew he was dying, even if we didn't face, or even discuss much, the immediacy of it. Once again, we respected his cues to us, that this was something he did not want to open up to his children about, or to wallow in. His friends who saw him during this period were pained, recognizing the end approaching for this man they loved. "He looked so dreadful," Bill Friend, Dad's colleague and good friend from their Berlin and Rome days, remembered. "He was somebody who had always been so energetic and funny, and it was just so hard to see."

"I was down at the Farm giving a talk not long before he died," Terry Douglas told me. Terry had worked with Dad in India as a case officer. "We took a very slow walk. He knew the end was coming, and we had a gentle, relaxed conversation about how, if they had mastered lung transplants at that time, he would have been a candidate. But as it was, there just wasn't any cure. He completely accepted the reality of it. He was in the present, satisfied with his life and family. He was at peace. Not an ounce of self-pity. He had no regrets."

Friends who saw him in his last weeks said that he faced death with his customary calmness and acceptance. Even though his deterioration was obvious we, his children, weren't prepared. That semester, I was studying out of the country, so I wasn't at home for those last few months and weeks. Besides, Dad had been in the hospital for treatment many times, and he had always come home.

My father went into Georgetown Hospital in late October 1980. Ben and Perky Pepper were among his last visitors. As they were getting ready to leave, Dad looked at Perky and, using the nickname he'd fondly called her over the years, said, "Good-bye, Perko." Later that day, on October 24, he died there.

"Paul was a wonderful, gentle, honest soul—a poet, not a technician," Terry Douglas told me. "He was seized with what he was doing in the moment. We'd be talking about some of the nonsense going on with the whole Angleton thing and about who was the mole, and he just dismissed that crap. Your father, he was listening to something else, to a different melody, and people were drawn to it. They wanted to hear a little of that music."

★

Sometime after Dad's funeral, Mom got a birth announcement from Viktor Belenko and his new American wife. They'd had a baby boy, and had named him Paul.

CHAPTER 16

AN UNMARKED GRAVE

Dmitri Polyakov after a hunting trip near Moscow, c. 1977.
(Courtesy of Sandy Grimes)

Gen. Dmitri Polyakov returned to Moscow from Delhi in the fall of 1976 and was assigned chief of the Third Faculty in the GRU's Military-Diplomatic Academy, the unit that trained intelligence operatives from both the USSR and Soviet Bloc countries. This gave him direct access to the names of all military intelligence agents preparing for overseas assignments. As Sandy Grimes and her colleagues back at Langley knew, Polyakov's return to Moscow as a general had the potential to pay even higher dividends. Back home, Polyakov again distributed gifts for his GRU associates and higher-ups. Such gestures were important to solidifying his relationships in Moscow, and as he was promoted, the quality of the gifts reflected his higher status: jewelry and watches, porcelain vases, silver tea sets, and other luxury goods, many not available in the USSR. All were bought for him by the CIA, of course, but the Agency considered the cost to be pocket change compared to the value of what they were getting.

Polyakov took a couple of months to settle into his new job and get familiar with the comings and goings of his Third Faculty officers and staff. Then, in early December, he took a trolley ride. In his overcoat pocket he carried UNIQUE, the transceiver my father had trained him to use in Delhi, which Polyakov had shipped back home in the interior of the specially designed, fully functional Panasonic three-in-one music player.

In his locked bathroom at home, Polyakov had loaded a packet of intelligence into UNIQUE via the tiny Cyrillic keyboard and accompanying stylus. The test in Delhi had worked perfectly; now he was making his first operational run with it.

As the trolley passed through Vosstaniya Square, across the street from the U.S. embassy, Polyakov slipped his hand into his pocket and pushed a button, sending a 2.6-second burst of energy toward the embassy. There the transmission was picked up by the base unit, which triggered a burst back to the device in Polyakov's pocket, illuminating the tiny red light that signaled "transmission received." Polyakov would see that confirmation when he got back to the privacy of his family bathroom.

Gathered in a room back in Langley for word of UNIQUE's first operational transmission, Sandy Grimes and the rest of the Polyakov support team had been on pins and needles. They had confidence in the device, but they knew that anything could happen—a snowstorm shutting the trolleys down or a malfunction of some sort. UNIQUE was brand-new, an expensive one-of-a-kind technological breakthrough, rushed to completion. The possibility of failure was on everyone's mind.

The news was cabled instantly from Moscow Station to Langley: "Transmission succeeded."

The team celebrated by opening the bottle of the Three Star cognac that Polyakov had given my father at their final meeting. "With a collective sigh of relief and thanks," Grimes later wrote, "the privileged few aware of the achievement toasted Polyakov, whose sacrifices required that we perform beyond what we imagined possible."

Polyakov sent and received communications via UNIQUE every few months. He knew how difficult the device's quick bursts would be for the KGB to pick up, and in any event, the encryptions were unbreakable. But he also knew the Soviet authorities monitored the airwaves carefully.

KGB radio counterintelligence did, in fact, notice strange bursts of electronic transmissions near the American embassy. They appeared, then they disappeared, then months later they appeared again. The Soviets tried to intercept them, but the bursts were too random and rapid for the airwave watchdogs to get a fix. The KGB communications specialists were frustrated at being unable to determine who was communicating with the American embassy, and never suspected that the culprit was wearing one of their own generals' uniforms.

UNIQUE was the answer to a spy's prayer. It provided much greater anonymity and security than the more rudimentary tradecraft used around the world in previous decades. But when the information Polyakov had to pass was too voluminous or urgent, he continued to use the dead drops he had arranged with the Agency. For those, another new, if less revolutionary, method for reducing his exposure came in the form of an electric wall clock he'd brought back with him from India and hung in his Kalininsky Prospect living room. A little red light on its face lit up in response to a radio signal informing him that a drop site had been cleared or loaded. Alexander pressed his father as to why he had the clock on the wall. It was clunky and ugly, and curiously, it operated on a voltage different from Russia's, so it never showed the right time. I keep it because I like it, Alexander's father said.

The Langley support team, already taken by the quality of the secret and top secret intelligence they were used to receiving from Polyakov, were amazed by what now began coming in to them. Polyakov photographed and sent the complete GRU training manual, known as the GRU Bible—"a comprehensive statement of GRU operational philosophy, modus operandi, and rules and regulations governing espionage activities outside the Soviet Union," wrote Sandy Grimes. He also shared the identities of three years' worth of graduating GRU officers, and their overseas assignments, "in effect," Grimes wrote, "eradicating their cover and that of their replacements for years."

Polyakov continued to copy and send the top secret issues of *Military Thought* and confidential Communist Party publications revealing the direction of Soviet domestic and foreign policy thinking. He kept the CIA up to date on what the Soviet military was buying. In scope and detail, the information he provided gave the Pentagon insight into the development of the USSR's military and industrial technology. The Langley support group was awash with information that needed to be decrypted, analyzed, translated, and distributed. To give their source additional layers of protection, even internally, it changed Polyakov's cryptonym numerous times. Previously TOPHAT and BOURBON, in turn he became SPECTER, BEEP, and ROAM.

★

By 1977, Polyakov's father, Fyodor, had died and Polyakov frequently went out for weekends in Shchelkovo to spend time with his mother, Alexandra, and devote himself to projects in the woodworking shop. By then, Petr had graduated from the Military Language Institute and joined the GRU himself, specializing in signals intelligence. The old hero Grandpa Petr Kiselev had also passed away, leaving his dacha to Nina and Dmitri. With her husband gone, Grandma Kiselev moved back into the Officers' House apartment to live with Dmitri and Nina, and when Alexander, Larisa, and their year-old baby, Marina, returned to Moscow in 1979, they moved into the empty co-op. It was small, but a big step up in comfort from their log "palace" in Kathmandu.

Back in Moscow, Alexander was put in charge of the Foreign Ministry's Nepal desk and was named personal aide to the chief of the ministry's Southeast Asia Department, a prestigious position. But with responsibility comes duty, and to Alexander's annoyance, the chief assigned him to be the secretary of the department's obligatory Communist Party meetings.

The ideological indoctrination Alexander had been subjected to all his life, from his time as a nine-year-old Young Pioneer onward, had been thorough and serious. Now, in the late 1970s, fifty years into the USSR's quest for pure communism, he was not surprised to see the party's grip appear to be slipping, the Communist spirit that had animated the believers and idealists seeming to lose its luster. People went through the motions, but with a bored acquiescence rather than conviction. He'd noticed that, quietly, the statue of Lenin that had dominated the Kalininsky apartment courtyard for so many years had disappeared, its upkeep having become a burden. "If you went to the twenty-third floor of our office building," Alexander said, "to the Party's offices, you would find absolute silence. No life."

Alexander himself could barely tolerate the Party meetings and their forced enthusiasm. As secretary, he found many of his tasks trifling and time-consuming. It was his job to track down party members for their monthly dues and to type up and distribute the minutes of the confidential meetings, since none of the clerk typists had the necessary clearances.

The meetings themselves went something like this, as recounted by Alexander with his characteristic sense of humor:

> First, the international situation of the Soviet Union . . . everyone sleeps through that. Second, how to boost production of the agriculture section . . . nobody cares that we work in the Ministry of Foreign Affairs, agriculture's still on the agenda. Third, the personal case of Anton Bogrov. Now everybody's interested!
>
> The party chief says, "Look, gentlemen, we have a bad sheep in our herd. Mr. Bogrov has divorced his wife. Anton Nikolayevich, come here and tell your comrades how you could let this happen in your family life."
>
> So Bogrov comes up. "I would like to say, comrades, forgive me, I was a bad husband."
>
> "Yes, okay, Bogrov. So, comrades, how do we propose to deal with him?"
>
> Of course, the Party section leader has assigned guys to give pre-prepared answers.
>
> "I've got a proposal!"
>
> "So, Ivanov, what's your proposal?"
>
> Ivanov takes out notes so as not to forget what his assignment was. "I think we should strongly discipline Mr. Bogrov and put a special notice in his Party book."
>
> "Okay, what other proposals do we have here? Komarov?"
>
> "We should strongly discipline Mr. Bogrov but without putting a notice in his book."

> Then, an unexpected third one: "I don't think we should discipline Mr. Bogrov at all."
>
> "Where are you from? Who are you? Sit down and shut up. Now let's vote."

"Okay, that last part's a joke," Alexander concluded, "but overall it wasn't funny. That's how it was then, these pretty sad meetings, just going through the motions. It had all become lax, just a kind of tradition."

The tradition that everyone tried especially hard to avoid was participating in celebratory parades. Every factory, institute, and organization in Moscow had to send contingents to the May First [International Workers' Day] Parade, the May Ninth Victory Day Parade, and the November Seventh Great October Socialist Revolution Parade. Given that these parades were conducted every year, finding volunteers was a thankless task. Everyone tried to avoid them, but all had to take a turn. Alexander recalled the typical experience, with one such May First parade he couldn't dodge. "At seven o'clock in the morning—it's damned cold in Moscow in May—you set out for Red Square and start looking for your column. You must find your section promptly because the most important thing is not to participate, but to report to your station leader that you're present; otherwise, be prepared for trouble. Then you start looking out for ways to escape. But you can't; the local police know all the tricks.

"You wait and wait, and finally a truck comes up loaded with flags and portraits of Party leaders on heavy poles. You rush to grab a flag instead of a portrait, because they're made of silk and are a lot lighter than the mounted picture of Brezhnev or the other Politburo members. Then, slowly, the silent, sad crowd moves hopelessly toward Red Square. Huge loudspeakers are broadcasting upbeat patriotic music. A party organizer rides by in a car with loudspeakers, shouting encouragement. 'Lift up your banners high, comrades!' You come to Red Square and wait forty-five minutes for the military parade to finish. Then you're moving in a long line with banners marching along Red Square, waving and smiling at Brezhnev and his closest cronies up on Lenin's Mausoleum. They're waving at you, and you're waving at them and you're wondering, when is this going to end? Mr. Brezhnev is wondering the same thing: it's time for him to have his first shot of vodka, so after receiving instructions from someone on high, the organizers are pushing you: 'Go! Move!' Your marching evolves from a slow pace to galloping through Red Square so Brezhnev can go home."

★

While Alexander and Larisa were sociable people with a circle of friends, Alexander's father, Dmitri, had always been more private. His favorite pursuits of woodworking, hunting, fishing, and photography were solitary pleasures, and his work as an intelligence officer severely narrowed the circle of people he could talk to about what he did professionally.

There were others, though, who couldn't keep their own counsel, among them James Angleton. After Angleton left the Agency, he became a deeply embittered man, still convinced that Polyakov and other supposed Soviet plants were doing the Agency and the country untold harm. Now on the outside looking in, Angleton couldn't do anything, at least officially, to unmask the purported impostors. But there were other ways.

In 1978, investigative journalist Edward J. Epstein published a book, *Legend*, about Lee Harvey Oswald and the Kennedy assassination. In the course of his research, Epstein learned of a Soviet agent in the USSR's UN Mission in New York who spied for the FBI, someone code-named FEDORA. In an interview that appeared in *New York* magazine on February 27, 1978, promoting the book, Epstein claimed that "90 percent of all anti-Communist cases in New York came from FEDORA (*and two other Soviets* [italics mine] who joined FEDORA in supplying the FBI with information)."

The Polyakovs' dacha, north of Moscow, undergoing renovations. *(Courtesy of Alexander Polyakov)*

Indeed, there was at least one agent besides Polyakov working for the FBI in the early 1960s, a KGB officer named Aleksy Kulak, whom the Bureau had code-named FEDORA. That his code name had been publicly revealed was a momentous breach of security, an unforgivable act within intelligence circles. Instantly, the identity of FEDORA, and of those "two other Soviets," became of paramount interest to KGB counterintelligence.

Two months later, *New York* magazine published another item, this one anonymous but known to have been provided by Epstein. This time the journalist revealed the code name of another FBI source who had worked for the Soviet Mission under diplomatic cover, a spy known as "TOP HAT [*sic*]." Years later I interviewed Epstein—he told me that his source for "TOP HAT" was Pete Bagley, Angleton's devoted disciple, the man who had handled the disgraceful incarceration of Yuri Nosenko.

Now, in addition to the existence of FEDORA and the "two

oviets," the KGB spy hunters had Polyakov's code name AT to compare to a fixed list of people who'd worked at the Soviet UN Mission in the early 1960s. Epstein's revelation cast a deep shadow of danger over Polyakov. For his part, Epstein was a writer looking for a good story—the sinister sources behind that story, though, were the Agency's master plan perpetrators, Bagley and his former boss, the retired James Angleton.

Angleton had always believed FEDORA and TOPHAT were plants, a fact that left many within the CIA to assume that he was the primary source behind the leak. Even Angleton's most scathing enemies, though, could hardly believe he would disclose details about two active agents.

The FBI's Ed Moody was incensed, saying bluntly, "Here's this guy [Polyakov] over there risking his life and they're talking out of school to get him killed. Angleton should have been taken to federal court and prosecuted for what he did."

New York magazine's "TOP HAT" article appeared in April 1978. Later that year, the Soviet military attaché in New Delhi suffered a stroke. With no one readily available to replace him, the GRU sent Polyakov back to Delhi for a second tour, suggesting that in its hunt for the spy TOPHAT, the KGB didn't consider him among their numerous potential suspects.

Shortly after Polyakov's return to New Delhi, the CIA reestablished contact with him. He met with a senior Russian-speaking CIA officer who had on occasion sat in on Dad's debriefings, and so was known to him. This officer introduced Polyakov to his new handler, Scotty Skotzko—the same case officer who'd approached Alexander in Kathmandu but had been waved off by headquarters, and who now understood why. Skotzko was a capable and experienced officer, but he was relatively young, twenty years or so Polyakov's junior. The Agency had some anxiety that a general, and one well up in the Soviet hierarchy, might construe being assigned a younger handler as a sign of disrespect. But Polyakov accepted his new handler without any apparent problem, except that he definitely did not like Skotzko's beard. GRU officers, he told Skotzko, were not allowed to wear beards. When Skotzko showed up early for the next meeting with Polyakov, he was still unshaven. The senior officer who was acting as the go-between for the two asked him why he hadn't taken off the beard. Skotzko replied that he hadn't realized that Polyakov expected him to take it off, that he thought the Russian had just been commenting that he didn't favor a beard for himself or his officers. "What our friend was telling you," the senior officer explained, "is that a GRU general is not comfortable being with someone wearing a beard. It could raise questions." Skotzko went immediately to a bathroom and used a borrowed razor to scratch it off as quickly and decently as he could.

Polyakov was pleased with Skotzko's newly shaven look, even complimenting him on his "neatness and appearance," but when Skotzko mentioned that he had met Polyakov's son Alexander in Kathmandu, Polyakov bristled. You stay away from my sons, he said. I don't want anyone approaching them.

After that, the relationship between Polyakov and Skotzko settled into one of businesslike efficiency. For the next eight months, they met—usually quick, surreptitious encounters. My father and Polyakov had been able to spend more time together, facilitated by the ruse that Dad was Polyakov's developmental source. Comparatively, Skotzko's situation didn't allow for that. An officer familiar with the case said that Dad spent so much time with Polyakov that he was essentially regarded within the agency as the heart and soul of the case.

In India, Polyakov continued to provide secret assessments of Soviet military capabilities and weaknesses as well as the Politburo's closely held foreign and domestic policy directives. He also gave the CIA a flow of information on Afghanistan, which, in December 1979, the Soviet Fortieth Army had invaded in order to support the beleaguered Russian-oriented government in its increasingly desperate fight against a Muslim insurgency.

Meanwhile, the KGB's "TOP HAT" investigation was winnowing the field of suspects, but with more than a hundred 1960s-era UN Mission intelligence officers to look at, progress was slow, and Polyakov was not among the leading suspects.

Then, a few months after Polyakov returned to Delhi, the ramparts of his cover started to crumble.

★

In early 1979, in New York City, an FBI special agent named Robert Hanssen walked into the Broadway office of Amtorg, the Soviet trading organization that he knew served as a front for the GRU, and volunteered that Gen. Dmitri Polyakov was spying for the United States.

Hanssen was a computer specialist who had been posted to the FBI's New York field office to create a database of Soviet intelligence agents. Living expenses in New York City were sky high, and supporting a wife and three children on an FBI salary was tough. Hanssen needed money, and with his knowledge of the FBI's counterintelligence operations, one obvious source presented itself.

Hanssen might have been surprised at the GRU's reaction to his revelation that Dmitri Fedorovich Polyakov was a spy for the Americans. The idea that Polyakov—a war hero with two Orders of the Red Star, a distinguished general with almost thirty years of service—might be a traitor stretched credulity. Wasn't it more likely that Hanssen himself was a provocation, a fake volunteer trying to spread false information and create havoc? Then again, what if Hanssen were right, improbable as it seemed?

The answer to that last question would prove to be unpalatable. The KGB was in charge of counterintelligence, but Hanssen had contacted the GRU. If it were known that Polyakov was a spy, it would be the KGB that would make the move on him. But Poly-kov belonged to the GRU. Spy or not, he was one of theirs.

Like the rivalry between the CIA and the FBI, there was little love lost between the KGB and the GRU. Hanssen had reported his explosive information to the GRU, and it was not inclined to share it with its rival. It wasn't just because of the competition. Polyakov's second Red Star had been recommended and signed by the GRU chief. The GRU Communist Party boss had given his approval, and his signature, to Polyakov's participation in the Party Committee. Polyakov's various promotions were larded with the signatures and approbations of the most important figures in the directorate. His disgrace would be theirs as well, his downfall their downfall.

Then there were the gifts. Polyakov had been good to his chiefs and colleagues over the years, and his presents could be construed as proof of illicit cronyism. The old boys were inextricably tied to him, and in their minds it was all too obvious that the KGB would relish their investigation into who had received what from Polyakov, with the ominous implication that those gifts had been provided by the Main Enemy itself.

Under these circumstances, maybe it would be best not to arrest Polyakov for this potential betrayal, but to retire him and let him descend into a peaceful old age, no one the wiser. Maybe, that way, pensions, ranks, and honors would remain undisturbed.

★

In New Delhi, Polyakov was not aware of the disaster of Hanssen's revelation. Then yet another exposure happened, in early 1980, placing his life in more imminent danger. Veteran intelligence reporter David Martin was picking up where Epstein had left off. "One KGB officer and one GRU officer," Martin wrote in his book *Wilderness of Mirrors*, "both ostensibly members of the Soviet delegation to the United Nations, contacted the FBI and volunteered their services as spies against their country. The two agents were christened

Scotch and Bourbon." "Scotch" was FEDORA's CIA cryptonym for Aleksy Kulak, and "Bourbon," of course, was Polyakov's.

Martin revealed that BOURBON had volunteered "within a few months of Golitsyn's defection." The KGB now had too many pieces to the puzzle of Polyakov's secret—his two primary code names, his UN Mission affiliation, the fact that he worked for the GRU, and a narrow period to focus on.

For what turned out to be their last meeting, Polyakov asked Skotzko to come to his private residence, which was unusual. An adversary's embassy and compound were normally strictly off base for an undercover agent. Coming into Polyakov's apartment, Skotzko was surprised to see all his possessions packed up. I'm going to Moscow, Polyakov told him in a calm, businesslike manner. He had, he said, been called back.

Knowing a return at this time was unexpected, Skotzko asked why.

One never knows, Polyakov said. But I will survive. Do not worry about me.

Skotzko, doing his duty to protect his asset, offered Polyakov exfiltration. His proposal: You don't owe us. We owe you. We'll get you out and resettle you.

Once again, Polyakov rejected the offer, this time angrily. "Don't wait for me," he told Skotzko. "I am never going to the United States. I am not doing this for you. I am doing this for my country. I was born a Russian and I'll die a Russian!"

It was the only time a handler saw the Soviet general flare up and lose his cool. For a moment there, the furnace door opened and you could see briefly the fire that was burning inside, and then it closed.

Skotzko wondered aloud to Polyakov what would happen if the Soviets were to catch him.

Bratskaya mogila, Polyakov told him. A common, unmarked grave.

CHAPTER 17

TOMORROW WILL BE TOO LATE

Polyakov's granddaughter, Marina, reciting at a school pageant, 1986. *(Courtesy of Alexander Polyakov)*

The American press had given the KGB a pretty present tied up in a bow: not one, not two, but three public disclosures about Soviets who'd worked for American intelligence in New York City in the 1960s. Epstein's two items revealed that the agents had worked undercover at the United Nations; Martin's book noted that one of them had been with the GRU. The KGB had never solved the mystery surrounding the exposure of its illegal agents in the 1960s (the Sokolovs, Egorovs, and others), and now it saw that linking a GRU officer to these leaks was likely within its reach. It was simply a case of coming up with a list of who worked at the UN Mission in New York City in the 1960s and starting a process of elimination.

Polyakov knew he was being called back to Moscow under a cloud, and he may have suspected that an upcoming conference of Southeast Asia *rezidentura* chiefs he'd been ordered to attend was merely a ploy to recall him and other GRU officers who fit the profile of the alleged mole. The KGB was working through its records, interviewing colleagues and bosses in its attempt to identify the penetration, but it needed to come up with an excuse for keeping the suspects who were attending the conference in the country afterward.

The excuse came in the form of a medical exam. All conference attendees, Polyakov's superiors said, were required to submit to one after the conference. The results of Polyakov's exam surprised him—his health situation, he was told, made it inadvisable for him to return to India. Delhi was too hot and humid for his condition and his age. He would not be going back.

Polyakov's health wasn't perfect—he was fifty-nine years old and had problems with high blood pressure and kidney stones, but why would those problems keep them from sending him back to Delhi? Suspicious, he scheduled his own private examination. The second doctor found no medical reasons that would have required keeping him out of the subtropical heat of India.

More disquieting news came through Polyakov's driver in New Delhi, who let him know through the grapevine that the KGB had searched his apartment. Though they didn't find anything, Polyakov understood that such an action meant the clouds of suspicion were thickening around him. He also understood that while the leaks in the American press were damaging, it would take more than circumstantial evidence to accuse a decorated general of treason. Of course, he didn't know that the FBI's Robert Hanssen had identified him as an American spy—that information was confined to the GRU, which was keeping it from the KGB.

Polyakov's reputation and status did have a powerful effect. Narrowing in on the leads from the American press, even KGB counterintelligence had difficulty accepting the fact that a Red Star hero of the Soviet Union, a distinguished general, could have committed treason. A KGB general intervened and effectively quashed the investigation on Polyakov—a Soviet general cannot be a spy, he said. Suspicion and anecdotal evidence were not enough to cause the arrest of such an august and respected figure.

Even so, those suspicions tainted Polyakov's reputation and had an effect on his career. His next appointment was to head the Pushkin State Russian Language Institute, the country's leading language teaching school. This was the first time in the institute's history that it was led by a full-rank general, and Polyakov knew the meaning behind his appointment to this nonsensitive and apolitical position.

His family, though, was in the dark and saw nothing untoward in his new appointment. Polyakov was close to retirement and he'd had some health problems normal for a man his age, so it didn't seem odd that his bosses would keep him from Delhi's insalubrious climate.

The Pushkin Institute job was Polyakov's swan song. It lasted for only a year, after which the GRU retired him with a full pension. Polyakov's career as an intelligence officer in service to the Union of Soviet Socialist Republics was now over. In both this, and his shadow life as one of the most valuable American assets in the history of the Cold War, he was now out of the game.

The elite at the GRU breathed a sigh of relief. They had gotten Polyakov out of the KGB's crosshairs and off the stage. And now that he was gone, interest in the case against him faded.

Dmitri Fedorovich Polyakov was a pensioner, free to enjoy his family, his dacha, and his hobbies, while his high-ranking friends and colleagues continued enjoying the benefits of their own positions and could look forward to their own dacha retirements and pensions.

Months passed, then years. By 1984, Polyakov's granddaughter Marina was six years old, and Polyakov spent much of his time with her, playing with the Legos and Lionel trains he'd brought back from the United States decades earlier for Alexander and Petr. With Alexander and Larisa both working, Marina spent the weekdays with her grandparents at the Kalininsky apartment and the weekends and summers with her parents out at the Chelyuskinskiy dacha. Polyakov built another woodworking shop there, installing the power tools he'd acquired over the years—power saws, lathes, and sanders, many of them given to him by the grateful Americans. He built furniture out of exotic woods he had shipped from Burma, some pieces with cleverly hidden secret compartments almost impossible for an outsider to detect or open, in which he kept a couple of old pistols and cartridges and Nina's good jewelry.

With his woodworking and carpentry expertise, Polyakov rebuilt the dacha from the ground up, with help from Alexander on the weekends. In the dacha's gardens, the elder Polyakov and his wife grew vegetables, berries, and flowers. They had apple and cherry trees, and they preserved fruit for the winter in a deep cellar Polyakov dug under the house. He made berry spirits, *samogon*, or Russian moonshine, enlisting Marina to help clean and sort the rowanberries.

Spending time with his granddaughter brought joy to Polyakov in retirement. He and Marina filled their days with swims and walks in the woods. In the winters, back in Moscow, they went sledding in the city's beautiful parks. To Marina's delight, each December, her grandfather put up a fir tree in the Kalininsky apartment, one that reached up to the ceiling. Back in the mid-1920s, the Party had officially banned Christmas, but a few years later it allowed New Year's trees as a nonreligious alternative to the traditional Christmas tree. Marina and her grandfather decorated the trees together, and on New Year's morning, Marina would wake up to see what kind of presents Ded Moroz and Snegurochka ("Grandfather Frost" and his granddaughter the "Snow Maiden") had brought her.

★

Marina Polyakova, in Moscow, c. 1984.
(Courtesy of Alexander Polyakov)

The Polyakov support team in Langley was aware that Polyakov had not returned to Delhi in 1980 to finish out his tour. Months went by with no contact, no UNIQUE transmissions, and no dead drops. As time passed, the silence grew increasingly ominous. Grimes and her colleagues fretted over a dozen possible reasons: maybe UNIQUE had broken down, maybe Polyakov was ill, or maybe something more insidious was going on in Moscow. Could the KGB have secretly arrested Polyakov without anybody from the outside world knowing?

Months of silence grew into a year, then two. Sandy Grimes had been working on the Polyakov case for thirteen years, and she and her colleagues were invested in the man himself. Like a family with one of its members off to war, incommunicado, and in potential danger, they lived with an undertone of anxiety for his welfare. Given the breaches to his security that had been leaked to the press, they had endless discussions as to what had happened to him and explored every avenue they could with guesses and speculations.

Searching for clues to Polyakov's silence, the CIA failed to see what was right out in the open. The headquarters support team knew that between his overseas postings, Polyakov was an occasional contributing writer to *Okhota*, a hunting and sporting magazine. They hadn't monitored *Okhota* for years, but now someone remembered to order up the back issues, and when they scanned through them, there he was: Artillery specialist D. F. Polyakov had been writing regularly since his return to Moscow—about bullets, their ballistic characteristics, their velocity, and their behavior in flight. He wrote mainly about American-manufactured bullets, using information from American magazines unavailable in the USSR. Judging from the number of letters to the editor, Polyakov's articles were popular.

Those working on the case were greatly relieved. Polyakov was apparently well, and after some debate, they decided not to attempt contact. "Our role would be to wait," Grimes wrote later, "reassured that knowledge of his secret past remained his and ours alone."

★

After his tour handling Soviet assets in New York City came to an end, Aldrich Ames, the case officer whom Sandy Grimes had gotten to know at Langley, returned to headquarters in January 1981 for a few weeks before being posted to a new assignment in Mexico City. He was pleased; his wife, with whom his relationship was increasingly strained, could stay in New York in the job she liked and visit regularly, he suggested. She agreed.

In Mexico City, Ames took over as the station's senior SE Division officer, the same position my father had held thirteen years earlier. Mexico City was still a hotbed of espionage activity, as it had been when Dad was there, but in his new posting, Ames was proving no more adept at recruiting Soviet agents than he had previously. Coincidentally, Diana Worthen, the intelligence analyst who had worked for my father in India, was sent to Mexico City to work with Ames.

Ames regularly attended luncheons hosted by the city's diplomatic association, and there he met the new twenty-nine-year-old Colombian cultural attaché Maria del Rosario Casas Dupuy. Rosario attracted a lot of attention among the men who dominated these luncheons, and she and Ames sparked on an intellectual level. Her father was from a prosperous Colombian family, but he had walked away from his family's wealth to pursue a career in teaching. Growing up, Rosario had been surrounded by academics. At a university luncheon, her father had introduced her to the president of Colombia, Julio César Turbay Ayala, and it was he who recommended her for the Mexico City attaché position.

Rick and Rosario started dating, but he didn't tell Rosario he was married, or that he worked for the CIA; in fact, she believed she was dating a State Department diplomat. To Ames, she was the best thing to happen to him in a tour that was not turning out as well as he had hoped. His new boss was concerned with his behavior. He'd watched Ames get into a loud drunken argument with a Cuban diplomat at an official function and, later, learned of a car accident in which the Mexican police found him heavily intoxicated. Ames's boss told Langley that Ames needed counseling for alcohol abuse when he returned to the United States, but that never happened.

Rosario was somewhat needy, and when she found out Ames was planning a weekend in Acapulco with a male colleague, she insisted on going. Ames acquiesced, even though his plan was to meet an old girlfriend there. He spent the weekend concocting stories to each of the women as to why he hadn't been available this or that morning, afternoon, or evening, as he juggled his time between the two. Eventually, Rosario figured out what was going on, and was furious, but after much pleading from him on the flight home she forgave him.

Ames's Mexico tour ended in the fall of 1983, and he was posted back to Langley. His analyst, Diana Worthen, had become friendly with Rick and Rosario in Mexico City, and after Ames left, the two women spent time together. Worthen found it curious that Rosario didn't appear to be affluent even though she came from a socially prominent family. "In Latin America if you are a wealthy woman, you don't work," Worthen said later. "I knew Rosario was putting in long hours at her job, so that told me that her family was not wealthy."

In the fall of that year, Rosario's father died. Devastated, she called Ames, and he flew to Mexico to console her. He invited her to come to Washington to live with him. Wounded and vulnerable, she said yes, asking him to promise that he would always take care of her.

He promised.

★

At Langley headquarters, Ames secured an impressive new job: head of the counterintelligence branch for Soviet operations within the SE Division, a position in which he headed the Agency's efforts to detect and prevent Soviet attempts to gather intelligence or spy on the United States. In retrospect, members of the intelligence communities wondered how Ames was chosen for such an important and sensitive position, given his lackluster career thus far, one that was blemished with behavioral problems. He did speak and write Russian passably, was known for creating good operational reports, and had experience working against the Soviets in Turkey and Mexico. Also, in an interview he could appear impressively intellectual. Somehow his drunken episodes and uneven performance hadn't played a role in the Agency's decision to promote him.

In this new position, Ames felt he had "finally arrived." As the Soviet counterintelligence head, he had access to the names of most of the Soviets' human assets in the United States. He knew of at least twenty active agents and one hundred covert operations. In time, he realized he was sitting on a gold mine.

In December 1983, he and Rosario moved into a small suburban apartment in Falls Church, Virginia. She had been devastated and angry when Ames confessed that not only was he married, but he worked for the CIA, not the State Department. But with a promise that he would get a divorce soon, the two shopped for furniture and stocked the kitchen with appliances. Still mourning her father's death, Rosario called her mother in Bogotá every day, and the monthly phone bills were soon exceeding four hundred dollars.

Ames used the credit card he shared with his wife to pay most of the bills. When Rosario wanted a car, he took a loan from a credit union. Rosario liked to shop in expensive boutiques and go to the finest restaurants, and Ames got a second credit card—which they promptly ran up to the limit. In love with Rosario and wanting her to be happy in her new life in the United States, Ames was digging an ever-deeper pit of debt for himself.

Diana Worthen, now posted back to Washington, visited her friend Rosario, noting that she seemed bored and lonely. Rosario wondered what had happened to the "old" Rick from the Mexico days, the Rick who'd been so fun and carefree. Worthen suggested going out shopping, but Rosario declined, saying she and Ames barely had enough money to buy groceries. His debts were piling up, including $34,000 on the credit cards he shared with his wife, who shortly filed for divorce.

In the fall of 1984, Ames took the train up to New York to meet with his wife and her divorce attorney. Rosario had coached him on not giving in to his wife's demands—to no avail. Ames capitulated almost completely, agreeing to cover the full credit card debt, give his wife outright ownership of their joint property, and pay her an additional three hundred dollars a month for forty-two months.

On the train ride home, Ames knew Rosario was going to be incensed by his lack of backbone, and he felt desperate. He needed about $47,000 to pay off his debts. His annual salary was $45,000. Where was he going to get $47,000 quickly?

Then, in November 1984, the opportunity to get out of debt presented itself. Always on the lookout for potential recruits, Ames's boss encouraged him to have lunch with Sergey Chuvakhin, a Soviet diplomat who specialized in arms control. It wasn't until April 1985 that Ames succeeded in getting Chuvakhin to accept a lunch date at the Mayflower Hotel, just a few blocks from the Soviet embassy. Ames reported his upcoming meeting to both the CIA and FBI, a requirement for all case officers meeting with Soviet contacts. Given what he intended to do at this lunch, Ames was pleased with his cover—he was following his boss's orders to recruit a Soviet, and had reported it appropriately.

Ames arrived early to the Mayflower. An hour and a half (and a number of vodkas) later, Chuvakhin had not shown up. With a determination fueled by alcohol, Ames decided to confront him in his lair. Walking the few blocks to the Soviet embassy, he entered the front door and handed the receptionist an envelope containing a note he'd prepared. It was addressed to the KGB *rezident* using the *rezident*'s internal code name—an indication to the Soviets that Ames had high-level intelligence access. The note explained that he was the branch chief of Soviet counterintelligence at the CIA, and that for fifty thousand dollars he would give the KGB the names of three Soviets the CIA was developing as assets.

He then asked for Chuvakhin, who reluctantly came down to the reception area. Ames asked him why he hadn't shown up for lunch. Chuvakhin claimed to have forgotten. Ames said he wanted to reschedule. Chuvakhin said he'd be busy.

"We'll see," Ames replied as he left.

A couple of weeks later, Ames called Chuvakhin again for lunch. This time the Russian showed up promptly. At lunch, he and Ames talked about arms control issues, and as they were wrapping up, Chuvakhin handed him a shopping bag. After they parted, Ames found $50,000 inside the bag in one-hundred-dollar bills wrapped tightly in brown paper. "I was totally exhilarated," Ames would later recall. "I had pulled it off."

He had originally planned a one-shot deal to cover his immediate debts, but on June 13, 1985, he again met Chuvakhin for lunch. The KGB had not asked for any more information, but Ames wanted to impress them: at his office before lunch, he'd loaded a shopping bag with seven pounds of classified intelligence and walked out through the CIA's security turnstiles.

The materials Ames handed to Chuvakhin at lunch that day, which the CIA later dubbed "the big dump," included information on top secret operations being run against the Soviets. They also included the names of almost every active Soviet agent who was spying for the Americans. Ames also gave them the name of an agent who had retired, the highest-ranking asset in the group: Gen. Dmitri Fedorovich Polyakov.

The KGB was delighted with this unexpected treasure trove of information, and with its source as well. A few months later, Chuvakhin passed Ames a written message: "Congratulations," Ames read, "you are now a millionaire!" Wishing to solidify the commitment from this most cherished new source, the Russians wrote Ames they'd set aside $2 million for him.

That same year, Rick and Rosario got married in a small, quiet ceremony.

★

In the fall of 1984 the Soviet Ministry of Foreign Affairs posted Alexander Polyakov to New Delhi as second secretary in the Russian embassy. This was a nice promotion for Alexander, and it gave him the opportunity to chat for hours with his now-retired father about the New Delhi station and Indian politics. Alexander, Larisa, and Marina moved into an apartment in the Russian embassy compound, close to Alexander's parents' former apartment. Alexander was assigned to the embassy's Foreign Policy Group, an important midlevel job.

But after less than a year, in the late summer of 1985, his career took a puzzling turn when he was assigned to the Bilateral Relations Group, which he saw as a step down. Not long after that, he found himself reassigned again, this time as second cultural attaché on the Mutual Cultural Exchange Group, working with troupes of performers. It was the type of job that got you nowhere. His work was as good as it had ever been. Why was he being demoted?

His boss claimed that the cultural work would broaden his background and be good experience. The embassy was working on a two-year artistic exchange program with India; it was important to get it right, and you, Alexander Dmitrievich, are just the man to do it, the boss said.

In June 1986, Alexander's boss informed him that he wanted him to take his vacation earlier than planned. Alexander had been scheduled to go back to Russia in August, but now they wanted him to go in July instead. You can stay in Moscow until September, his boss said, then come back to New Delhi when the delegations arrive to negotiate the upcoming cultural agreement.

While unexpected callbacks to Moscow were potentially ominous for intelligence officers, Alexander was a diplomat, and his boss's explanation made the vacation switch seem sensible. So, in early July, he, Larisa, and eight-year-old Marina boarded an Aeroflot jet for Moscow.

The six-hour flight from Delhi was uneventful, but at Moscow's Sheremetyevo Airport, the passengers were held up by a delay in unloading the luggage. No bags appeared, and the Aeroflot staff offered no explanations. It took four hours before the first suitcases began arriving in the claim area. Typical Soviet inefficiency, Alexander thought, unaware that it was his bags that had caused the delay. The KGB had been searching his suitcases specifically and had held up everyone else's, too, in order to not give away that it was investigating Alexander.

The length of the delay, it turned out, was caused by an unusual item found in one of Alexander's suitcases: a gas converter that a friend in Moscow had asked him to bring back from India. The converter allowed cars to run on liquefied natural gas, which was far cheaper than the standard automobile gas that was becoming exorbitantly expensive in Moscow. The suspicious KGB inspectors puzzled over the unfamiliar tanklike device. A specialist came to the airport to examine it, Alexander later learned. Once he got his suitcases hours later, Alexander wondered how the tank had gotten so dented up in transit.

Petr had come to the airport to pick up Alexander and the family, and during the long wait for their luggage, he explained that Nina and Dmitri were out at the dacha getting ready for Dmitri's sixty-fifth birthday party that Sunday. Local neighbors were invited, and friends from Moscow would be taking the train out.

It was going to be a simple party in the backyard, and their mother had been busy preparing food for the occasion. But their father, Petr told Alexander, seemed a little anxious. It wasn't anything specific; he just appeared a little down—not like him at all.

That morning, Friday, there had been a call from Col. Gen. Valentin Meshcheryakov, Petr said, chief of the Military-Diplomatic Academy where Polyakov had headed the intelligence training faculty between his tours to India. The colonel general had asked Polyakov to deliver a speech at the academy's graduation ceremony the following Monday. Maybe their father was stressed about giving a speech, the brothers speculated. Picking up the delayed luggage at last, Petr, Alexander, and his family drove to Moscow for the night. The next day, Saturday, they would head out to the dacha to get ready for their father's birthday party on Sunday. First, though, Alexander stopped by the Kalininsky apartment to pick up his father's Panasonic three-in-one music player; he had some new tapes with him that he wanted to listen to while on vacation.

The next morning, Saturday, July 5, Alexander, Petr, and their families drove out to join the family at the dacha. Coming into the village of Chelyuskinskiy, they noticed something unusual: two ambulances parked just down the street from their dacha. Alexander saw that the ambulances had Moscow plates, not the regional plates from Chelyuskinskiy. Strange, he thought.

At the cottage, Nina was making a big Olivier salad, everyone's traditional favorite, with the potatoes and most of the vegetables coming from their own garden. Married thirty-eight years, Nina had followed her husband through his distinguished and demanding career. Now she was enjoying spending time with him in his retirement. There was a lot to celebrate.

Outwardly, Polyakov was composed, but on alert. Being asked on short notice to go into the city to speak at the Military Academy and the presence of the ambulances parked down the street were both clear signals to an experienced intelligence expert.

That afternoon, the family was sitting outside in the garden talking about plans for the next day's party. Mikhail Gorbachev, the reforming party general secretary, had been in office for a year. His most controversial reform so far was his anti-alcohol campaign, which was raising prices and clamping down hard on sales. Yes, we live in cruel times, the family joked: no vodka! Fortunately, Polyakov had a good supply of his handcrafted *samogon* down in the cellar. He didn't drink much himself, but he knew the duties of a good Russian host, and no one at the party was going to go thirsty.

While they were talking, two young men walked by, along the dacha's fence. In Chelyuskinskiy, everyone knew everyone else, but no one in the garden had seen these men before. Oddly, given the village's friendly rural character, the two men didn't stop to chat or even wave hello. They walked by several times, looking straight ahead. Another strange occurrence, Alexander thought.

Walking down their lane later in the afternoon, Larisa bumped into a former school friend, Helen Tretyakov. Helen's husband, Sergei, was at the same stage in his career with the KGB as Alexander was at the Foreign Ministry, and the two couples were friendly and visited each other often at their nearby dachas. Returning to the house, Larisa told her husband that Helen had seemed somewhat uneasy, and that she, Larisa, had seen the same two strange men standing not far off.

The next day, Sunday, the sixth, friends started arriving shortly after noon. The food was plentiful, the *samogon* a hit. Everyone happily joined in the many toasts to Polyakov's health. Toward evening, as the party was winding down, a neighbor, a KGB officer whose summer cottage was down the street, stopped at the fence and looked in. Invited in for a drink, he chatted with Dmitri and Alexander about Moscow politics and commuting nightmares. The neighbor raised his glass. "Za zdorov'ye," he said, "to your health, Dmitri." They all drank.

"You know," the KGB neighbor said, pointing to a flowering bush, "you promised to give me that plant over there for my garden."

"Of course," said Polyakov, "but not now. The party's still going on. Besides, how would you carry it? Come over with your car tomorrow."

"Tomorrow," Alexander heard the KGB neighbor say to his father, looking steadily at Polyakov, "will be too late."

The neighbor paused for a moment, his eyes still on Dmitri. Then he left.

★

Decades later, sitting in the living room of his home in suburban DC, Alexander told me what he eventually realized the neighbor meant by "Tomorrow will be too late." This was a punctuation mark on the message that was being sent to Polyakov. The obvious surveillance, the ambulances in plain view, the call to come to Moscow and give a speech—they were overt hints to the seasoned intelligence operative, an invitation to spare his family and colleagues the anguish and consequences of an arrest for treason.

"There was this last hope by the KGB and GRU that my father would take his officer's gun and kill himself," Alexander told me flatly. "And it would be a great weight off all of them. 'Tomorrow will be too late.' If he committed suicide that night, he would be buried as a full-fledged general, everything quiet, nobody revealing the suspicions. Can you imagine what a political drawback it would be to reveal that an important member of the party, a general in the Red Army, a war hero, worked on an ideological basis for the Americans for twenty years?

"If he'd killed himself," Alexander continued in a gush of suppressed anguish, "he would have saved them and his family from all problems. Mother? She would have lived as a widow of a general. Our family would not have been disgraced, his fellow officers' careers would have been spared. Father was not a religious person, so there was no religious reason not to commit suicide. But father would not do it. Perhaps he wanted to prove his beliefs to himself. Perhaps he wanted to do it for history. I don't know what his motivations were. Yes, he was a loving father, a perfect husband. He knows what the fate of the family will be, so how could he save his family? Yes, that's a way out, perhaps I will try it. But he did not. No. He was absolutely sure about his fate. He did not believe that he could be saved."

CHAPTER 18

UPWARD MOBILITY

The CIA's mole hunt team that discovered that Aldrich Ames was selling secrets, including the identity of Dmitri Polyakov, to the KGB. *Left to right:* Sandy Grimes, Paul Redmond, Jeanne Vertefeuille, Diana Worthen, and Dan Payne. *(Courtesy of Sandy Grimes)*

In January 1986, the SE Division chief called Sandy Grimes into his office to discuss a disturbing development. Grimes sat dumbfounded as he tallied up in detail the recent inexplicable loss of many of the division's Soviet assets. In the previous four months, he told her gravely, five active Soviet sources had either been arrested or had disappeared altogether. Numerous operations against the Soviets had been compromised. Something was seriously wrong.

In fact, the division was not yet aware of the true enormity of the problem. Acting on the information Aldrich Ames had passed to the KGB the day of "the big dump," the Soviets had rolled up more agents than the Americans knew of, one after another. The KGB managed to conceal many of these arrests, and it would often be months or even years before the Agency learned of them. By the time it did, the magnitude of the losses would be devastating.

The bad news was only background to the main reason for Grimes's visit to the division chief's office. He was assigning Grimes to a small deep-cover team to make sure that newly recruited assets stayed safe and uncompromised. To do this effectively, the team (later to be known as "the back room") would be operating under unprecedented security procedures. It didn't take long before Grimes found herself stretched by the amount of work this took, and she recruited her old friend and colleague Diana Worthen to join her.

There were two prominent theories about what was causing the ongoing losses of the CIA's Soviet assets. One theory was that the Soviets had somehow tapped into the Agency's communications system, which had given them the ability to read and decode cables that went back and forth between the Agency's stations around the world and Langley headquarters. The more obvious one was the existence of a mole, an Agency employee who had access to SE Division records or who had handled these compromised cases at some point.

Of the two theories, the tapped communications system was the easier and more palatable one to explore, and two probes were conducted. Cables were sent to Langley and the CIA Moscow Station, identifying KGB officers in Nairobi and Bangkok whom the CIA had supposedly recruited. (This was untrue.) If Moscow recalled the "recruited" KGB officers for interrogation, it would prove the Soviets had intercepted the cables. But the two officers remained in their posts unaffected, so that hypothesis was ruled out.

Determining if there was a mole to blame was a more complicated problem—no one wanted to search for a traitor among their own ranks. Even after then CIA director William Casey was briefed on the losses, he was reluctant to begin an exhaustive mole hunt within the SE Division ranks. Angleton's mole hunt, with all its destructive consequences, was still embedded in the Agency's institutional psyche.

Instead, Casey asked an experienced senior Agency officer to investigate each of the known cases of compromised agents and look for the cause. After a three-month review, the officer produced a report that concluded that rather than a single common denominator being responsible for the lost assets, each of the cases could be blamed on "sloppy work by the Soviet agents or their case officers." The conclusion was comforting as well as convenient, as it appeared unlikely that the problem was a traitor inside Langley headquarters.

Yet, every passing month brought news of more Soviet sources disappeared, arrested, or executed. In October 1986, a year after the CIA first became aware that its Soviet assets were disappearing, the Agency finally ordered that a task force be formed to look for a mole within the CIA. The special task force reported to counterintelligence staff chief Gus Hathaway, who then recruited Ben Pepper. (They had both been pallbearers at my father's funeral.) Hathaway appointed Jeanne Vertefeuille, a veteran Soviet specialist who'd spent much of her Agency career in research and counterintelligence, to head up the task force. Jeanne knew and worked well with Sandy Grimes, and Grimes and Diana Worthen cooperated with Vertefeuille's team, aware that sources found in the "back room" would be useful in hunting down the potential mole responsible for the ongoing loss of their assets.

★

In the summer of 1986, Aldrich Ames was posted to Rome. He and Rosario were thrilled. It was a plum assignment for Ames, and Rosario, who hadn't adjusted to life in the suburbs of Washington, DC, felt she would be much more suited to living in the glamorous, vibrant city. There, Ames took up the job of chief of the Enemy Targets Branch, responsible for operations against the Soviets, Eastern Europeans, North Koreans, and Chinese. As with my father sixteen years earlier, his cover title was first secretary in the U.S. embassy. Ames quickly realized that the quantity of valuable information that flowed through the Rome Station, which included the identities of and interactions with foreign agents, would keep him abundantly relevant to his Soviet masters.

Ames asked the station chief for permission to court a diplomat from the Soviet embassy, a potential recruit he wanted to develop. The station chief had no way of knowing that far from being a likely target, this particular diplomat was in reality a KGB contact, assigned to Ames by his new handler in Moscow, "Vlad." Ames's supervisors once again gave him permission to meet frequently with someone to whom he would hand over reams of top secret information. Agent and handler would again swap shopping bags

Aldrich Ames and Rosario Casas Dupuy, Puerto Vallarta, Mexico, 1984. *(Courtesy of Diana Worthen)*

under a table at lunch every six to eight weeks, a six-inch stack of documents for one, $20,000 in cash for the other.

Rick and Rosario started spending the money, and didn't try to hide their affluence. Rosario shopped at the best boutiques. They dined at the priciest restaurants. Ames wore expensive Italian suits, had his teeth capped, and sported more fashionable eyeglasses. He also drove an expensive sports car and wore a Rolex watch.

But the excitement Ames felt that spring about being in Rome was overshadowed by his worry over the news of arrests of the SE Division assets, and the quickening pace of investigations over who or what was causing them. Starting in the fall of 1985, the revelations seemed to continue nonstop. He had expected that the KGB would space out its arrests over a much longer period in order to protect him. Instead, it appeared to be snatching up every source he gave them in a rush, thus placing Ames in danger by making it obvious to the CIA that it likely had a mole in active operation.

In October, Ames's handler, "Vlad," came to Rome for a meeting, and Ames asked him for the $2 million the KGB had promised. "Vlad" told him it was too risky to give him such a large amount all at once, but at their next lunch meeting, the shopping bag contained $60,000. To deal with all the cash, Ames opened two checking accounts in Zurich, at Credit Suisse, one of which was in his mother-in-law's name. This helped to corroborate the story he was telling his friends and coworkers: that the wealth he was displaying, obviously above the means of his salary, was coming from Rosario's family.

At his meeting with "Vlad," Ames planned to bring up the question of why the KGB was putting him in danger by arresting so quickly all the agents he'd turned over. But "Vlad" brought it up himself.

"My friend, I have some unfortunate news to share with you. We have been forced to close everyone down on the list that you provided us."

"Jesus Christ!" Ames replied. "You're going to get me arrested! Why not just put up a big neon sign over the agency with the word *mole* written on it?"

"Vlad" explained to Rick that the KGB had been forced by the Politburo to make the arrests. The Soviet leadership did not have the patience to space out the arrests of the shockingly large number of traitors Ames had unveiled. Protecting the agent, the Politburo said, was the KGB's job. "Vlad" told Ames that the KGB was leaking information to the CIA suggesting it had gotten the intelligence by tapping into the Agency's communications system in Warrenton, Virginia (playing into one of the CIA's mistaken assumptions).

Despite their new riches, Rosario would later claim that their marriage began to unravel during this period. "The myth that Rick would take care of me quickly began to crumble in Rome," she was quoted as saying later, noting that she had to "prod him" for things she wanted. Perhaps hoping it would help their marriage, she and Rick decided to have a baby. Rosario asked Diana Worthen to send her pregnancy vitamins from the United States. In return, Rosario sent Worthen a Salvatore Ferragamo scarf, an inappropriately extravagant gift, Worthen thought. The Ameses' baby boy was born in November 1988.

Acknowledging the birth, the KGB gave Ames a large bonus.

★

Aldrich Ames's tour in Rome was up in July 1989, and he and Rosario returned to Washington, DC. Diana Worthen met the Ames family at the airport on their return to Washington and noted how fashionably dressed the two were. Later that year, Rick and Rosario bought a five-bedroom house in Arlington, Virginia, paying the $540,000 asking price. Ames told friends and colleagues that the house was a gift from his wealthy mother-in-law. He also bought a Jaguar for $49,500, and drove it to work daily.

When Ames arrived back at Langley, Sandy Grimes was astonished by his new appearance and demeanor. "There was an air of confidence that I'd never seen before," she recalled. "He exuded it, and I couldn't believe it, because he certainly wasn't getting his ego stroked professionally by the agency."

Once again, despite a substandard job performance while in Rome, Ames was given an important and sensitive job at Langley: chief of the European Branch of the SE Division. This was a position of great interest to the KGB as it gave Ames access to all the developmental cases and recruited assets the CIA was running against the European Soviet target. Had it not been for the "back room" where Grimes and Worthen were employing draconian security measures, especially internally, to protect newly recruited sources, Ames could have exposed more agents. But there was plenty else to share operationally, and again he regularly stuffed stacks of confidential material into his briefcase and walked out Langley's front door.

CHAPTER 19

DO SVIDANIYA

Dmitri Polyakov at his dacha outside Moscow with granddaughter Marina, Nina *(far left)*, and neighbors, c. 1983. *(Courtesy of Sandy Grimes)*

The morning after the birthday party, Monday, July 7, 1986, Dmitri Polyakov got up early, put on his full-dress uniform, took out his box of medals and ribbons, and arrayed them across the chest of his tunic. Alexander and Petr were up early, too, to get into Moscow for work. They thought their father would drive in with them, but at breakfast he said he'd take the train. With the usual rush-hour traffic jams it would be faster than driving, he said.

Eight-year-old Marina was at breakfast, too, surprised to see her grandfather dressed in his uniform. "Why are you wearing that?" Marina asked. Her grandfather smiled at her. "I am giving a speech," he said.

Marina was proud of him in his impressive uniform, her important grandfather. As he left, he turned to look at her, smiling again. "Do svidaniya," he said. Good-bye.

Marina had no idea it was the last time she would ever see him.

★

A little before 10:00 a.m., Gen. Dmitri Polyakov walked through the front door of the Military-Diplomatic Academy and showed his ID to the guard. A moment later, four men in suits, members of the KGB's elite Alpha Group unit, grabbed him. Polyakov was instantly immobilized, two men pinioning his arms and another wrapping an arm around his throat in a headlock, keeping his head erect. They hustled him into a guard room off the lobby, where they methodically pulled off his uniform jacket and stripped back his shirt, feeling the seams for anything suspicious.

Nine years earlier, Aleksander Ogorodnik, a Foreign Ministry official who was spying for the United States, had been arrested but had managed to slip a CIA-issued cyanide pill into his mouth and die on the spot. Since then, arrest procedures had changed, and special Alpha teams were trained to prevent suicides.

Polyakov didn't resist. He had prepared himself for this emotionally, and as they stripped him, he was calm. When they finished their search, the agents dressed him in a jogging suit and drove him in a car with covered windows to the KGB's Lefortovo

Prison, a special place of detention for political prisoners. Lefortovo had once been notorious as the site where brutal interrogations and torture took place. In more recent years, though, it became considered one of the more humane Russian prisons, with decent meals and civil guards.

That same morning, Alexander dropped Petr off at his GRU office building. There was a meeting that morning at the Foreign Ministry that didn't require Alexander's attendance, so he dropped Larisa off at the apartment and went to buy a new muffler for his car.

At the auto parts store, he noticed four men watching him, but he didn't pay them much mind. He then headed home to drop off the muffler and change into office clothes—he was still wearing the jeans he had worn at the party the day before. His apartment was on a quiet tree-lined street, and as he parked in front of the building, the four men he'd noticed at the store suddenly materialized and surrounded him. They flashed their IDs. KGB.

"Come with us," one of them said.

"Where?"

"To Chelyuskinskiy."

"Why?"

"We need to make a search there."

"For what?"

"Your father has been arrested. We are going to search the dacha."

"Arrested?" Alexander said, barely believing them. "On what charge?"

"Article Sixty-Four-a."

Alexander felt despair wash over him. He had graduated with a degree in law and was well aware of the notorious Article 64-a of the Soviet criminal code: Treason in the form of espionage.

"Something broke inside of me," Alexander described the moment later. "Emptiness. Life stops."

The KGB men put him in their car and drove him to Chelyuskinskiy. Driving out of Moscow, Alexander got over his initial shock and was a little surprised to find himself calm. "What papers do you have?" he asked the men. "What warrants?"

One of the agents produced the prosecutor's permission to search the dacha and explained that Alexander would be the family witness to the procedure.

While Alexander was on his way to the dacha, another KGB team picked up Petr at his office in the GRU building—he would be the witness to the search at the Kalininsky apartment. A third team rang the doorbell at Alexander and Larisa's apartment. Larisa opened the door to find three serious-looking men. "Sorry," she said, "Alexander isn't home." The three came in anyway and looked around, asking her strange questions about her husband and their apartment.

Okay, enough of this, she thought. "May I see your IDs, please?" They produced them.

"We're going to Shchelkovo," one of the men said. "To your husband's grandmother's house. Dmitri Fedorovich has been arrested. Please come with us."

The KGB men drove Larisa to the house that Grandfather Fyodor and Grandmother Alexandra had built with Polyakov's combat pay after the end of the Great Patriotic War. Grandmother Alexandra was ninety years old and almost blind. Larisa was shaking with nerves as she arrived with the three KGB men, explaining that Dmitri Fedorovich had been arrested. Alexandra hardly seemed fazed—she had lived through Stalin's purges, and knew how to deal with these grim and purposeful men. "Fine," she said, with a steely dignity as they told her they had a warrant to search the house. "Do what you please."

As Alexander was being taken to Chelyuskinskiy, Petr to Kalininsky, and Larisa to Shchelkovo, Polyakov was under interrogation at Lefortovo Prison. He had no regrets about what he had done or why he had done it, and he knew his course by then; he was prepared to cooperate fully. He would reveal everything, he told his questioners, but under one condition: that he first speak directly with Viktor Chebrikov, the chairman of the KGB.

Polyakov knew the value of his offer. The KGB was committed to finding out every detail of his many years of treason. It wanted to know what the Americans knew. It needed to determine the extent of the damage his treason had caused the Soviet Union, and who had greased his way.

At the meeting, Polyakov told Chebrikov that he would admit to spying and that he would tell his interrogators everything. In turn, he wanted Chebrikov's promise that his wife and sons would be spared arrest. They knew nothing, he told the KGB chief. Chebrikov quickly accepted the deal.

With that done, Polyakov signed a confession stating that he had been a spy for the United States of America since 1962. Once the papers were signed, he was taken to a cell. He knew he was facing a long, grueling interrogation, and he knew with equal certainty what was going to happen when the interrogators were finally done with him.

★

Not long after Polyakov's meeting with Chebrikov, the KGB team with Alexander in tow arrived at the Chelyuskinskiy dacha. "I have some company with me," Alexander told his surprised mother and Marina. "They've come to make a search. Father has been arrested."

Nina went into a state of shock; Marina stood next to her, wondering what was happening, who these stern-looking men were.

"You have to come with us back to Moscow," one of them said to Nina.

"But what about my granddaughter?" Nina asked. "Can she stay here with my son?"

"No. She'll come with us, too. She's going to Petr Dmitriyevich's apartment in Moscow. His wife will take care of her."

The KGB had organized the day meticulously.

From the dacha, the KGB men drove Nina to Lefortovo and questioned her for hours, but it was clear she knew nothing. Eventually, they showed her a paper, written in a hand she knew well: "I have been working in the interests of the United States of America since 1962," it read. It was signed, "Dmitri Fedorovich Polyakov."

Late that night the family gathered at Alexander and Larisa's apartment. Walking in the door pale with distress, Nina put her finger to her lips, afraid there might be listening devices. Alexander found paper and pencils so they could write notes to each other. Marina still understood nothing. No one offered any explanation for these strange things that were happening. But she could feel the fear that pervaded the family. Her father was the only one not crying.

Marina didn't understand, but the others did. No one comes back from Lefortovo.

★

Nina, Alexander, and Petr were told to sign confidentiality agreements, forbidding them to speak to anyone about what had happened to Polyakov. To do so would result in a six-month prison sentence. If anyone asked, Dmitri Fedorovich was ill. The Polyakov affair was secret; there was no public announcement about the arrest. Those within the KGB, the GRU, and the Ministry of Foreign Affairs who knew were ordered to keep their mouths shut. The KGB was determined to avoid compromising Aldrich Ames, who was continuing to provide priceless information from Langley.

For seven days, Alexander was taken to the dacha to witness the searches. The KGB men tried to talk to him, good cop/bad cop style, but he knew better than to respond. Whenever the searchers found something of interest, they showed it to him and had him sign an affidavit: Yes, I see it.

The first few days, they discovered little of importance. There was a moment of excitement when the secret compartments in Polyakov's furniture were discovered, but they contained only Colonel Kiselev's rusted wartime Tokarev TT pistol and some of Nina's jewelry. They were more interested in Polyakov's Spanish Astra Cadix .22 caliber nine-shot revolver he had acquired in India; they had never seen one like it. It was in its original box along with cartridges, and the box had foreign markings. A curious and potentially suspicious item. Yes, I see it, Alexander signed.

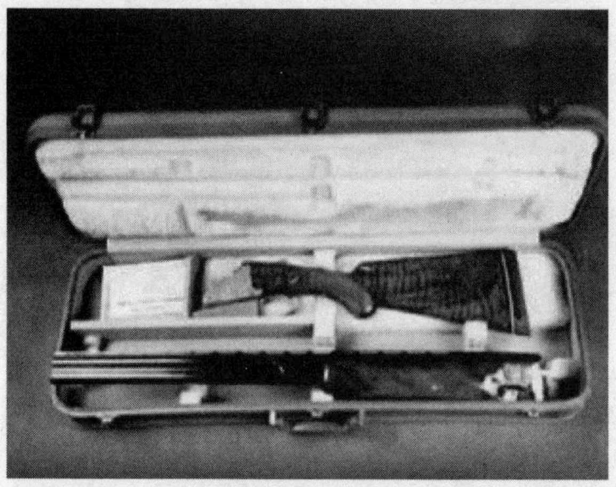

This shotgun and case confiscated from Dmitri Polyakov by the KGB was likely given to him by my father as a gift.

While Alexander was witnessing the dacha search, Petr was doing the same at Kalininsky. There, the KGB confiscated almost everything in the apartment: the carpets, the art, Polyakov's guns, Nina's jewelry, the books, all the family photographs, the TV and other electronics, even the toys and bows and arrows Polyakov had bought for the boys when they lived in New York. When the search was finished, only the furniture was left.

Initially, the investigators found nothing incriminating in the apartment, or out in Shchelkovo, where Larisa was the family witness. But that changed when the interrogators back at Lefortovo turned their questions to the spy paraphernalia the Americans had given Polyakov, and he revealed where he had hidden the items left over from his spying days. The Shchelkovo house held the most incriminating items. Jammed into a crack in the log-built wall up in the attic they found a small lead tube with microfilm and cipher notebooks—onetime pads. Yes, I see it, Larisa signed. The searchers also found paper for secret writing, dissolvable tablets to reveal secret writing, and a shortwave radio. Yes, I see it, Petr attested at the Kalininsky apartment, when the KGB men showed him incriminating finds. Yes, said Alexander at the dacha, when they showed him a key chain with instructions for making contact with the United States underneath the leather binding. I see it.

The KGB asked Alexander to bring the Panasonic three-in-one music player from his apartment to Lefortovo. Clearly Polyakov had revealed what its more clandestine purpose was. Alexander could not imagine why they'd be so interested in the music player—probably they just wanted to take it for their own use, he thought sarcastically.

Alexander, Petr, and their wives were called in for their own interrogations. Alexander remembers his as being perfunctory, an official declaration for the record that he knew nothing about the espionage his father had been engaged in. Larisa was asked about the jewelry Polyakov had given her. But it was clear they all knew nothing.

Polyakov's colleagues and superiors at the GRU had more extensive explaining to do. They were at last being called to account for the gifts Polyakov had offered around strategically over the years. The KGB demanded that anyone who'd received presents from Polyakov relinquish them. There was no hiding them—or the commendations, promotions, and awards they had bestowed on him in return for the gifts. As Polyakov's interrogation continued, more and more people went under. The Aquarium's halls became littered with ruined careers—high-ranking officers were pushed out, demoted, or sent off to distant army posts. The head of the GRU was removed. The chief political officer and a close ally of Polyakov's pretended to be insane in order to prevent his being sent to the gulag. In time, a hundred or more people lost their jobs. The fears of the GRU officials who earlier were given Polyakov's name by Robert Hanssen but chose to look the other way came true.

KGB chairman Chebrikov had made a bargain with Polyakov to spare his family from prosecution, but it did nothing to spare them of suspicion or indignity. Shortly after their father's arrest, Alexander and Petr found themselves out of jobs.

"The son of a traitor cannot work at the Ministry of Foreign Affairs," Alexander acknowledged. "It was a nightmare. After the arrest, I was looking for a job in newspaper classifieds. It was still the Soviet Union then, when employers required all prospective employees to fill out a form, an *anketa*: Name? Place of birth? Are you a member of the CPSU? When did you become a member? Have you ever been expelled from membership? Then, the most important thing, your parents: Where were they born? Were they ever detained or on trial? Under which article of the penal code? Article Sixty-Four. Every enterprise, state firm, and plant has KGB representatives on staff, and the human resources chief will run next door to the KGB guy and say, 'Look at this, do we need these troubles? No, we don't need this guy.'"

Alexander's apartment was near the Foreign Ministry. In the mornings, he boarded the tram on his daily travels around the city looking for a job. Encountering him on board, his former colleagues would avert their eyes and jump off at the next station, afraid to be seen in close proximity to the traitor's son. Alexander was able to laugh about it later. "I always had a seat," he said.

It was best to stay away from the Polyakovs. Many of their friends melted away. Sergei and Helen Tretyakov, the couple who also had a dacha at Chelyuskinskiy, where Larisa had run into a nervous Helen out in the lane, were among them. Sergei at the time was chief of his department's Young Communist League, a small party boss. "He could have called if he wanted to commit political suicide," said Alexander. "Just pick up the phone and say, 'How are you, Alex?' And the next day, he wouldn't be Komsomol chief anymore."

Little Marina missed her grandfather and didn't understand where he'd gone. "The rest of the summer I spent at the dacha with my grandmother Nina," Marina remembered. "She told me Grandfather was in the hospital. But as time was passing by, I kept asking to see him, and they didn't know what to tell me."

Marina knew that she was being kept from the truth. "One day I tried to test my grandmother. I was playing with a toy, a little car, and the wheel broke off. And I said, 'Hey, can you fix it for me?' And she tried to fix it but couldn't, and I said, 'Well, let's wait for Grandpa. He'll fix it.' She got frustrated and grabbed the toy back, saying, 'I'll fix it!' And she was angry. I think she was angry at him for what had happened. I could feel that."

Marina's parents and grandmother gave her mysterious instructions, too. "'Don't tell people your grandfather was your grandfather, that he was a general, and don't mention his name.' When I went to school, my grandmother said, 'Don't tell that your dad worked for the Ministry of Foreign Affairs.' Many of my classmates' dads worked for the MFA, so they knew what happened, and my parents and grandma were trying to protect me so people wouldn't know who I was. But of course, everyone knew."

Eventually Marina stopped asking her elders about her grandfather. "It was kind of a forbidden topic, and I understood well enough that it brought sadness and bitterness."

Soon, money became a challenge for the whole family. Alexander and Petr were suddenly without incomes, and Nina had lost Polyakov's pension. Although she continued to teach school, her salary wasn't nearly enough to make ends meet. When (mother Alexandra died shortly after the arrest, they were able to sell the Shchelkovo house, which helped everyone get by for a while.

Meanwhile, Polyakov's interrogation went on, day after day, month after month. The family was not allowed to visit, and was told only that Polyakov was healthy. No other questions were answered.

Polyakov confessed his story without reservation. "He told it all, in great detail, and with an element of pride that unsettled his interrogators," wrote Milt Bearden in *The Main Enemy*. "Polyakov offered no apologies. He declared that he'd had ample opportunities to leave the USSR, but he'd never considered that an option. Everything he had done had been *for* the Russian people, not against them. Whatever was to become of him, he told his interrogators without emotion, was his own cross to bear. And he would bear it with honor. That, too, would be part of his contribution to bringing about a revolution in thinking in the USSR. He was a social democrat of the European sort, he said. That had been the reason for his struggle over the decades. Now his death would be another part of his struggle."

Polyakov's account of how and why his views had changed rang with authenticity and had a disconcerting cogency to it. In former times, such political thinking would not have unsettled members of the Party. But by the time of Polyakov's arrest, Mikhail Gorbachev had been general secretary for more than a year, and the Russian president's thinking about reform was shaking the old establishment. In October 1986, four months after Polyakov's arrest, Gorbachev had proposed to President Reagan at their meeting in Reykjavik that both nations' strategic arms be reduced by half. Reagan had countered with a proposal to eliminate all ballistic missiles. No one in the Party could possibly mistake how the wind was blowing—political pluralism, transparency, changes in the economic system, and a drastic reduction in the nuclear weaponry aimed at the Main Enemy were all on the table.

And here was Dmitri Polyakov, a respected and influential general turned traitor, declaring that he was a social democrat in the European style who had done what he had done in an effort to prevent nuclear war. *That* was discomfiting.

Polyakov's chief interrogator, Alexander S. Dukhanin, was only a KGB colonel, and thus at too low a level to consider anything but the task before him, namely to solicit and document all Polyakov's traitorous activities and prepare materials for his upcoming trial. But Dukhanin's boss, KGB chief Chebrikov, was a member of the Politburo. The new political environment was his reality, and Dmitri Polyakov's case was a part, however large or small, of that reality.

★

The Polyakov trial opened on November 24, 1987. Polyakov, who had been in custody for sixteen months, walked into the courtroom that morning accompanied by two guards, who seated him in the prisoner's dock, a partitioned-off half-height box of wooden uprights. Polyakov looked diminished. Before his arrest he had the strong muscles and robust appearance of a hunter and builder. Now he seemed older, thinner.

The presiding judge, a lieutenant general, announced the charges: Article 64-a, treason in the form of espionage; and Article 78, illegal transportation of goods or objects across the Soviet border. "In the interests of national security," he said, "the court has decided to operate in secret."

"Who would listen to him during this trial?" Alexander said about his father's lack of a meaningful legal defense. "It was a secret affair. He had a KGB lawyer, government prosecutor, chief judge, two associate judges, security guards, that's all. No audience, an empty hall. You can say anything you want, but you won't be heard. They don't need any revolutionary statements in the Supreme Court of the USSR. It's not an American court."

On November 27, three days after the start of the trial, the chief judge read the sentence: "In the name of the Union of Soviet Socialist Republics, Dmitri Fedorovich Polyakov is sentenced by the Supreme Court to capital punishment . . . for treason in the form of espionage and deliberate hostile actions to the detriment of the USSR's national security and defense capabilities."

Polyakov was stoic during the reading of the sentence, and even Colonel Dukhanin was impressed. "There were no pleas, appeals, or anything else," Dukhanin said. "No tears, no signs of weakness on his part. He held himself very confidently."

Gen. Dmitri Polyakov in the prisoner's dock at his sentencing hearing before a secret military court, November 1987.

After the trial, the family was allowed to visit, the first time since his incarceration—one visit each, for Nina and each of the sons, separately. Alexander remembered his visit as being uncomfortable—he and his father sat across a table from each other, with the prison chief, a KGB colonel, and four other officers in attendance, too.

"We talked for an hour," Alexander said. "He was trying to act normal, I was trying to act normal. He wasn't looking bad, though he had lost weight. But his vision was damaged, maybe because of the bad light and [from] reading so much. He was smiling, asking about my future, what I was going to do in the new environment. I told him how I was looking for work, how important his advice had been about going to law school so I could have another profession to fall back on." They talked about Marina, what she was doing; about the dacha. With the KGB guards present, an intimate and genuine exchange was impossible. Polyakov seemed composed and self-possessed, facing his fate calmly, with a sense that he had done with his life what he had to do and was now ready to take the last, inevitable step.

Sometime after his visit, Alexander applied to see his father again, and the court gave him permission. On the morning of March 16, 1988, he presented himself at Lefortovo and handed his permission document to the duty officer, who took it with him into the back office. Alexander heard loud voices coming from that room, though he couldn't make out what was being said. A moment later the officer emerged and threw the permission slip down in front of him. "Your meeting is declined," he said.

"But this is a permission from the Supreme Court," Alexander insisted. "I am permitted this meeting."

"Just leave," the officer told him, "or I'll have you escorted out."

That afternoon, Nina found in her mailbox an envelope with no stamp; it had been hand-delivered. Inside the envelope was an official form: *By this letter we inform you that Mr. Dmitri Fedorovich Polyakov died on March 15, 1988.* Under "cause of death" there was a blank space.

Dmitri Polyakov had been executed in Lefortovo Prison the day before Alexander arrived for his second visit. The manner of his execution has never been disclosed. The most common method in those days was with a close-range revolver shot to the back of the head.

Where he is buried is also not known.

Bratskaya mogila. An unmarked grave.

★

Shortly thereafter, Alexander's friend Sergei Tretyakov attended a dinner party hosted by KGB deputy chief Vladimir Kryuchkov. As the toasting began, Kryuchkov stood up to make an announcement to the assembled party. He was happy to inform them, he said, that the traitor general Dmitri Fedorovich Polyakov had been executed. Everyone in the room dutifully rose and applauded, Tretyakov along with everyone else, but he was stunned. Tretyakov came home that night—as his wife, Helen, described it to Larisa years later, after she and Sergei had defected to the United States—his skin without color, his shirt soaked through with sweat. "They've shot Alexander's father," he told Helen. "They executed Dmitri Fedorovich." (Helen also explained that, the day in 1986 when she ran into Larisa in the lane in Chelyuskinskiy near the dacha, the KGB men surveilling the dacha were using her as an informant. She knew then that she would not be able to be friends with the Polyakovs any longer.)

The CIA would learn of Polyakov's death two months later, when President Reagan came home from the 1988 Moscow Summit with the news from General Secretary Gorbachev.

"To many who had never met Polyakov," Sandy Grimes wrote, "but who supported the operation, to his case officers who remained, the loss of this man was inexpressible. Polyakov, his contributions, and the sheer number of years of his service had become legend . . . It was difficult to accept that he was gone."

Grimes's sense of loss was palpable, as was her anger toward Aldrich Ames. "Rick could have gotten millions from the KGB without telling them anyone's name," Grimes is quoted in *Confessions of a Spy.* "He could have just told them about technical operations . . . Look at Polyakov. The guy was a grandfather. He was retired! He wasn't even spying anymore! He was living in his dacha playing with his grandchildren! Why did Rick have to tell the KGB about him? Why?"

Time magazine reported on Polyakov's death. "The CIA has confirmed that the most important of Ames' victims by far was Polyakov, whose briefing transcripts and photocopies of secret documents fill 25 file drawers in the agency's innermost sanctum."

Among all the secret agents recruited by the United States during the Cold War, "Polyakov," said James Woolsey, CIA director under President Clinton, "was the jewel in the crown . . . What General Polyakov did for the West didn't just help us win the cold war, it kept the cold war from becoming hot. Polyakov's role was invaluable, and it was one that he played until the end—in his own words—for his country."

CHAPTER 20

NIGHTMOVER

Maj. Gen. Dmitri F. Polyakov, official military portrait, Moscow, 1970s.

I heard rumors that half the interrogators thought he should be kept alive longer," Alexander told me about his father's execution. "Everything was changing—perestroika, glasnost—there were more changes coming, and he could be forgiven."

The conjecture about why the KGB executed Polyakov was that Viktor Chebrikov, the Politburo member and KGB chairman who struck the deal keeping Polyakov's family from arrest, was among those demanding his death. By 1988, Chebrikov was in a growing conflict with Mikhail Gorbachev and his radical reformist agenda. In October of that year, seven months after Polyakov's execution, Gorbachev sacked Chebrikov from his KGB chairmanship and later from the Politburo as part of an effort to remove conservatives from positions of power. Some believe that Polyakov's death order was linked to Chebrikov's persistent Cold War mentality and his desire to demonstrate that the KGB was still a force on the side of old-style Soviet law and order.

By 1989 the Soviet Union's hold over its client states was disintegrating, most dramatically symbolized by the fall of the Berlin Wall. Gorbachev had indicated that he would not use force to help Russia's client states preserve their Communist systems, which resulted in a procession of Eastern Bloc nations shaking off their Soviet-modeled governments and embracing more democratic political systems. The old Cold War world order was coming apart, yet in every Communist nation there were intense struggles between those fighting a rearguard action to preserve the Party's supremacy and the forces of change.

That conflict was perhaps sharpest in Russia itself. *Pravda*, the official Communist Party newspaper, did what it could to shore up the Party's position and assert its continuing reach and power. The newspaper demonstrated this resolve by publishing an article on January 14, 1990, about the Polyakov case. Its purpose was a not-so-subtle warning to anyone who might think the KGB was loosening its grip. Even then, a year and a half after Polyakov's death, the article did not directly identify Polyakov, whose case was still secret because Aldrich Ames was continuing to hand over precious American secrets. But it made Polyakov's identity obvious to the insiders who mattered, Soviet and American both. And its meaning was emphatic enough to everyone, whether in the know or not. The headline read, "KGB Organs Have Neutralized a Dangerous Spy." The author of the article, writing in first person, warned his readers not to be fooled by ordinary citizens in their midst:

> He has a Russian surname, given name and patronymic. I may have traveled with him on the same subway car or sat next to him at the theater. It is this man, whom I subsequently will call "Donald" (a pseudonym given to him by the U.S. special services) who became a spy.

("Donald" was Polyakov's code name in the *New York Times* personal ads placed by the FBI.) *Pravda* didn't identify Polyakov by name, but it did identify an American involved in his case.

> In the early seventies "Donald" went to work in India. Here he met with a U.S. intelligence agent, Paul L. Dillon, who would introduce him to new espionage equipment—a high speed R/T [radiotelephone] set designed for use in urban areas. In Moscow "Donald" used it to transmit information to the Americans from a streetcar traveling past the embassy.

So Polyakov had revealed my father's identity to his interrogators. "Donald," the writer asserted, was fiendishly clever and practiced in the arts of intelligence. But the KGB had tracked him down. Their skilled investigators had sifted through "a thousand pieces" of information to find their man, to locate the proverbial "needle in the haystack." In the end, the traitor was brought to justice:

> A trial took place which concluded the matter (with the death penalty).

And then another warning:

> The ultimate punishment and long prison terms are the price that our fellow citizens have paid for their intrigues.

★

In November 1989, Rosario Ames invited Diana Worthen over to help her pick out new drapes. She told Worthen she was having the whole house done at once. She and Rick were also renovating the kitchen and landscaping the yard, and besides the new Jaguar, Rick had bought Rosario her own new car.

Worthen became uncomfortable. She could see that Rick and Rosario were spending a lot of money, and she knew that in Mexico, as well as when they returned to Virginia before their Rome posting, the couple had been barely getting by. The Ameses were Worthen's good friends, and she wrestled with her conscience for a while before bringing the matter up with Sandy Grimes.

When Grimes heard about Rick and Rosario's lavish spending, it was as if she had been given a key piece to a puzzle. Ames's sudden change in style, personality, and attitude was peculiar, but the appearance of unexplained wealth sent her suspicion levels soaring, and she told Worthen that the source of the Ameses' purchases needed to be investigated quickly. Grimes had believed for some time that a mole might be the cause of the Agency's security problems, and Ames was increasingly fitting the description of one. She sent Worthen to talk to Jeanne Vertefeuille and their boss, Paul Redmond, and Worthen told them about Ames's outsize spending, and that he had access to each of the compromised cases. They then brought in Dan Payne, an officer in the Agency's Office of Security. Payne listened to Worthen's full story and immediately started an investigation.

Ames's security and personnel files revealed two DUI citations and a number of issues with drinking too much at the office and at parties, but nothing suspicious in the way of counterintelligence. Payne then went to the Arlington County Courthouse to investigate the mortgage on Ames's new house. He was surprised to find no record of one. Jeanne Vertefeuille ordered him back to the courthouse two more times to be sure, but still he found no mortgage on file. His investigation did turn up three currency transactions made by Ames from 1985 to 1989 of more than $10,000 each, but those were hardly a smoking gun.

Diverted by other security matters, Payne didn't return to the investigation of Ames until late 1990, a year after Worthen first rang the warning bell to Sandy Grimes. Payne checked into Ames's credit card statements and found nothing unusual in the couple's spending. This turned out to be simple bad luck—he had chosen a rare month when Rick and Rosario hadn't made any excessive purchases.

Ames's job as head of the European Branch lasted only three months, and from late 1989 through 1990 he was assigned to three other offices. In each of these jobs he had access to sensitive material, which he continued to pass on to his Soviet handlers via dead drops around the Virginia suburbs.

★

When Dan Payne returned to his investigation in November 1990, he asked the Office of Security to schedule a routine polygraph test and background examination for Ames. It was CIA policy that all employees be tested every five years, and Ames was due. In preparation for the polygraph and background check, Payne wrote a memo asking the investigator to focus on Ames's finances and spending habits—the half-million-dollar house paid for in cash, the expensive renovations, the Jaguar, and the cash deposits over $10,000. (Cognizant of the years when Angleton smeared the reputations of innocent people he suspected of being a mole, Payne also mentioned that Ames's money could possibly have come from Rosario's mother.)

Incredibly, someone in the Office of Security decided that

Payne's memo contained too much personal information, and all mention of Ames's spending was redacted from it. When Ames underwent his polygraph test in April 1991, he wasn't asked a single question about his finances. The only hiccup was when the polygrapher asked him about his foreign contacts, and his response registered as deceptive. Ames explained that he had many foreign contacts in Colombia, where his wife's family lived, and perhaps that was the reason for the reaction. The polygrapher accepted his answer. Ames had beaten the machine.

Jeanne Vertefeuille and Sandy Grimes were not convinced, and sent an officer to Bogotá to find out if Rosario's family was wealthy, as that could be the only reason left to explain the money. The officer came back a week later with a report saying that Rosario's family was indeed well off. Given Ames's successful polygraph and the report from Bogotá, the Office of Security closed its file on him.

Months later, Vertefeuille and Grimes would find out that the investigation in Bogotá had been a travesty. Its conclusions were based on a single source, a paid informer who, like others, figured that so prominent a family had to be rich. The information he gave was based entirely on hearsay—no research whatsoever had been done by the informant, the CIA station in Bogotá, or the officer sent to investigate. The fact was that though Rosario's family was financially comfortable, they had no real wealth to speak of.

Even after the report from Bogotá, Vertefeuille and Grimes never lost their conviction that Langley was harboring a mole, and that Ames was probably it. But many at the Agency had doubts—Soviet sources recruited after the 1985 losses had not been arrested, and the Agency's recent operations against the Soviets had not been compromised. The counterintelligence staff went through a reorganization, further diffusing efforts to investigate the source of the doomed Soviet assets. To some, the 1985 losses were a historical anomaly that had come and gone.

★

At the beginning of 1991, Jeanne Vertefeuille was approaching mandatory retirement. She'd worked for the CIA for forty-five years, a productive, successful career. But as she contemplated retirement, she was "plagued by a sense of guilt." The failure to solve the 1985 losses had left a bitter taste in her mouth.

As she neared the end of her time with the Agency, she decided she had to make one final effort. "Our agents who were executed deserve someone giving it one more 'good old college try,'" she said, and she asked her boss if she could dedicate her remaining months to working on the case. Her boss agreed, and recruited Paul Redmond, who then formed another group, the Special Investigations Unit, the sole purpose of which was to hunt for a mole within their ranks. When the FBI heard that Redmond and Vertefeuille were taking up the cause again, they asked to join in and dedicated two agents to the mission.

At the same time, Sandy Grimes was also planning to retire. She had dedicated herself to her work for almost twenty-five years. Now, she thought, it was time to devote herself to her husband and two teenage daughters. But like Jeanne Vertefeuille, she felt a persistent, gnawing regret about the agents they had lost—all of them, but one in particular.

Knowing how she felt, and aware of her retirement plans, Redmond asked Grimes if she wanted to join the unit and help Vertefeuille once again investigate the 1985 losses. As she later wrote, "Without hesitation, I replied that he had made the only offer I could have never refused."

This time, the newly formed unit made no effort to keep the investigation secret within the agency. Rather, they hoped someone would come forward with information. On her first day on the job, Sandy Grimes walked into the Counterintelligence Center and bumped into Rick Ames. What are you doing here? he asked, surprised to see her there. "We've formed another task force to look at the 1985 losses," Grimes replied honestly. Without missing a beat, Ames offered to help, and gave her a lecture on how to properly conduct a counterintelligence investigation.

The four-person unit, comprising Vertefeuille, Grimes, and the two FBI men, started by putting together a list of current and former CIA employees who knew about one or more of the cases that had been lost. After they culled the list, it still had 160 names on it, too many for the small team to investigate thoroughly. In order to fine-tune it, Vertefeuille came up with a system that was criticized by some within the Agency for not being scientific enough, but that eventually proved that human intuition has its value. Members of the unit, along with a few trusted others who were familiar with most of the names on the list, each selected five or six names that "made them uneasy for one reason or another." They were to rank them from most suspicious to least, and Vertefeuille and Grimes would then weight the names: six points to the first name, five to the second, and so on. After all the tallying was done, a name emerged at the top of the list, with twenty-one points: Aldrich Ames.

About twenty other names had made the list, some scoring seventeen and sixteen points, which meant the investigations team could not focus solely on Ames. And while his name had the most accumulated points, Sandy Grimes was the only team member who had designated him as number one.

Part of the investigation was a tedious and painstaking effort Grimes took up to compile a database of every detail of where Ames had been and whom he had met with, eventually folding into her data the financial information that the Office of Security's Dan Payne was collecting. "It was mind-numbing work," the journalist Pete Earley wrote, "but Grimes didn't complain. She was going to catch a mole."

★

Despite his taking the top spot in their informal survey of selected CIA officers, the special investigations unit still didn't have any firm evidence on Ames. But there was enough suspicion surrounding him that the Agency finally moved him into a position considered nonsensitive. In late 1991, in the same month that the Soviet Union was disbanded—six years after he started spying for the Soviets and two years after Diana Worthen first rang the warning bell—Ames was assigned to the agency's Counternarcotics Center. It was not a prestigious position, aptly located in the building's basement, and he had little access to operational information of interest to his handlers. Nonetheless, he could still pass on in-house information, which he continued to do via dead drops and at meetings with his handlers outside the country.

In the spring of 1992, Dan Payne and the investigations unit used a special provision to the Right to Financial Privacy Act that allowed access to personal financial records in cases involving foreign counterintelligence. They now collected full copies of the Ameses' credit card receipts and bank statements. What they saw astonished them.

Ames and his wife were spending enormous amounts of money, up to $30,000 a month, on luxury items and fine dining. Ames's annual salary was less than $70,000, so something was clearly amiss. While it was possible the money was coming from Rosario's family, the special unit investigated further. Credit card receipts revealed undeclared trips that Ames had taken to Caracas and Vienna—very suspicious, and a violation of Agency policy. The unit members even wondered if Ames's frequent trips to Colombia were to run drugs—immoral and illegal, surely, and a potential explanation for the money, but not a connection to the Soviets.

It was Sandy Grimes who identified that link. Using information collected in the team's database, she compared the dates that Ames met overtly with Sergey Chuvakhin (the Soviet diplomat to whom he'd handed over "the big dump") to the dates of his bank deposits. They matched. Ames deposited $9,000 the day after meeting Chuvakhin in May 1985, and twice in July of that year he deposited thousands of dollars on the very same days he met with the Russian.

After years of suspicion and frustration at not being able to nail the man she believed was responsible for the disappearance and execution of her assets, Grimes was finally vindicated by this evidence, at least in her mind. She marched into Paul Redmond's office and produced her time line, telling him, "Rick is a goddamn Russian spy!"

The unit's financial research also discovered that from 1985 to 1991 Ames had deposited $1.3 million in Swiss bank accounts from unidentified sources. Then, in 1993, additional (still classified) information was reported that, together with the other evidence pointing to Ames's guilt, prompted the FBI to apply for the necessary warrants.

Finally, in May 1993, a full eight years after Ames started handing over top secret information to the KGB, the FBI opened a full-scale investigation on him. The operation was code-named NIGHTMOVER.

★

So began the FBI's massive surveillance effort on Aldrich Ames. He was put on a twenty-four-hour live watch, starting with a tap placed on his home and car phones, and another, with the CIA's assistance, on his desk phone at Langley. Hidden cameras were installed in his office ceiling and on a telephone pole across from his house, and a transmitter was planted on the underside of his Jaguar. The FBI's team of surveillance experts posed around his neighborhood as landscapers, garbage collectors, and telephone linesmen. It got its first big break when agents searched the trash Ames had put out on the street and pieced together a torn-up note he'd drafted for his Russian handler regarding an upcoming meeting with him in Bogotá.

A few weeks later, the listeners heard that Ames and his family would be going to Florida soon to attend a wedding. It was the first time since the NIGHTMOVER operation got under way that all the family would be out of the house, the opportunity the FBI had been waiting for.

At 1:45 a.m. on October 9, 1993, an FBI surveillance team picked the lock on a side door and entered the empty house, where they installed listening devices throughout the rooms and made a thorough search. In one of Ames's drawers, they found a note with details of his trip to Bogotá. Apparently unaware that his word-processing program made automatic backups, Ames's computer hard drive provided a trove of letters he'd written to his handlers. Later, the FBI would find a nine-page letter Ames had received five years earlier from the KGB detailing the money it had paid him and promising land on a riverbank in Russia for his retirement dacha, complete with pictures.

From a printer ribbon pulled out of his trash they reconstructed another incriminating letter he'd written to his Russian handlers that implicated Rosario: "My wife has accomodated [*sic*] herself to what I am doing in a very supportive way."

The bugs the FBI planted in the house yielded more information implicating Rosario as a knowing collaborator. In conversations it recorded, she hectored Ames about his sloppy tradecraft and got after him to make his drops and meetings on time.

The FBI now had enough evidence to accuse Ames of spying and Rosario of being an accomplice, but the FBI team leaders wanted to be sure their case was airtight and argued among themselves whether to pick the two up immediately or give it more time in order to catch Ames in the act.

On the CIA side, frustration was growing. Sandy Grimes,

increasingly impatient, went to Paul Redmond and said, "Rick is a spy, why don't they just arrest him?"

Finally, the Justice Department decided to take action. The time had come.

Aldrich Ames FBI mug shot, February 1994.

On the morning of February 21, 1994, almost nine years after Aldrich Ames started spying for the Soviet government, Aldrich and Rosario Ames were arrested by the FBI. (Fairly or unfairly, the CIA would be taken through the wringer by the press and Congress—an intelligence agency unable to collar a mole under their own noses . . . for almost nine years!) Two months later the Ameses appeared in front of Judge Claude Hilton for sentencing, dressed in prison drab green. During the interrogations, Rosario had claimed to be innocent, that she knew nothing about her husband's spying. But when her lawyer, advising her to make a plea deal, played the tape of her reminding Rick to make a dead drop, she agreed to plead guilty. She received a sentence of five years and three months.

Afterward, she was quoted by a journalist as saying, "Not too many people are real men. They don't have the guts, the courage, the honor to be called a man, and I thought he was. He was not man enough to stop this from happening to me, to protect me."

At his sentencing, Ames was given the opportunity to make a statement, and used it to lash out at the Agency. Espionage was a self-serving sham, he said, carried out by careerist bureaucrats, a monstrous effort that had no ultimate significance.

Judge Hilton sentenced him to life imprisonment without the possibility of parole.

Jeanne Vertefeuille, Diana Worthen, Dan Payne, and other CIA officers were in the courtroom listening that day. (Sandy Grimes had gone out of town.) They were waiting for an explanation from Ames as to why he had sent so many people to their deaths.

It wasn't a question Aldrich Ames answered in Judge Hilton's courtroom that day. But, later, he said, "Let's be frank. The men I betrayed knew what they were doing. They knew the risks. Do you believe that any of them would have hesitated to have reported me if they had learned my name? So their deaths, while sad to me, are not really my responsibility. They have no one to blame but themselves."

CHAPTER 21

WELCOME

Alexander Polyakov with his mother, Nina, at their dacha outside Moscow, c. 1975. *(Courtesy of Alexander Polyakov)*

A few months after Rick and Rosario Ames were arrested, Alexander Polyakov's mother, Nina, was diagnosed with stomach cancer. "She was never sick a day in her life," Alexander said. Four months after her diagnosis, she died. She was sixty-eight years old. "We did everything we could to help her, to manage the pain—the best doctors and medicine we could find. But it was a hurricane cancer. She was absolutely healthy before that. I'm sure that it was brought on by stress."

★

The arrest of Aldrich Ames meant that the KGB no longer needed to protect the identity of its star mole, so the secrecy surrounding Gen. Dmitri Fedorovich Polyakov and his fate gave way to the beginning of his official demonization as the greatest modern traitor to the Russian homeland. One night, his granddaughter Marina, then in her teens, was cooking dinner for the family. The television was on in the background, and when she heard the name Polyakov, she turned to look. There, on the small screen, was her grandfather in the grip of four KGB men, one holding him in a headlock, two pinioning his arms, a fourth pulling off his shirt. They had videotaped his arrest, the clip now part of a documentary on the traitor general. She saw in her grandfather's eyes the stoic acceptance of his fate. It was as if he were looking directly at her.

Marina was in shock—no one had ever told her frankly what had happened to her grandfather. By then she knew, at least in general terms, why she had never seen him again after he said good-bye to her that morning at the dacha, but suddenly there he was, his face exactly as she remembered it, while being held, stripped, and searched. The clip was short, a little over a minute. She watched, mesmerized.

★

In 1996 the American writer and journalist Pete Earley went to Moscow to do research on a book he was writing about Aldrich Ames, *Confessions of a Spy*. Earley had obtained an agreement with Ames and his lawyer for exclusive rights to Ames's story, and he had spent weeks privately interviewing Ames in an Alexandria, Virginia, detention center before Ames began serving his life sentence at a federal penitentiary in Allenwood, Pennsylvania. Ames wanted Earley to go to Moscow to talk with the KGB about him and his case. After the fall of the Soviet Union, the United States and Russia had an awkward relationship, but they were no longer enemies. It was unlikely the reconstituted KGB would agree to talk with Earley about Ames's case, but it wasn't beyond the realm of possibility, either. Ames had a personal motive for sending Earley. "If you go to Moscow," he said, "the FBI and CIA will never be certain if I told you something that was classified or if you learned it on your own from the Russians. No one will be able to trace anything back to me."

Ames also had a financial motive for getting his exclusive biographer to Moscow—he wanted him to check on whether the Russians would keep their word about giving him the $2 million they were holding for him. Perhaps, Ames thought, they could find some surreptitious way to get it either to him or to Rosario. "I laughed," Earley told me in an interview years later, "and said, 'They're not going to pay you,' and Ames said, 'Oh yes they will, because there's somebody else doing it [spying] right now and [that person is] going to watch and see how I'm treated to know how they'll be treated.' And I didn't know then, but [Robert] Hanssen was that person."

Earley wanted to talk with the KGB, the men who had been Ames's handlers. As a journalist, he welcomed the opportunity to ask them about the money Ames claimed they owed him, but he had no intention of acting as an illegal courier in the unlikely event that the Russians handed over a large bag of cash.

With a letter from Ames in his pocket asking the Russians to cooperate, Earley did get an interview, with Boris Solomatin, a retired KGB general who had supervised the notorious John Walker spy case about which Earley had written a book. Solomatin introduced Earley to "Yuri," an obviously fake name. Given what "Yuri" knew about Ames, Earley figured he must have worked on the case. In a meeting in "Yuri's" apartment, which Earley determined was likely being videotaped, Earley listened in frustration as his host read prepared statements that in essence claimed that Ames had not worked for the Soviets.

After the meeting, though, in the privacy of the elevator going down, "Yuri" stopped the car and said, "The two million, does Ames want his two million? We have it." Earley replied that indeed Ames wanted it, and the Russian asked Earley if he'd consider taking it to him. Earley knew it was a trick. "They were trying to see if I could be bought, if I could be manipulated. I gave him the name of a U.S. lawyer." The money, needless to say, was never forwarded to Aldrich Ames.

While in Russia, Earley also looked up the families of the spies whom Ames's revelations had doomed. Ames had given him a complete list of names, together with cryptonyms, and over time Earley tracked down quite a few of the family members. He met people who, like the Polyakovs, had lost their incomes, possessions, and friends, people who had been hounded and traduced by the KGB, who had essentially become nonpersons in the old USSR and were still suffering in the new Russia.

A newspaper editor who was one of Earley's sources happened to know Alexander and Petr Polyakov. The editor called them to say that an American writer wanted to interview them, and they agreed to meet Earley and talk about their father and the impact his arrest had had on their lives.

By 1996, Alexander and Petr had finally secured jobs. By the late 1980s, perestroika was changing Russia's economy, and with the state's stranglehold loosening, small businesses were starting up. Others were privatizing or semiprivatizing, which required unfamiliar legal procedures such as registering, documenting, and verifying contracts in ways that hadn't previously existed. Lawyers were in heavy demand, and with the fall of the Soviet Union, *anketas*, the application forms on which prospective employees provided information on their party membership, were no longer required.

When Earley arrived in Moscow in 1996, Alexander was a lawyer with an international insurance company, and Petr was working as a salesman for a car dealership.

Yet, as the 1990s progressed, the initial rush of business growth in Russia began spiraling downward. Failed economic liberalization policies had brought with them high inflation, massive corruption, and the concentration of wealth in the hands of the oligarchs. The black market, and with it, organized crime, was now consuming about half the economy, and honest businesses couldn't compete. The Communist Party, vilified and diminished by the death of the Soviet Union, was now making a strong political comeback. By 1996, the Party controlled the parliament, known as the Federal Assembly, and it looked as if a Communist might take over the presidency as well. To many Russians, the future seemed bleak.

Economic challenges aside, Alexander and Petr had striven to make the best of their new lives, both personally and professionally. But the reality was that their lives in Russia were not what they had been.

When they met with Earley, they asked the American writer for a favor. Could he get a message to the U.S. government letting them know they wanted out of Moscow, that they wanted to start a new life in the United States?

"They had no way of contacting anyone in the U.S.," Earley explained, "and were apprehensive because they didn't want to compromise themselves. It was after the collapse of the Soviet Union, but everyone was still nervous."

Conducting interviews at the CIA for his upcoming book about Aldrich Ames, Earley relayed the message. The officers still there who had familiarity with the Polyakov case were moved. One CIA officer reminisced with me in an interview about the Agency's efforts to get Alexander and Petr into the United States and recalled how Polyakov had never asked for anything in all his years of service to the country. Most assets, he said, asked for regular monthly payments, or to get their kids into an American college. But Polyakov had been different. He hadn't asked for any of that. Now the Agency put together a resettlement plan for Alexander and Petr and their families, and asked Earley, who was returning to Moscow for more research on his book, to assure them (unofficially since, by law, journalists cannot work for the CIA) that they were prepared to assist Alexander and Petr in resettling in the United States.

Petr arrived with his family in 1998, and a year later, Alexander and Larisa decided to go, too. "By then," Alexander said, "I was getting on toward fifty years old. I decided it was the right time to start a new life. Otherwise, it would be too late." At the U.S. embassy in Moscow, he waited in line for five hours. He was granted a business visa, valid for ninety days. He had no intention of coming back.

★

Today, Alexander and Petr Polyakov are American citizens. Marina came over in 2005. Dmitri Polyakov's three American great-granddaughters are learning to speak Russian.

Alexander Polyakov and Eva Dillon, 2016.
(May Goren Photography, 2016)

ACKNOWLEDGMENTS

I wish to first acknowledge my wonderful husband, James L. Fritsch. This book would never have come to fruition had he not supported it, and me, in generous ways, big and small. His advice and encouragement; assistance in research, copyediting, photo restoration; and role as household chief of information technology were invaluable—and lovingly appreciated.

My sincerest thanks go to my exceptionally talented, hard-working, and steady writing partner, David Chanoff, whose word-smithing kept me on track, and whose advice, charm, and humor kept me sane.

My agent, Laura Yorke, from the Carol Mann Agency, recognized the potential in this story and championed it from beginning to end. Thank you, Laura, for your confidence in me and for the energy and enthusiasm you exuded every step of the way.

At HarperCollins, Luke Dempsey adroitly edited the manuscript and, simply, made it better. My thanks go to Jonathan Burnham and Claire Wachtel for realizing the book's concept.

I cannot thank enough the many of my father's former colleagues and friends at the CIA who shared their memories and stories, or explained the labyrinth of spy-think, intrigue, and diplomacy which are the essence of intelligence work. Sandy Grimes, especially, the officer who supported Dmitri Polyakov's case for over twenty years, championed my work, gave me advice, and encouraged my efforts throughout the process. Her book, *Circle of Treason*, was invaluable to the further telling of Polyakov's story, and I admit to borrowing liberally from it. My thanks also go to the other case officers and analysts—each one more interesting than the next—who talked with me about my father, General Polyakov, and the CIA during the Cold War: Richard Allocca, John Bogart, Dick Corbin, Terry Douglas, Bill and Louise Friend, Jay and Anne Gruner, Gus Hathaway, Ed Juchniewicz, Walt Lomac, Bill Lonam, Tom Mills, David Murphy, Bob (and Moni) Rayle, Dick Stolz, and Diana Worthen. A few others asked not to be identified.

Special thanks go to former FBI Special Agent Edward Moody, whose years of dedication to General Polyakov's case and sharp, detailed memory were invaluable to the telling of the early years of TOPHAT's story; to Viktor Belenko, whose courage, chutzpah, and devotion to this country, and to my father, are treasured by me; and to Pete Earley, whose assistance to Polyakov's sons was honorable.

I'd also like to thank my two Russian translators, Mark Gomer and Leigh Millard, for their hard work and dedication to the project; Keith Melton, for showing me his fabulous private spy museum and for sharing pictures of memorabilia related to General Polyakov; Melton's coauthor Bob Wallace, for talking with me about spy technology and devices; Jackie Leo, for introducing me to Laura Yorke; and Dwight Williams, Rob Evans, Chat Whitmore, Jo Ellen Gold, Lou Hammond, Laurie Seese, and Firth Griffith for their support and input on the manuscript. Thank you, Perky Pepper, Joan Vogel, and Natalie Basso Ryan for your memories and love for my father.

What can I say about the best sisters and brothers a person can have? Maria Nodolf; Clare Finn; Julia Zenone; and Leo, Paul, and Jacob Dillon were my best friends growing up as we moved from country to country, adjusting to new environments and cultures. Their memories are recorded in this book, and their support in my efforts has been constant. Leo, especially, turned out to be a skilled and creative editor. Thank you, Leo, for your artistry, time, and zeal. Thanks go to all my cousins who shared their memories, especially to Paul Dillon; to my sharp-witted uncles Tom Dillon and Sal Truscello; and to my wonderful aunt Priscilla McNeil, whom

I love and admire greatly. All of your memories added details that enhanced the book.

I have two mentors who were my biggest cheerleaders throughout my publishing career and the writing of this book, to whom I owe a debt of gratitude: the brilliant, funny, and ever-energetic doer Mary Berner; and the savvy, entertaining, and passionate insider Wenda Millard. Thank you both for your unflagging support and encouragement.

And finally, my most earnest and profound thanks go to Alexander Polyakov; his wife, Larisa; and their daughter, Marina, for sharing with me their beautiful, potent, and heart-wrenching memories. Alexander's brother chose not to be interviewed for this book.

NOTES

PROLOGUE: SO CLOSE

ix "A certain chemistry does exist between us": Ronald Reagan, *The Reagan Diaries* (New York: HarperCollins, 2007), p. 613.

ix "I was talking about another time, another era": *The Moscow Summit 20 Years Later,* National Security Archives Electronic Briefing Book No. 251, http://nsarchive.gwu.edu/NSAEBB/NSAEBB251/.

x "Your generation is living in one of the most exciting, hopeful times in Soviet history": Ronald Reagan, Moscow State University speech, May 31, 1988, Reagan Presidential Library, https://reaganlibrary.gov/archives?catid=2016&id=9373:moscowsp.

x "Mr. President, I will have to disappoint you": *GRU* General—*American Agent,* Russian television documentary, Telecompaniya Ostankino, http://my.mail.ru/mail/ilya_isaev_1994/video/18424/18435.html#video=/mail/ilya_isaev_1994/18424/18435.

INTRODUCTION: *PULVEREM PULVERI*

xv His code name: TOPHAT: David Wise, "Our Man in Moscow," *George,* October 1997, pp. 118–21.

CHAPTER 1: AMERIKA

4 Dmitri Polyakov's diplomatic cover didn't fool the FBI: Author interviews with Edward Moody, former special agent of the FBI, February 2015. Most of the reporting on Dmitri Polyakov concerning his early years of spying for the United States

comes from interviews with Moody and his collection of documents concerning the case.

7 Nina and Dmitri had all the medical assistance they needed: Author interviews with Polyakov's son Alexander. Contrary to widespread reporting that Igor died in New York City at the age of three due to the GRU leadership's denying Polyakov money for medical treatment, Alexander reports that Igor was afflicted with polio while in New York and lived to the age of seventeen.

CHAPTER 2: REDSOX

13 One class was called Introduction: Personal Qualifications of a Conspirator: REDSOX, internal CIA operational summary, June 4, 1952, CIA Digital Library Reading Room, https://www.cia.gov/library/readingroom/docs/AESAURUS%20AENOBLE%20%20%20VOL.%201_0032.pdf.

14 A declassified secret CIA report: Ibid.

15 "We've entered history": Ibid.

16 "I was puzzled": Author interview with John Bogart, former CIA officer, December 6, 2012.

16 "It was hoped that these guys were getting established": Ibid.

17 "It is my opinion that the mental demands": CIA Fitness Report (performance evaluation), May 6, 1952, for Paul Dillon, obtained via FOIA request.

19 "Philby was responsible for passing on the timing and geographical coordinates": Ben Macintyre, *A Spy Among Friends: Kim Philby and the Great Betrayal* (New York: Crown, 2014), p. 138.

19 "I do not know what happened to the parties concerned": Kim Philby, *My Silent War: The Soviet Master Agent Tells His Own Story* (New York: Grove Press, 1968), p. 159.

19 "They were met by Soviet security people": Author interview with John Bogart.

CHAPTER 3: THE GENERAL AND THE SPY

21 "He's back!": Conversation as recalled by Edward Moody, former FBI special agent, in private interviews, February 2015.

22 "Polyakov is an astute, intelligent, shrewd, and fully Americanized Soviet intelligence officer": Internal FBI memo from Edward Moody, former FBI special agent, to Director, FBI, dated December 7, 1960, courtesy of Edward Moody.

23 "He has been identified as a Staff Officer": Ibid.

24 "Robert Baltch": Nigel West, *Historical Dictionary of Cold War Counterintelligence* (Lanham, MD: Scarecrow Press, 2007), p. 317.

24 "Later on, [the Soviet handlers]": Author interviews with Edward Moody.

27 They even got the police to write: Vladimir Chickov, *Mole in the Aquarium* [Чиков Владимир Матвеевич КРОТ В АКВАРИУМЕ] (Moscow: Detective Press, 2013), section 21, http://www.x-libri.ru/elib/chikv000/index.htm.

28 "Polyakov commented that he was very sorry": Internal FBI memo from Edward Moody.

29 "I would be convicted of treason . . . I would probably never be set free": Kaarlo Tuomi, *Spy Lost: Caught Between the KGB and the FBI* (New York: Enigma Books, 2014), pp. 117–19.

30 "I struggled senselessly with myself": Ibid., p. 117.

30 "The double agent's life is, in fact, quite free": Ibid., p. 119.

35 "He couldn't bear the man": Author interviews with Alexander Polyakov.

35 "I want to apologize": Internal FBI memo from Edward Moody.

36 "Polyakov again made remarks to": Ibid.

38 "I was pleased that you would have enough confidence": Tape recording of the conversation, courtesy of Edward Moody.

40 "It would mean all-out war": Conversation as recalled by Edward Moody, in author interviews.

CHAPTER 4: THE WALL

44 "Paul thought it was all bullshit": Author interview with Gus Hathaway, former CIA officer, October 18, 2012.

45 "We'd ask him that. But he was his own man": Ibid.

47 "a bone in my throat": Evan Thomas, *Ike's Bluff: President Eisenhower's Secret Battle to Save the World* (New York: Little, Brown, 2012), p. 318.

48 "target room": David E. Murphy, Sergei A. Kondrashev, and George Bailey, *Battleground Berlin: CIA vs. KGB in the Cold War* (New Haven, CT: Yale University Press, 1997), p. 256.

49 "Your dad was pipin' hot mad": Author interview with Gus Hathaway.

50 "Paul had a good case": Ibid.

50 "We had another great case": Ibid.

51 "They used to kid him": Author interview with David Murphy, former chief of Soviet operations, CIA, October 20, 2012.

52 "We had to do what was de rigueur": Author interview with Louise Friend, former CIA officer, October 19, 2012.

53 Then, in 1957, *Doctor Zhivago* was smuggled: Peter Finn, *The Zhivago Affair: The Kremlin, the CIA, and the Battle over a Forbidden Book* (New York: Pantheon Books, 2014), pp. 12–13.

54 "Berlin is the testicles of the West": John Lewis Gaddis, *The Cold War: A New History* (New York: Penguin Books, 2014), p. 71.

55 "If we had listened to him": Author interview with Gus Hathaway.

56 "It was pandemonium": Author interview with John Bogart.

56 "We had one hundred eighty officers in Berlin": Author interview with Gus Hathaway.

57 "It's not a very nice solution": Gaddis, *The Cold War: A New History*, p. 115.

CHAPTER 5: MOODY AND MABEY

61 "I am a military intelligence officer": Chickov, *Mole in the Aquarium*, sec. 15.

62 "He knew what the consequences were": Private interviews with Edward Moody.

62 "It was the first time we had ever developed an inside agent": John Mabey, interview transcript for episode 21 of *Cold War*, CNN, National Security Archive, http://nsarchive.gwu.edu/coldwar/interviews/episode-21/mabey1.html.

64 "It would be inaccurate to characterize his comments": Sandra Grimes and Jeanne Vertefeuille, *Circle of Treason: A CIA Account of Traitor Aldrich Ames and the Men He Betrayed* (Annapolis, MD: U.S. Naval Institute Press, 2012), p. 42.

64 "began to view the Soviet leaders as corrupt thugs": Ibid.

65 "I want to warn you": Chickov, *Mole in the Aquarium*, sec. 26.

65 "the cause of freedom, justice, and democracy": Grimes and Vertefeuille, *Circle of Treason*, p. 43.

65 "Then they made a big show of kicking the tires": David Wise, *Nightmover: How Aldrich Ames Sold the CIA to the KGB for $4.6 Million* (New York: HarperCollins, 1995), p. 61.

66 "If you ever took an aerial view": John Mabey, interview transcript for *Cold War*.

67 "the whole kettle of information": Ibid.

68 "He could go in the store": Author interviews with Edward Moody.

68 "cheap, cheap, cheap": Ibid.

68 "He did it for what he saw went on": Ibid.

72 "When a visitor entered Angleton's office": Tom Mangold, *Cold Warrior: James Jesus Angleton—The CIA's Master Spy Hunter* (New York: Simon & Schuster, 1991), p. 56.

73 "Monster Plot": Grimes and Vertefeuille, *Circle of Treason*, p. 21.

73 "Angleton's destruction of the credibility of this squadron of defectors": Mangold, *Cold Warrior*, pp. 231–32.

CHAPTER 6: HOME AND AWAY

78 "Do you believe the evidence in this book": Author interview with Ed Juchniewicz, former CIA officer, August 23, 2014.

80 "They were like a bunch of monks going off to the priory": Ibid.

80 "the Agency had probably missed out on a goldmine of secrets": Milt Bearden and James Risen, *The Main Enemy: The Inside Story of the CIA's Final Showdown with the KGB* (New York: Random House, 2000), p. 23.

80 "Careers were destroyed, reputations smeared": Mangold, *Cold Warrior*, pp. 246–47.

80 "Such was the paranoia within the division": Author interview with Ed Juchniewicz.

81 "He showed a marked degree of paranoia": Mangold, *Cold Warrior*, p. 85.

82 "in a psychological *folie a deux*": Ibid., p. 158.

83 "Subject must be broken at some point": David C. Martin, *Wilderness of Mirrors: Intrigue, Deception, and the Secrets That Destroyed Two of the Cold War's Most Important Agents* (New York: HarperCollins, 1980), p. 158.

84 "Paul managed to avoid scrutiny": Grimes and Vertefeuille, *Circle of Treason*, p. 41.

CHAPTER 7: TO THE MEXICO STATION

91 "a city of intrigue like Vienna or Casablanca": Jefferson Morley, *Our Man in Mexico* (Lawrence: University Press of Kansas, 2008), p. 88.

92 "He was a mouthpiece of Angleton's": Author interview with Gus Hathaway.

93 "virility astonished both the girl and the station": Philip Agee, *Inside the Company: CIA Diary* (New York: Farrar, Straus and Giroux, 1975), p. 544.

95 "the CIA station had reported fifteen differing and sometimes flatly contradictory": Morley, *Our Man in Mexico*, p. 271.

95 "The puppet master had become a puppet": Ibid.

96 "If Paul Dillon ever invites you for coffee": Author interview with Richard Allocca, former CIA officer, July 23, 2014.

CHAPTER 8: THE PERSONALS

106 "MOODY. Donald F.": *New York Times* Public Notice, September 19–30, 1962, courtesy of Edward Moody.

106 "had to bow to the rules of the *New York Times*": Wise, *Nightmover*, p. 63.

108 "MOODY, Donald F. Everything O.K. with Brother Bob and Aunt Betty": *New York Times* Public Notice, April 1963, courtesy of Edward Moody.

109 including the names of the entire Soviet General Staff command: *GRU General-American Agent* Russian television documentary Telecompaniya Ostankino, http://my.mail.ru/mail/ilya_isaev_1994/video/18424/18435.html#video=/mail/ilya_isaev_1994/18424/18435.

109 "It can only be suggested": Author interviews with Edward Moody.

110 "It is noted in [the] referenced CIA memorandum . . . is of paramount importance": Internal FBI memo from Edward Moody, former FBI special agent, to SAC (Special Agent in Charge), dated July 28, 1965, courtesy of Edward Moody.

110 "CIA makes a great deal of the fact": Ibid.

111 "Letter from brother Bob received in August": *New York Times* Public Notice, September 19–30, 1963, courtesy of Edward Moody.

111 "U.S. Frees Red Spy Couple": *New York World Telegram and Sun*, October 11, 1963.

112 "Our business will re-open August 28": *New York Times* Public Notice, June 19–30, 1965, courtesy of Edward Moody.

112 "please write as promised": *New York Times* Public Notice, May 20–30, 1964, courtesy of Edward Moody.

112 "Traveling? When? Where?": *New York Times* Public Notice, May 20–30, 1964, courtesy of Edward Moody.

112 "Presumably, Russia still does not know of his defection": Edwin Ross and Lester Abelman, "Ex-Soviet Mystery Agent Key to Monday Spy Trial," *Sunday News*, September 27, 1964.

113 "Other Russians mentioned as members of the spy ring": David Anderson, "Finn Disclosed as Double Agent at Spy Trial Here," *New York Times,* September 28, 1964.

113 "SPIES FREED: Why U.S. Stopped the Trial": Robert Walsh and Sidney Kline, *Daily News*, October 3, 1964.

CHAPTER 9: HANDOVER

118 "All this time I was supposed to be CIA, not FBI": Wise, *Nightmover*, p. 65.

118 "all bullshit": Ibid., p. 67.

119 "had been the guy in touch with Polyakov from the very beginning": Author interview with David Murphy.

121 "turned every fact around to fit their premise": Author interview with Walt Lomac, former CIA officer, August 15, 2014.

122 "bound by civilized rules of behavior": Grimes and Vertefeuille, *Circle of Treason*, p. 43.

122 "A Soviet naval commander would have fought to the death": Ibid.

122 "special delight ": Ibid., p. 36.

123 "Over time he had developed a distrust of CIA spy gear": Ibid.

CHAPTER 10: EXIT THE MOLE HUNTER

132 "Jim Angleton went over to Paris . . . suspect him of being a Soviet agent": Author interview with Walt Lomac.

132 "Angleton was mad as a hatter by then, in my opinion": Author interview with Gus Hathaway.

132 "We know it's bullshit, but we got a free trip out of it": Ibid.

133 "Murphy thought I'd be one of the Black Hats": Author interview with Walt Lomac.

133 "They were all talking about a big plot going on": Ibid.

135 "Polyakov had become my first teacher on the Soviet Union": Grimes and Vertefeuille, *Circle of Treason*, p. 13.

135 "He never demanded the respect . . . affectionately called him Father Paul": Ibid., p. 41.

136 "I am so happy for you": Conversation as recalled by Sandy Grimes, former CIA officer, in author interview, September 3, 2012.

137 "The sorcerer would have been proud of his apprentice": Mangold, *Cold Warrior*, p. 300.

137 "baloney": Ibid., p. 303.

138 "I had never seen a man . . . when I turned a corner": Ibid., p. 319.

CHAPTER 11: BACK IN THE USSR

145 "The Americans are bastards": Ross Terrill, *Mao: A Biography* (New York: Harper and Row, 1980), p. 283.

148 "Although he was issued a two-way plan": Grimes and Vertefeuille, *Circle of Treason*, p. 37.

149 "Let's recruit all over the world": Mangold, *Cold Warrior*, p. 314.

149 "Aggressiveness and risk-taking would be the norm": Grimes and Vertefeuille, *Circle of Treason*, pp. 37–38.

150 "witchcraft": Ibid., p. 38.

CHAPTER 12: ENTER THE MOLE

154 "while silently laughing at his goofy physical appearance": Grimes and Vertefeuille, *Circle of Treason*, p. 178.

154 "was being groomed for another promotion": Pete Earley, *Confessions of a Spy: The Real Story of Aldrich Ames* (New York: Putnam, 1997), p. 53.

CHAPTER 13: YOU DON'T SEE ONE OF THOSE EVERY DAY

159 Gupta: Name has been changed for privacy.

161 "Where's his uniform?": Conversation as recalled by Alexander Polyakov.

163 "Little did I know he had concrete reasons for being careful": Victor Cherkashin, *Spy Handler: A Memoir of a KGB Officer—The True Story of the Man Who Recruited Robert Hanssen and Aldrich Ames* (New York: Basic Books, 2004), p. 111.

165 "Paul's case was extraordinary": Author interview with Richard Allocca.

166 "I knew it was very discreet": Author interview with Terry Douglas, former CIA officer, July 30, 2014.

166 King invited Polyakov to his house, where Dad was waiting for him: Chickov, *Mole in the Aquarium*, sec. 108–12.

166 "Don't ever do that again!": Grimes and Vertefeuille, *Circle of Treason*, p. 40.

166 "He carried himself confidently . . . and there was nothing contrived about him": Chickov, *Mole in the Aquarium*, sec. 108.

166 "Paul D[illon] and Polyakov were the perfect match": Grimes and Vertefeuille, *Circle of Treason*, p. 42.

167 "sanctuary": Ibid., p. 43.

167 "had finally gotten it right": Ibid., p. 40.

167 "was the pinnacle of our long and productive association": Ibid.

167 "which gave him access to state secrets": Ibid., p. 35.

168 a code name: PLAID: Chickov, *Mole in the Aquarium*, sec. 112.

169 "fishhooks, sinkers, fly rods, shotguns": Grimes and Vertefeuille, *Circle of Treason*, p. 45.

169 "He had a good sense of humor": Earley, *Confessions of a Spy*, p. 263.

CHAPTER 14: THREE STAR

174 "Immediately recognizing the significance and importance of the information": Grimes and Vertefeuille, *Circle of Treason*, p. 36.

175 "subscription to a favorite magazine": Ibid., p. 44.

176 "that was the American defense establishment's best judgment": William Crowe Jr. and David Chanoff, *The Line of Fire: From Washington to the Gulf, the Politics and Battles of the New Military* (New York: Simon and Schuster, 1993), p. 249.

176 "gave us insights into how they talked to each other . . . touched off a shooting war": Elaine Shannon, "Death of the Perfect Spy," *Time*, August 8, 1994, pp. 32–34.

177 "We found there were 5,000 separate Soviet programs": Ibid.

177 "Christmas came early and often": Grimes and Vertefeuille, *Circle of Treason*, p. 43.

182 "MYSTERY DOCUMENT IDENTIFIES CIA MEN IN INDIA": *Times of India*, May 28, 1975, courtesy of the University Archives and Records Center, University of Pennsylvania.

185 "short-range, high-speed, two-way communications device": Grimes and Vertefeuille, *Circle of Treason*, p. 46.

186 "a technical leap in covert communications": Robert Wallace and H. Keith Melton, *Spycraft: The Secret History of the CIA's Spytechs, from Communism to Al-Qaeda* (New York: Dutton, 2008), p. 116.

186 "The cryptography in the equipment was revolutionary": Grimes and Vertefeuille, *Circle of Treason*, p. 46

186 "the world's first text message exchanges": Wallace and Melton, *Spycraft*, p. 116.

188 "The last meeting between Paul and Polyakov was bittersweet": Grimes and Vertefeuille, *Circle of Treason*, p. 47.

CHAPTER 15: ENDGAME

196 "The value of what he gave us": John Barron, *MiG Pilot: The Final Escape of Lieutenant Belenko* (New York: McGraw-Hill, 1980), p. 190.

198 "I was like a dry sponge soaking up new experiences . . . I felt like he was *my* father, too": Author interview with Viktor Belenko, former MiG pilot, November 19, 2012.

199 "Your father never talked down to me": Ibid.

201 "We *will* get you back": Ibid.

204 "I simply lost my senses . . . That I had to go home": Ibid.

204 "Your father saved my life": Ibid.

207 "He looked so dreadful": Author interview with Bill Friend, former CIA officer, October 19, 2012.

207 "I was down at the Farm giving a talk . . . He had no regrets": Author interview with Terry Douglas.

208 "Paul was a wonderful, gentle, honest soul . . . They wanted to hear a little of that music": Ibid.

CHAPTER 16: AN UNMARKED GRAVE

211 "With a collective sigh of relief and thanks": Grimes and Vertefeuille, *Circle of Treason*, p. 49.

212 "a comprehensive statement of GRU operational philosophy": Ibid., p. 50.

212 "eradicating their cover and that of their replacements": Ibid., p. 50.

214 "Third, the personal case of Anton Bogrov": All names in this anecdote are fictitious.

216 "90 percent of all anti-Communist cases in New York came from FEDORA": Susana Duncan, "The War of the Moles," *New York Magazine*, February 27, 1978, p. 36.

217 but known to have been provided by Epstein: Mangold, *Cold Warrior*, p. 234.

217 he told me that his source for "TOP HAT" was Pete Bagley: Author interview with Edward Jay Epstein, May 9, 2014.

218 "Angleton should have been taken to federal court": Private interviews with Edward Moody.

219 "a GRU general is not comfortable being with someone wearing a beard": Wallace and Melton, *Spycraft*, p. 114.

219 "neatness and appearance": Ibid.

221 "One KGB officer and one GRU officer": David Martin, *Wilderness of Mirrors: Intrigue, Deception, and the Secrets That Destroyed Two of the Cold War's Most Important Agents* (New York: HarperCollins, 1980), p. 111.

222 "I was born a Russian and I'll die a Russian!": Shannon, "Death of the Perfect Spy," *Time*, August 8, 1994, pp. 32–34.

CHAPTER 17: TOMORROW WILL BE TOO LATE

225 a Soviet general cannot be a spy: Chickov, *Mole in the Aquarium*, sec. 158.

229 "Our role would be to wait": Grimes and Vertefeuille, *Circle of Treason*, p. 52.

230 "In Latin America if you are a wealthy woman, you don't work": Earley, *Confessions of a Spy*, p. 110.

231 "finally arrived": Ibid., p. 116.

233 "We'll see": Ibid., p. 140.

233 "I had pulled it off": Ibid., p. 142.

234 "you are now a millionaire": Grimes and Vertefeuille, *Circle of Treason*, p. 169.

238 "to your health, Dmitri . . . will be too late": Conversation as recalled by Alexander Polyakov.

CHAPTER 18: UPWARD MOBILITY

243 "sloppy work by the Soviet agents or their case officers": Tim Weiner, David Johnston, and Neil Lewis, *Betrayal: The Story*

of Aldrich Ames, an American Spy (New York: Random House, 1995), p. 86.

245 "My friend, I have some unfortunate news to share with you": Earley, *Confessions of a Spy*, p. 213.

246 "Jesus Christ!": Ibid.

246 "The myth that Rick would take care of me": Ibid., p. 212.

247 "There was an air of confidence that I'd never seen before": Ibid., p. 258.

CHAPTER 19: DO SVIDANIYA

250 "Why are you wearing that?": Conversation as recalled by Marina Polyakova Finch.

250 keeping his head erect: Video of Dmitri Polyakov's arrest, in *Cold War*, CNN documentary series.

251 "Come with us . . . Article Sixty-Four-a": Conversation as recalled by Alexander Polyakov.

252 "Alexander isn't home . . . Do what you please": Conversation as recalled by Larisa Polyakova.

253 "I have some company with me . . . His wife will take care of her": Conversation as recalled by Alexander Polyakov.

254 "I have been working in the interests of the United States of America since 1962": Document language as recalled by Alexander Polyakov.

259 "He told it all, in great detail . . . Now his death would be another part of his struggle": Milt Bearden and James Risen, *The Main Enemy: The Inside Story of the CIA's Final Showdown with the KGB* (New York: Random House, 2000), p. 188.

260 Polyakov looked diminished: Video of Dmitri Polyakov's trial, in *Cold War*, CNN.

260 "In the interests of national security": Chickov, *Mole in the Aquarium*, sec. 245.

261 "In the name of the Union of Soviet Socialist Republics": Ibid., sec. 249.

261 "There were no pleas, appeals, or anything else": *GRU General—American Agent*, Telecompaniya Ostankino, 1994.

262 "Your meeting is declined . . . or I'll have you escorted out": Conversation as recalled by Alexander Polyakov.

262 "*By this letter we inform you that*": Content of letter as recalled by Alexander Polyakov.

263 Alexander's friend Sergei Tretyakov attended a dinner party: Pete Earley, *Comrade J: The Untold Secrets of Russia's Master Spy in America After the Cold War* (New York: Putnam, 2007), p. 71.

263 "They've shot Alexander's father": Conversation as recalled by Larisa Polyakova.

263 "To many who had never met Polyakov": Grimes and Vertefeuille, *Circle of Treason*, p. 53.

263 "Rick could have gotten millions from the KGB": As quoted in Earley, *Confessions of a Spy*, p. 285.

264 "The CIA has confirmed that the most important of Ames' victims": Shannon, "Death of the Perfect Spy," *Time*, August 8, 1994, pp. 32–34.

264 "What General Polyakov did for the West didn't just help us win the cold war": Ibid.

CHAPTER 20: NIGHTMOVER

266 "KGB Organs Have Neutralized a Dangerous Spy": *Pravda*, January 14, 1990, via the Foreign Broadcast Information Service, January 17, 1990.

271 "plagued by a sense of guilt": Grimes and Vertefeuille, *Circle of Treason*, p. 127.

271 "Our agents who were executed deserve someone": Earley, *Confessions of a Spy*, pp. 289–90.

271 "I replied that he had made the only offer I could have never refused": Grimes and Vertefeuille, *Circle of Treason*, p. 19.

272 "We've formed another task force to look at the 1985 losses": Quoted in Earley, *Confessions of a Spy*, p. 291.

272 "made them uneasy for one reason or another": Grimes and Vertefeuille, *Circle of Treason*, p. 129.

272 "She was going to catch a mole": Earley, *Confessions of a Spy*, p. 297.

274 "Rick is a goddamn Russian spy!": Ibid., p. 301.

275 "My wife has accomodated [*sic*] herself to what I am doing": Weiner, Johnston, and Lewis, *Betrayal*, p. 213.

276 "Rick is a spy, why don't they just arrest him?": Quoted in Earley, *Confessions of a Spy*, p. 311.

277 "Not too many people are real men": Ibid., p. 286.

277 "So their deaths, while sad to me": Ibid., p. 284.

CHAPTER 21: WELCOME

281 "If you go to Moscow": Earley, *Confessions of a Spy*, p. 6.

281 "I laughed": Author interview with Pete Earley, December 6, 2012.

282 "The two million, does Ames want his two million?": Ibid.

282 "They were trying to see if I could be bought": Ibid.

BIBLIOGRAPHY

Agee, Philip. *Inside the Company: CIA Diary*. New York: Farrar, Straus and Giroux, 1975.

Anderson, David. "Finn Disclosed as Double Agent at Spy Trial Here." *New York Times*, September 28, 1964.

Andrew, Christopher, and Vasili Mitrokhin. *The Sword and the Shield: The Mitrokhin Archive and the Secret History of the KGB*. New York: Basic Books, 2001.

Bagley, Tennent H. *Spymaster: Startling Cold War Revelations of a Soviet KGB Chief*. New York: Skyhorse Publishing, 2013.

———. *Spy Wars: Moles, Mysteries, and Deadly Games*. New Haven, CT: Yale University Press, 2007.

Barron, John. *KGB: The Secret Work of Soviet Secret Agents*. New York: Reader's Digest Press, 1974.

———. *KGB Today: The Hidden Hand*. New York: Reader's Digest Press, 1983.

———. *MiG Pilot: The Final Escape of Lieutenant Belenko*. New York: McGraw-Hill, 1980.

Bearden, Milt, and James Risen. *The Main Enemy: The Inside Story of the CIA's Final Showdown with the KGB*. New York: Random House, 2000.

Brown, Archie. *The Rise and Fall of Communism*. New York: Ecco, 2009.

Cherkashin, Victor. *Spy Handler: A Memoir of a KGB Officer—The True Story of the Man Who Recruited Robert Hanssen and Aldrich Ames*. New York: Basic Books, 2004.

Chickov, Vladimir. *Mole in the Aquarium* [Чиков Владимир Матвеевич КРОТ В АКВАРИУМЕ]. Moscow: Detective Press, 2013. http://www.x-libri.ru/elib/chikv000/index.htm.

Crowe, William, Jr., and David Chanoff. *The Line of Fire: From Washington to the Gulf, the Politics and Battles of the New Military*. New York: Simon & Schuster, 1993.

Duncan, Susana. "The War of the Moles." *New York Magazine*, February 27, 1978.

Earley, Pete. *Confessions of a Spy: The Real Story of Aldrich Ames*. New York: Putnam, 1997.

———. *Comrade J: The Untold Secrets of Russia's Master Spy in America After the Cold War*. New York: Putnam, 2007.

Epstein, Edward Jay. *Legend: The Secret World of Lee Harvey Oswald*. New York: Reader's Digest Press, 1978.

Finn, Peter. *The Zhivago Affair: The Kremlin, the CIA, and the Battle over a Forbidden Book*. New York: Pantheon Books, 2014.

Fursenko, Aleksandr, and Timothy Naftali. *Khrushchev's Cold War: The Inside Story of an American Adversary*. New York: W. W. Norton, 2006.

Gaddis, John Lewis. *The Cold War: A New History*. New York: Penguin Press, 2005.

Galayko, Vladimir. *The Spy Who Was Chased for a Quarter of a Century*. Interview with Gen. Leonid Aleksandrovich Gulev, *Mirror of the Week* (Moscow), March 24, 2001. http://gazeta.zn.ua/SOCIETY/shpion,_za_kotorym_ohotilis_chetvert_veka.html.

Grimes, Sandra, and Jeanne Vertefeuille. *Circle of Treason: A CIA Account of Traitor Aldrich Ames and the Men He Betrayed*. Annapolis, MD: U.S. Naval Institute Press, 2012.

GRU General—American Agent. Russian television documentary. Telecompaniya Ostankino, 1994. http://my.mail.ru/mail/ilya_isaev_1994/video/18424/18435.html#video=/mail/ilya_isaev_1994/18424/18435.

Harris, Steven E. *Communism on Tomorrow Street: Mass Housing and Everyday Life After Stalin*. Washington, DC: Woodrow Wilson Center Press, 2013.

Kalugin, Oleg. *Spymaster: My Thirty-Two Years in Intelligence and Espionage Against the West*. London: Smith Gryphon, 1994.

Mabey, John. Interview transcript for episode 21, *Cold War,* CNN, National Security Archive, http://nsarchive.gwu.edu/coldwar/interviews/episode-21/mabey1.html. Video of episode 21 (*Spies 1944–1994*): http://www.infocobuild.com/books-and-films/social-science/cold-war-cnn.html.

Macintyre, Ben. *A Spy Among Friends: Kim Philby and the Great Betrayal.* New York: Crown, 2014.

Mangold, Tom. *Cold Warrior: James Jesus Angleton—The CIA's Master Spy Hunter.* New York: Simon & Schuster, 1991.

Martin, David C. *Wilderness of Mirrors: Intrigue, Deception, and the Secrets That Destroyed Two of the Cold War's Most Important Agents.* New York: HarperCollins, 1980.

Montefiore, Simon Sebag. *Stalin: The Court of the Red Star.* New York: Knopf, 2004.

Morley, Jefferson. *Our Man in Mexico.* Lawrence: University Press of Kansas, 2008. www.kansaspress.ku.edu. Used by permission of the publisher.

The Moscow Summit 20 Years Later. National Security Archives Electronic Briefing Book No. 251. http://nsarchive.gwu.edu/NSAEBB/NSAEBB251/.

Murphy, David E., Sergei A. Kondrashev, and George Bailey. *Battleground Berlin: CIA vs. KGB in the Cold War.* New Haven, CT: Yale University Press, 1997.

Philby, Kim. *My Silent War: The Soviet Master Agent Tells His Own Story.* New York: Grove Press, 1968.

Reagan, Ronald. Moscow State University speech, May 31, 1988, Reagan Presidential Library, https://reaganlibrary.gov/archives?-catid=2016&id=9373:moscowsp.

———. *The Reagan Diaries.* New York: Harper, 2007.

REDSOX. "Transmittal of Final Report on First Cycle of CACCAOLA 1." Internal CIA memo dated June 4, 1952. CIA Digital Library Reading Room. https://www.cia.gov/library/readingroom/docs/AESAURUS%20AENOBLE%20%20%20VOL.%201_0032.pdf.

Remnick, David. *Lenin's Tomb: The Last Days of the Soviet Empire*. New York: Random House, 1993.

———. *Resurrection: The Struggle for a New Russia*. New York: Random House, 1997.

Shannon, Elaine. "Death of the Perfect Spy." *Time* 144, no. 6, August 8, 1994, pp. 32–34.

Smith, Hedrick. *The Russians*. San Antonio, TX: Quadrangle, 1976.

Suvorov, Viktor. *Inside Soviet Military Intelligence*. New York: Macmillan, 1984.

———. *Inside the Aquarium: The Making of a Top Soviet Spy*. New York: Macmillan, 1986.

Taubman, William. *Khrushchev: The Man and His Era*. New York: W. W. Norton, 2003.

Terrill, Ross. *Mao: A Biography*. New York: Harper and Row, 1980.

Thomas, Evan. *Ike's Bluff: President Eisenhower's Secret Battle to Save the World*. New York: Little, Brown, 2012.

Trento, Joseph J. *The Secret History of the CIA*. New York: Basic Books, 2001.

Tuomi, Kaarlo. *Spy Lost: Caught Between the KGB and the FBI*. New York: Enigma Books, 2014.

Wallace, Robert, and H. Keith Melton. *Spycraft: The Secret History of the CIA's Spytechs, from Communism to Al-Qaeda*. New York: Dutton, 2008.

Weiner, Tim, David Johnston, and Neil A. Lewis. *Betrayal: The Story of Aldrich Ames, an American Spy*. New York: Random House, 1995.

Wise, David. *Molehunt: The Secret Search for Traitors That Shattered the CIA*. New York: Random House, 1992.

———. *Nightmover: How Aldrich Ames Sold the CIA to the KGB for $4.6 Million*. New York: HarperCollins, 1995.

———. "Our Man in Moscow." *George*, October 1997, pp. 118–21.

INDEX

Page numbers in *italics* refer to illustrations.

ABOUT THE AUTHOR

Eva Dillon spent twenty-five years in the magazine publishing business in New York City, including stints at *Vogue*, *Harper's Bazaar*, *Glamour*, and the *New Yorker*, and as president of *Reader's Digest*, U.S. Growing up, Dillon and her six siblings moved around the world for her father's CIA assignments in Berlin, Mexico City, Rome, and New Delhi. She holds a bachelor's degree in music from Virginia Commonwealth University and lives in Charleston, South Carolina.